Makers and Milestones of the Middle Ages

P. Gordon B. Stillman

Illustrated by
John B. Severance

Longman/Independent School Press

Longman Inc.
95 Church Street
White Plains, New York 10601

Associated companies:
Longman Group Ltd., London
Longman Cheshire Pty., Melbourne
Longman Paul Pty., Auckland
Copp Clark Pitman, Toronto
Pitman Publishing Inc., New York

PRINTED IN THE UNITED STATES OF AMERICA

88899091
ISBN 0-8013-0214-5   12345678

Contents

Maps

Illustrations

Dynastic Tables

Preface

This book is a revised and expanded edition of *Men and Milestones of the Middle Ages*, which was first published in 1960. The old chapters have been edited; two new chapters, about Justinian and Theodora and Eleanor of Aquitaine, have been added. The changes have been made with the express intention of broadening our view to take better note of the role and influence of women.

The idea for this book grew from the teaching of a secondary school course in Medieval History. Many students working with a conventional textbook were losing track of the main story in a maze of factual details that, even when carefully memorized, seemed as confusing as they were unimportant.

Fortunately, it appeared that numerous topics — for example, the quarrels of Germanic dynasties or Saxon monarchs — could be eliminated without doing damage to our understanding of the essential progress of humanity in the Middle Ages. We may pass over many little principalities and minor potentates. Much that the specialist would deem indispensible — about Guelphs and Ghibellines, gelds and fyrds, stem duchies and appanages — has, therefore, been omitted from this history. One cannot learn from it all about the lives of the kings of Castile and Sicily, the dukes of Bavaria and Burgundy, the bishops of Bremen and Mainz. The emphasis, rather, is on the major trends of human activity in the Middle Ages.

For, clearly, one cannot understand modern men and women, or the evolution of western civilization with its joint centers in Europe and in Christianity, without knowing something of events and accomplishments from 500 to 1300 A.D. Many medieval conflicts — Church against State, the individual against the institution, mystical faith against rational argument — are fascinating to study because they continue to have relevance in our own times.

Ideas are like natural resources. To be of use people have to discover and develop them. To gain vitality, an abstract principle needs to be embraced and interpreted by the person who gives it practical application and proves it in action. The word must be made flesh.

All of us are accustomed to reading stories of heroes, and we are attracted to them. These heroes may be spiritual or political leaders, athletic champions, even comic strip or television paragons. We can identify best with these people if we can become familiar with their personalities and imagine ourselves in their positions, contending with daily difficulties, dreaming dreams and suffering doubts, confronting opposition and misunderstanding, ending in glory or disaster.

So this book is biographical in organization. It selects a handful of important people, each with a personal claim to fame. It tells their life stories, each one of which elucidates a critical aspect of medieval history. People did not lie dormant during the Middle Ages but attacked the problems of their times in the context of their thinking and their abilities. By concentrating on certain actions of enduring significance in the history of western people, I hope both to identify the essential developments of the Middle Ages and to explore the dimensions of human greatness. Because there is much more of interest to learn, I would like this book to stimulate wider reading and independent research.

In John B. Severance I had the pleasure and benefit of a colleague whose artistic talents were matched by his friendly interest in the production of this book. I would like to express to him again my appreciation for the creation of the imaginative and striking portraits that imparted so much life to the earlier edition, and now to add my admiration of his portraits of the new heroes of this edition and of the exciting design for the cover.

The other illustrations are reproduced from their extensive collection by courtesy of The Bettmann Archive in New York City. These illustrations were selected to enable the reader to visualize some of the people who play important parts in our story and some of the arts and material objects with which they were familiar, as they were depicted or designed by the artists and artisans of their own day. We gain a more lively idea of the Middle Ages by looking at things which medieval people saw and read, touched and used. It is important to realize how much we know about a civilization from sources other than history books.

Gordon Stillman

New York City
July 1987

Introduction

If we were to return to the Middle Ages for a day, we would find people much like ourselves, but we would immediately be struck by evidence of the lack of industry and technological skills. This lack forced life into a pattern of sparse population, small-scale organization, limited education, and an appalling scarcity of material goods. These had to be produced by hard manual labor using the simplest of machinery and the power of animals, wind, or water. In such an age major changes in purpose and method were closely bound to the working of personal genius. Thought was redirected, policy determined, and history made by the likes and dislikes, ambitions and jealousies, talents and frailties, of the individual. Leaders like those Thomas Carlyle described in *Heroes and Hero-Worship* dominated the public arena and shaped the age in their own image.

The qualities of greatness

A fundamental question for us as we explore any particular era is how to recognize and evaluate greatness in people. To begin with, "heroes" are representative of their time. We cannot and should not expect people of the 12th century to see with the eyes of the 20th. According to Milman, the famous historian of Christianity, people are "great in relation to the state and to the necessities of their age, engrossed by the powerful and dominating principles of their time, and bringing to the advancement of these principles surpassing energies of character, inflexible resolution, the full conviction of the wisdom, justice, and holiness of their cause, and in religious affairs of the direct and undeniable sanction of God." They exemplify the aspirations of their age, and their devotion and singleness of purpose lead thousands of others to share in their beliefs and endeavors. Their influence depends on their "gift for expressing the thoughts that lie, more or less consciously, in the minds of all their contemporaries."

We require, further, that the principles to which great leaders give their allegiance be principles we can deem valid or commendable even if we cannot personally share them. Great people must be representative of much, if not all, of the best of their time. Not everyone today is concerned with individual salvation. But we can agree that saving a person from a life of crime is more important than winning a joust, or providing justice for poor peasants more important than taking a castle. We may not agree with the monks that the way of salvation was fixed and that the best place to find and follow that way was a monastery. But we cannot fail to note that when monasticism was in need of reform, the fervent and zealous monk, Bernard of Clairvaux, brought to it a fresh inspiration. In his 12th century, which has been called "the century of the monks," the greatest monk of all was Bernard.

So we come to a third requirement for greatness, the advancement of principles or the setting of new standards. The most memorable people of the Middle Ages, as of all eras, transcended the limitations of vision or action that restricted their contemporaries. Not only did they bring to fullest effectiveness the reputable thoughts and policies of their times, but also they conceived new ideas and established new institutions. Their thinking was original, their lives unique. They created the world in which they lived by reshaping its purposes and redirecting its energies, and they came to symbolize a people or a force in history.

Great people, then, point the way and persuade others to follow. Their vision makes them prophets; their personality makes them leaders; their work alters the pattern of their times. The world would not be the same without people of their stature and dynamism. In describing Mohammed, Carlyle wrote that he came to the Arab world "as lightning out of heaven; the rest of men waited for him like fuel, and then they too would flame." Like a spark to combustible material, people of greatness come to their divided, confused, disillusioned world, offer a glimpse of how it can be made better, and move their society forward in the unending quest for a satisfying way of life.

History deals with people, their words and deeds, hopes and fears, achievements and failures. By nature, people are fallible: sometimes they set selfish goals, make errors of judgment, fail to do what they know to be right. In the pages of history, therefore, we shall not find any individual person who attains ideal greatness. But it should be interesting to measure the prominent personages of the Middle Ages against our concepts of what great men and women should be like and can accomplish. Did these leaders in their time personify the best in thought or policy or morality? Were they effective in putting their new ideas into practice? In what ways and to what extent do the people we shall meet in this book deserve to be called great and their actions beneficial to humankind?

Part One

Reactions to the Fall of the Roman Empire in the West

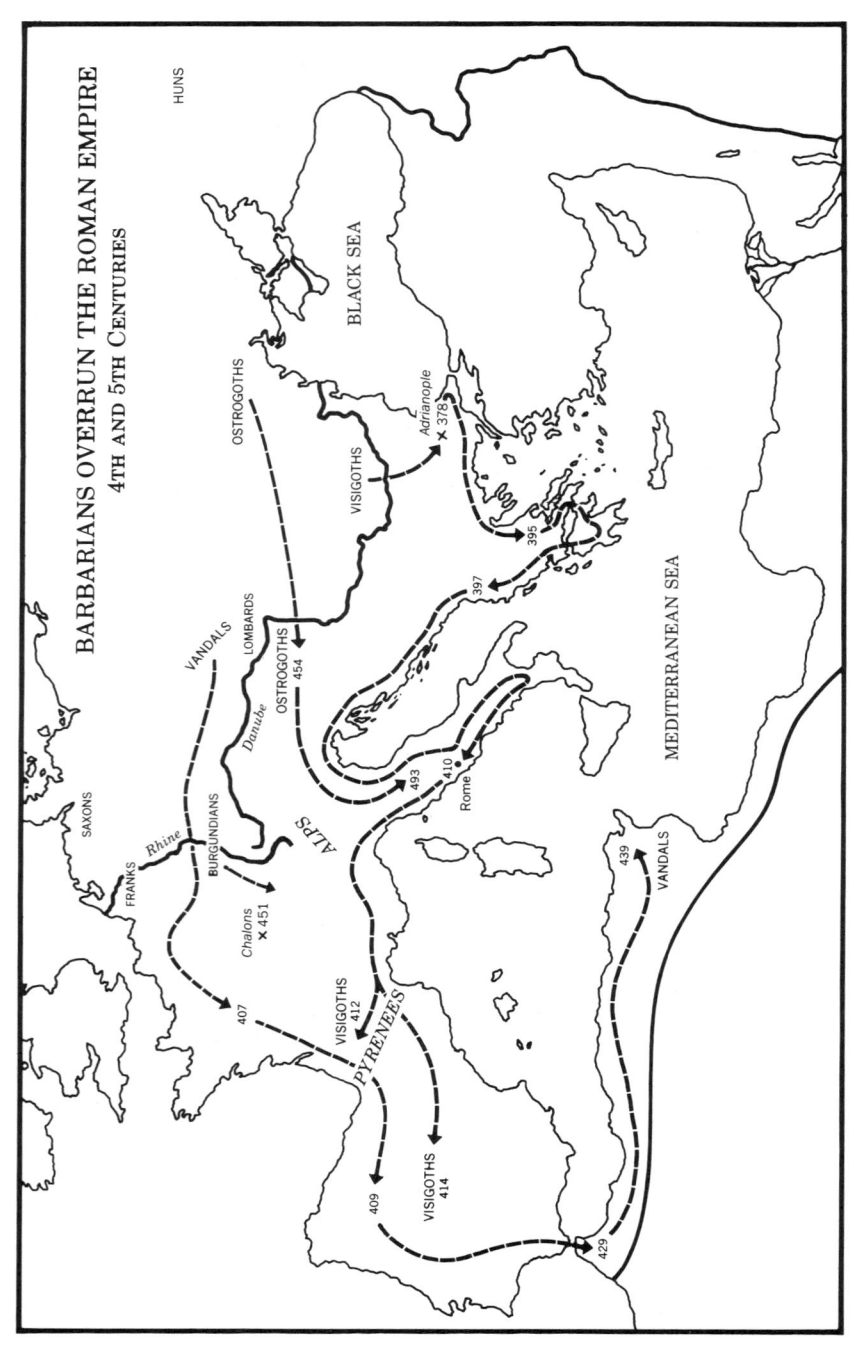

BARBARIANS OVERRUN THE ROMAN EMPIRE
4TH AND 5TH CENTURIES

HUNS

BLACK SEA

OSTROGOTHS

VISIGOTHS

Adrianople
× 378

395

397

VANDALS

LOMBARDS

OSTROGOTHS
454

Danube

MEDITERRANEAN SEA

ALPS

SAXONS

FRANKS

Rhine

BURGUNDIANS

493

410

Rome

Chalons
× 451

439

VANDALS

407

VISIGOTHS
412

PYRENEES

409

VISIGOTHS
414

429

Chapter One

PARTITION: CLOVIS (466-511)

In 476 A.D. a pathetic little boy with a great name, Romulus Augustulus, was put off his throne by a barbarian named Odoacer; and the Roman Empire in the West ceased to exist. For a thousand years the inhabitants of Europe would be stirred by the dream of re-establishing a single political state upheld by a single religious faith. The man who first demonstrated the potential strength of such a combination of Roman governmental unity and the Christian religion was Clovis.

1. Barbarian invasions; the Franks in Gaul

When Clovis was born in 466, there was nothing to indicate that he would become such an important man. He belonged to a race of people called the Franks. Along with the Ostrogoths and the Visigoths, the Burgundians and the Vandals, these Franks were, in the eyes of the Romans, barbarians. They lived outside the borders of the empire, "beyond the pale." They did not understand the language of Rome; their laws were crude and harsh; they were idol-worshipers. They were not included in the civilized world. But, since early in the 3rd century, the rich lands and the luxuries of the empire had attracted these barbarians. In steadily increasing numbers, they had been infiltrating from northern and eastern Europe across the Rhine and Danube Rivers into the border provinces of the empire. Some had come to settle down as laborers or soldiers of a Roman lord, and many of these had prospered and become educated to Roman ways. Like them or not, the Romans could not stop them; the pressure on the frontiers was irresistible.

The inflow of barbarians was accelerated in the 4th century when the fierce Huns from the area near the Caspian Sea began to push them from behind. The imperial government decided to allow great masses of Goths to occupy lands south of the Danube. Then the officials made the stupid mistake of callously cheating and mistreating the new residents. Unhappy and desperate, the Visigoths rose against their hosts. In 378 a barbarian army faced a Roman one at Adrianople. Long marches and a shortage of water had rendered the legions unfit for action, and reinforcements were on the way, but Emperor Valens rashly offered battle. Deserted by their weak force of auxiliary cavalry, the legionaries were overwhelmed. Two-thirds of their number were slaughtered, including the emperor himself.

The effect of this battle, both physical and moral, was shattering. A barbarian host had annihilated the disciplined army of the mistress of civilization. Overnight, the Danube barrier ceased to exist. Hordes of barbarians flowed unchecked into the empire. Although pacified temporarily by Emperor Theodosius, the Visigoths soon reasserted their vigor and ambition under a young leader named Alaric. In 410 they captured and sacked the city of Rome itself. Carrying their plunder, they moved back out of Italy. In Gaul they found the Vandals, who had crossed the frozen Rhine River in force on a December night in 406 and swept the Roman garrisons from their path. Pushing the Vandals in front of them, the Visigoths passed the Pyrenees and won a domain for themselves in Spain. The Vandals moved on into North Africa, where they quickly overran the Roman province. In 455, under Gaiseric, they returned briefly to raid and loot Rome, from which event comes our word "vandalism." A little later, the Ostrogoths, too, made a westward movement and established a kingdom in Italy. Theodoric, king of the Ostrogoths, replaced Odoacer in power at Rome and calmly approved the murder of his predecessor.

Like most of the other barbarians, the Franks had started to immigrate into the empire in the 3rd century. Unlike the more adventurous tribes we have mentioned, they did not come in as conquerors nor did they penetrate deep into Roman territory. Crossing the Rhine from their original homeland in what today is western Germany, they chose to settle down near the river in northern Gaul. Their loose confederacy split into two groups: the Salian Franks centered in the lowlands west of the lower Rhine around the modern cities of Cambrai, Arras, and Tournai; the Ripuarian Franks centered farther up the river and on both banks, around Cologne and Metz. The Roman authorities in Gaul accepted the Franks as allies.

Romans and Franks, as well as Burgundians and Visigoths, fought together in 451 under Aetius at the bloody battle of Châlons on the Marne River. There they halted the Asiatic invasion of Attila, the "Scourge of God," and his ferocious olive-skinned and beady-eyed Huns. It is perhaps significant that after the withdrawal of the invaders, the Franks, rather than the Romans, took over control of several of the Gallic cities. But in the middle of the 5th century there were few portents of a great destiny for the Franks. They were politically disunited; they had paid little attention to the culture and learning of the Romans; they were still unconverted to Christianity. Other people accused them of a dishonesty and disloyalty surpassing that of the average barbarians. But they seemed to present no particular threat to the Roman power, against which they apparently harbored no designs.

Clovis himself was the son of Childeric, a king of the Salian Franks, but this was a less exalted position than we might suppose. There were a number of petty Frankish kings, none of whom had at that time much real authority over his people. He usually owed his title, which was not normally hereditary, to the will of the assembly of independent warriors. These accepted a king as their spokesman and leader in time of war, unless indeed a more accomplished military leader won over their loyalty. In time of peace, however, the king counted for little and was bound by the laws equally with his subjects. In such a kingship Clovis, at the age of fifteen, succeeded his father and began to reign at Tournai. He did not, in fact, command the allegiance of more than 5000 warriors, and he must have realized that his rule, and indeed his life, depended not on legal right or ancient custom but on his own personal strength and skill.

Although in 481 Clovis' position was neither secure nor powerful, the times were ripe for changes which might much benefit both the new king and his people. The Visigoths had extinguished the Roman power in southwest Gaul, but now their king died and was succeeded by a less capable and less warlike Alaric. For a while the Visigoths would make no effort to advance beyond their existing northern boundary, the Loire River. Stretching between the Loire and the Somme and Meuse Rivers, which marked the extent of the Frankish settlements, was all that remained of Roman Gaul. Included in this area were the centers of the Catholic Church—Paris, the city of St. Genevieve, and Reims, the seat of the learned bishop Remigius—and the center of Roman administration, Soissons. But with the downfall of the imperial government at Rome, Gaul was cast politically adrift. No longer did orders and instructions for its rule come out from Rome; no longer were Roman legions prepared to march north for its protection. Gaul was a province without a capital, a body without a head. In the troubled era of the late 5th century, with the Roman world collapsing, could Gaul establish its independence? What was to be the position of Syagrius, the last provincial governor appointed from Rome? Could he transform himself into a king?

Now their earlier lack of wanderlust proved beneficial to the Franks. On the Somme and the Meuse, they were adjacent to the most highly-civilized of all the old Roman provinces. They commanded the level routes to the center of that province, which—in all history through our 20th century—have commended themselves to an invading army. At the same time their lands stretched back to their native bases beyond the Rhine, whence they might draw fresh contingents of hardy Frankish warriors. Clovis had the wit to recognize these strategic advantages which geography had placed in his hands. And he had ambition. He would not rest content with his meagre and doubtful inheritance; he would conquer Gaul for himself. Wisely, he made all possible preparations for his campaign. He secured his rear as well as he could by alliances with the other Frankish kings; he trained and equipped his fighting men. In 486, his aggressive purposes clear in his own mind, Clovis was ready to advance into Gaul.

One battle settled the question of Syagrius. His was not the army of tough and disciplined legionaries with which Julius Caesar had originally subdued Gaul. He commanded Romanized barbarians, who had the superficial organization but not the spirit of a Roman army, and they had neither the fortitude nor the mobility to withstand the furious onslaught of their less civilized but more determined foes. After the battle, the Franks entered Soissons and looted, each warrior taking an equal share of the spoil, as was their custom.

Two acts of Clovis following his first great victory throw interesting light on the character of the barbarian chieftain. His defeated opponent Syagrius fled in desperation to the Visigothic court to beg asylum. Clovis immediately sent an embassy to demand that Syagrius be surrendered to the Franks, and cowardly Alaric acceded to this request. Given over to the victors, Syagrius was put to death. No doubt it was convenient for Clovis thus to be rid of the last legal representative of the Roman power in Gaul, although it would seem he had little to fear from the discredited Syagrius. Clovis permitted no quality of mercy to moderate his barbarian ferocity or to interfere with considerations of politics. The loser must suffer the punishment to which fate had exposed him. Clovis kept his eye on the main chance, he was inflexible of purpose. And we may rightly assume that he did not forget how easily Alaric had given in to the Frankish threats.

Then there was the episode of the Soissons vase. After the city's churches had been despoiled of their treasures, Bishop Remigius begged the king that a special vase should be returned. Clovis agreed to give back the vase, but it was first necessary for it to be included in the king's share of the plunder, contrary to the Frankish custom of equal shares for all, distributed by lot. All the Franks were willing to bow to the king's desire save one, who promptly took his axe and shattered the vase. Making no sign of anger, Clovis handed the broken pieces to the bishop. But here was a critical moment. Clovis' control over his army was at stake. Beyond that, the newly-conquered Gauls, accustomed to the absolute power of Roman officials could not be expected to live quietly subject to a king whose wishes could be successfully flouted by one of his own soldiers. For some time Clovis took no action. But it was the Frankish practice for a great review of the entire army to be held each March for inspection of equipment and organization for the summer campaign. On the next such occasion, Clovis walked down the ranks until he reached the soldier who had broken the vase. Inspecting him carefully, Clovis found fault with the state of his weapons and threw his battle-axe to the ground. As the soldier bent to retrieve the weapon, Clovis raised his own axe, and broke the soldier's skull, crying "Thus did you to the vase." The letter of the law must not be allowed to stand in the way of a conqueror. Clovis would be a king in fact as well as in name. At a blow he gained the respect of soldiers and subjects alike. His bold showmanship created one of those legends which add glamour and terror to the figure of a monarch.

With the battle at Soissons, Roman Gaul as far as the Seine fell into the hands of the Franks, and Clovis soon extended his sway to the Loire. He shifted his capital from Tournai to Soissons, and the Catholic bishops had to acknowledge the rule of the heathen barbarian over their cities. But there arose among the Ripuarian Franks rumblings of discontent that a single Salian king should have amassed so much authority. Campaigning against them in the next few years, Clovis forced the Ripuarians to accept his overlordship, and the Franks were at least in theory united again in a single race.

2. Conversion to Catholic Christianity; Church and State

Having overwhelmed Roman Gaul and subdued the Ripuarians, Clovis now enjoyed a short rest from his military labors. He employed some of his leisure in the search for a wife with whom he could perpetuate his branch of the family descended, tradition said, from the ancient Frankish king Meroving. His choice fell upon Clotilde, a niece of the king of neighboring Burgundy. This selection of Clotilde, which might normally be expected to be of no particular importance, turned out to be a second decisive step in the life of Clovis. It was the religious situation which made it so significant.

The Franks, as we have seen, were still heathen. The Romanized Gauls were Catholics. Their highly organized Church adhered strictly to the doctrine of the Trinity as it had been enunciated by the first great Church Council at Nicaea in 325. The vast majority of the barbarians who had preceded the Franks into Gaul, the Visigoths and the Burgundians, had been Christianized; but they had almost all been infected with what was called the Arian heresy. They denied the Trinity, and accepted only God the Father as divine. For this reason the Gallic and the barbarian Christians had never been able to come to a friendly understanding; they looked upon each other as hopelessly misguided and wicked. But to the ordinary rule that Burgundians were Arians, Clotilde was an exception—and a very remarkable exception. She was a Catholic, a most devout and sincere Catholic, who was to devote many of her eighty years to austere living and works of charity and finally to be made a saint by the Church. It is difficult to imagine such a lady married to the harsh and relentless Clovis, but their marriage took place in 493 and had a marked effect on history. For Clotilde was unwilling that her husband should be damned by continuing in his present ignorant ways. In the words of the Church chronicle, she "never ceased to persuade him that he should serve the true God," who was naturally the God in Three Persons of the Catholic Church.

Clovis as a husband was not immune to his wife's influence. Their first son was baptized in the Church. Although his death in infancy raised some doubts as to the wisdom of such baptism, Clovis consented that their second son should also be baptized. Such foolish, womanly fancies, while acceptable for children, were not suitable for a warlike king. So Clovis resisted Clotilde's efforts to convert him to Christianity.

Domination over the Ripuarians made Clovis responsible for the eastern frontier of the Frankish territory, which was open to attack by other barbarians. A Teutonic tribe from central Germany, known as the Alemanni, now proceeded to swarm across the Rhine into modern Alsace-Lorraine and advance on the Frankish city of Cologne. Here was a threat not only to the Franks, but also to the Gauls, who could imagine their lands overrun by a second wave of barbarians. Clovis collected his forces and met the invaders at Tolbiac, near Strasbourg. Despite his personal courage and cool generalship, the battle was fierce and, for a long time, indecisive. Desperate, in the heat of his desire for victory, Clovis thought of Clotilde's God and called on him for assistance:

"O Christ, Jesus, I crave as a suppliant Thy glorious aid; and if Thou grantest me victory over these enemies, I will believe in Thee and be baptized in Thy name."

Immediately, so the story goes, the Alemanni gave ground and were swept from the field in utter defeat.

Clovis was as good as his word. But the baptism of a king was not lightly to be passed over. It was not a matter of personal conviction only, but of public policy. It must be solemnized with the most stately ceremonies, it must be a shining example to the people. So Clovis came to the Cathedral at Reims and was baptized by Bishop Remigius. It was an enormous transition the bishop saw the king undergoing — from heathen idolater and bloodthirsty plunderer to Christian father of his people — and Remigius spoke words to signalize the momentous occasion: "Adore that which thou has burnt, and burn that which thou hast adored." Three thousand warriors were baptized with their commander, and within a single generation most of the Franks had followed their example. They became Catholic Christians.

We must examine this conversion of Clovis at length because it was the most crucial event in his life. First of all, we must admit that Clovis did not become a good Christian. In character Clovis the Christian mirrored Clovis the heathen. Where he had before been cruel and false and heartless, he was cruel and false and heartless still. Nor did Clovis really understand the meaning of Christianity. Neither in his heart nor in his mind could he appreciate the life of Christ, his mildness, his self-sacrifice. Of the Crucifixion, Clovis is reported to have said with warmth: "Had I been present at the head of my Franks, I would have avenged His injuries." One may wonder what would have happened to Christianity had Clovis been there at Golgotha.

What then made this conversion so crucial, for Clovis and for history? No doubt Clotilde had planted the seeds of the Christian idea in her husband's mind. Then, in a desperate juncture, he had been moved — like Constantine — to call on the Christian God for the express purpose of gaining a vital victory, and this God seemed to have answered his call. But all this was temporary and inconclusive, done in a moment, capable of being revoked. It was the formal baptism at Reims of which the world took note. We may be sure that Clovis did not undergo this definitive act without carefully weighing all the pros and cons. Here was a deed not of inflamed emotion but of considered judgment. In the cold afterlight of the battle, Clovis deemed it wise to be baptized into the Catholic Church. His conversion was a matter of statecraft, from which Clovis expected to derive political advantage.

Let us look at the political situation in Gaul late in the 5th century. With the collapse of the imperial government, there was created what we would call a power-vacuum. Local rule fell into confusion because there was no central authority to direct it, no central force to uphold it. In such a situation, individuals of ability and reputation may exercise power temporarily and locally. Such people existed in Gaul, chiefly churchmen, of education and experience in affairs, who from their urban centers could exert their influence over the surrounding territory.

The Church as an organization, however, was not then interested in temporal power. What it desired was a strong political authority which would respect religious institutions and ensure the good order under which it might expand its moral influence. So Gaul lay open to seizure by the first powerful group which might appear. The inhabitants found this situation intolerable. Rich, cultivated as they were, with their Roman legal system and their highly-developed commercial life, they had become accustomed to the firm control of a Roman governor. As much as the Church, Gaul desired peace and security and feared the anarchy of repeated barbarian invasions.

At this point Clovis and his Franks entered. The victory at Soissons made further resistance to the barbarian general obviously absurd, and so the best must be made of the existing situation. Here, calculated the Church, was a man of power. If his government could be firmly established, the Church might carry on its important work of converting the heathen and saving souls. Clovis, to be sure, was an idolater, but was that any worse than being a heretic? With the Arian Visigoths and Burgundians pressing on its borders, the orthodox Church in Gaul needed above all a strong-armed protector. And the idolater might be converted to the true faith.

Meanwhile, Clovis surveyed the opportunities which Soissons opened to him and made his own calculations. He, too, sought security and permanence for his own rule. Far better to be ruler in the absolute Roman tradition over the Gauls than to enjoy the limited authority accorded to a Frankish king. Far wiser to have the generous support of the Gauls against potential rivals than to be required to exercise police power over unwilling subjects. Such history as was recorded, was recorded by the Church, which monopolized learning. Education of the young was in the hands of the Church. If Clovis was to win the heart of Gaul, he must gain the favor of the Church.

So the independent reasoning of Remigius and Clovis drew them to the same conclusion. Neither could lose, each should gain, from an alliance of Church and State. The field of Tolbiac presented the opportunity, which the ceremony at Reims confirmed. His conversion at such a crucial moment, says the French historian Bainville, "made Clovis irresistible in Roman Gaul." In a day, Clovis became the protector of the orthodox Church against heathen and heretic alike and the defender of Gaul against barbarian surges from across the Rhine. Shortly afterward, Bishop Avitus of Vienne said to Clovis: "Whenever you fight in these lands, it is we who conquer." In the wake of Clovis' armies, the Catholic Church spread its doctrines. Nor did Clovis fail to benefit from being the first barbarian king to embrace Catholicism. He gained the devotion of the Gallic population, a fresh source of support. He transformed himself from a hated usurper into a legitimate champion. Wrote the English historian Gibbon in the 18th century: "The eldest, or rather the only, son of the Church was acknowledged by the clergy as their lawful sovereign, or glorious deliverer; and the arms of Clovis were strenuously supported by the zeal and favor of the Catholic faction."

3. Victory over the Visigoths

After 496, therefore, Clovis found himself in a new position. No longer only a military leader, he had filled the power-vacuum and was now a king. No longer a conqueror, he was now a national hero. He had repulsed the Germanic invaders. He had recognized the validity of the orthodox Church. He had kept the loyal respect of the Franks by his unbroken string of victories. From now on, public opinion was on Clovis' side. In the ambitious schemes which began to form themselves in his mind, he was to have need of popular support. It was no longer enough for Clovis to order the effective but small band of Frankish warriors into action; he must also carry with him the common people of his new kingdom of Gaul. All future expeditions must be planned with an eye to their political as well as their military aspects. Would they excite Clovis' new subjects to enthusiastic support? To the brilliant ardor of his generalship Clovis must add the cool prudence of statesmanship. By far his greatest political asset proved to be his position as the champion of orthodox Christianity. As such, he was unique among barbarian leaders. As such, conservative Gaul rallied to his banner and the Church served gladly as his propaganda agency. As such, orthodox Christians in other lands looked to Clovis as their possible deliverer. The pope called him "a helmet of salvation for the Church."

With Roman Gaul on his side, Clovis was strong enough to face the older barbarian powers as an equal. Burgundy naturally commended itself to him. It was Clotilde's homeland; it was a prey to the ignorance of the Arian heresy; it contained rich farming land. Burgundy might well be assimilated into the domains of Clovis and the Catholic Church. The attack was made in 500. At first sweepingly victorious, Clovis found the Burgundians unexpectedly resilient. When they raised new forces against him the following year, Clovis was content to make a treaty by which the king, Gondeband, retained his throne but agreed to pay the Franks an annual tribute. Several years later, the Alemanni showed signs of a restless and aggressive spirit, and Clovis led a punishing expedition to complete their subjugation. But the climactic campaign of Clovis' later career was that against the Visigoths.

These heretic barbarians were hated by the Gauls, whom they had terrorized in earlier decades, and by the Catholics, whose religion they had scorned. Never was Clovis so popular, never was his orthodoxy proven a more valuable policy, than when in 507 he announced his intention of chastizing the Visigoths. Clovis had become a clever politician, able to exploit any advantage which fell to him. "I cannot bear," he declared, "that those Arians [the Visigoths] should hold any part of Gaul. With God's aid we will go against them and subdue their land beneath our sway." What orthodox Christian could resist the summons to such a worthy cause? It was not immediately apparent to the people of Gaul that Clovis, even more than the Church, would profit from a Visigothic defeat.

Clovis led his invading host across the Loire River, and all the omens pointed to a great Frankish victory. When Clovis entered the shrine of St. Martin at Tours, a psalm was being sung proclaiming the victory of God's champions. When the Visigoths were found strongly entrenched behind a river, a pure white hart led Clovis to a ford by which the visigothic position could be turned. When the Franks needed to make a night march to Poitiers, a flaming meteor in the sky served as their beacon. In those days omens were made much of, and on this occasion, they prophesied aright. Alaric had always feared Clovis. Now, on the field near Poitiers, Clovis slew Alaric with his own hand and the Visigoths were routed. The remnants of their army fled to Spain, and their kingdom from the Loire to the Pyrenees fell into the hands of Clovis.

Who could doubt that God was on the side of this true believer? Clovis himself made rich gifts of thanks to St. Martin, although in his practical hardheadedness, Gibbon tells us, he muttered that St. Martin was "an expensive friend." Now that all of ancient Gaul was at least tributary to him, Clovis' reputation began to spread abroad. News of his exploits reached Constantinople, where the Roman Empire survived.

The prestige of the eastern emperor was still high in the west, and Anastasius desired to keep alive the idea that all the world was still united under his sway. Clovis was now a power which he must recognize and, if possible, attach to himself. So Anastasius sent an embassy to Tours, bearing to Clovis the insignia of a proconsul—the empire's chosen representative in Gaul—and the purple robe of a patrician. For Anastasius the practical results of this mission were nil. Clovis acknowledged neither his inferiority to, nor his dependency on, the eastern emperor. Anastasius was too far away to give effect to his words. For Clovis, on the other hand, the mission was significant. His importance, his grandeur, was publicly proclaimed by the greatest earthly ruler. The proconsular insignia were an honor that had come to no other barbarian leader. His position was recognized and exalted by the favor of the emperor. His royalty, that of his family the Merovingians, was made legitimate. No longer could he be slighted or opposed as a barbarian usurper. The Roman world had formally accepted Clovis.

4. A new nation: government and culture

Since the fall of Rome the internal situation of Gaul had changed radically. The collapse of the source of authority had undermined the centralized provincial administration. For a time anarchy had threatened and it appeared that Gaul would be divided into many parts, each perhaps dominated by a fortified city. The strongest person would be the one who could subdue and control several cities, become a sort of local tyrant. Into this power-vacuum, as we have called it, had come the Frankish army, strong enough to subjugate all of Gaul that had not already been swallowed by the Visigoths and the Burgundians. The movable plunder might be apportioned equally among the victorious troops, but all Gaul could not logically belong to the Frankish army. Gaul had been ruled by a Roman governor; such a vigorous and unified administration it continued to need and demand.

So it was the victor rather than the vanquished that was transformed by the Frankish conquest. All the power amassed by the occupation of the Gallic cities fell naturally into the hands of the Frankish general, Clovis. The Gauls looked to him for orders. A territory the size of Gaul could not be governed by the voice vote of several thousand uneducated Franks gathered in what we might today call a mass meeting. Day-by-day administration required the decisions and supervision of a single, dominant authority at the top. This could only be provided by Clovis, the ruler—in fact, the owner—of conquered Gaul. Their homeland might belong to the Franks collectively; Gaul belonged to Clovis. And so we see the battle leader of a rude and jealous soldiery transformed into a real king of a civilized state. In ruling Gaul he would not be the representative of the Frankish community or of the Eastern Emperor; he would reign by and for himself.

The Frankish tribes had never had the organization of a national kingdom, because national kingdoms did not exist in the 4th and 5th centuries. There was no Frankish precedent for the personal, absolute rule of Clovis over Gaul, and so the Franks had no machinery by which such government could be carried on. Fortunately, the Roman machinery of government was still functioning and Clovis possessed himself peacefully of the lands and the prerogatives which had belonged to the emperor. Court was held; taxes and tolls and customs duties were collected; money was coined and a coinage fee paid to the treasury.

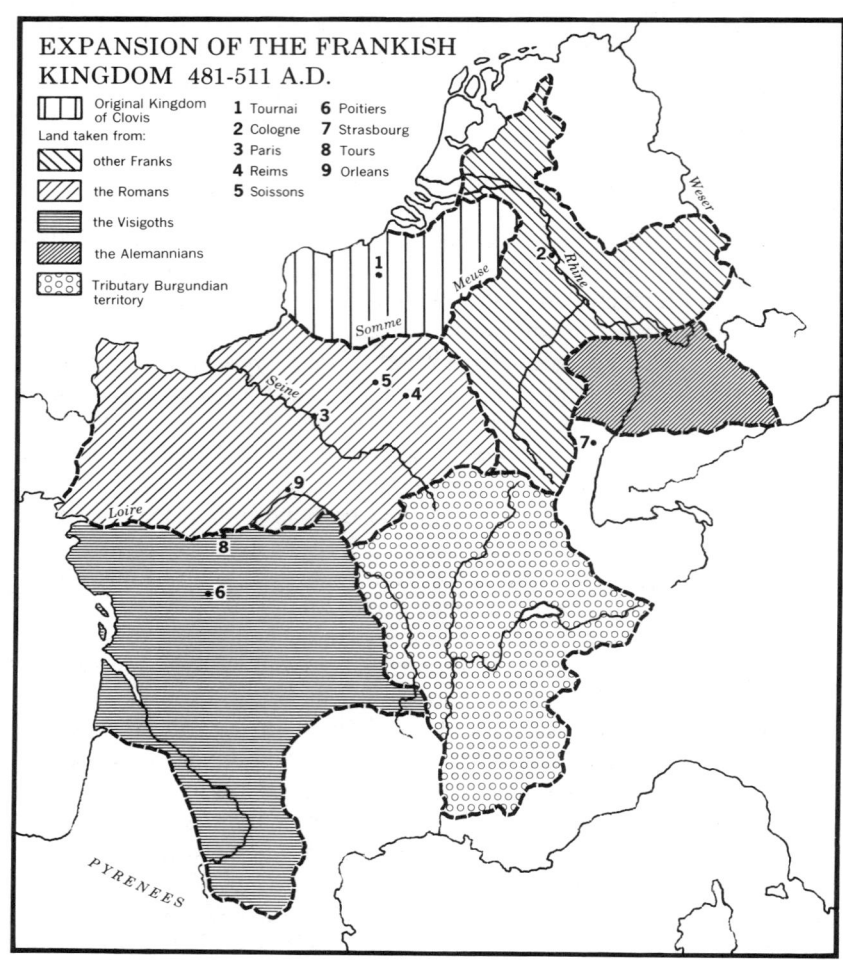

EXPANSION OF THE FRANKISH
KINGDOM 481-511 A.D.

Original Kingdom
of Clovis

Land taken from:

other Franks

the Romans

the Visigoths

the Alemannians

Tributary Burgundian
territory

1 Tournai   6 Poitiers
2 Cologne   7 Strasbourg
3 Paris   8 Tours
4 Reims   9 Orleans
5 Soissons

Weser

Rhine

Meuse

Somme

Seine

Loire

PYRENEES

Government went on as before, but what had been done for a governor as deputy of the emperor was now done directly for the king. The profits and the prestige belonged to Clovis. The king's commands had special significance because if they were not obeyed he was on hand with his soldiery to inflict penalties. What had been known in the flourishing days of the empire as the Pax Romana was now, in Gaul, the king's peace, and woe be to the offender who should break it.

Meanwhile Clovis maintained the firm control over the Frankish army which was indispensable to his security. By his victories and by the rich plunder he had shared among his soldiers, he had gained their favor and loyalty. Now that his lands were pacified, no further exploitation of the inhabitants was permitted. Military justice was swift and sure and fearful. The annual inspections in March were continued, and regular standards of discipline were maintained on a year-round basis. Clovis had the good sense not to try immediately to pour Frank and Gaul into one mold. Gauls were treated in the Roman way to which they were accustomed; Franks were satisfied by the preservation of their native traditions. Within his realm Clovis permitted to survive many local differences of custom. A person accused of a crime might choose the manner of trial which he or she would undergo. Thus both Gaul and Frank felt "at home" under Clovis' rule.

Neither Frankish warriors nor Gallic municipalities, however, retained quite the independence that had been theirs before the battle of Soissons. As general, conqueror, and owner of the land, Clovis exercised a close dominion over them. Slowly but surely a power was being felt among them which they had not experienced before—the power of a king and lord. This power might be new, it might be crudely administered, but it was a fact. The force of Clovis' arms had prevented the disintegration of Gaul and had consolidated the Franks. Now he sent counts throughout the land as his personal representatives, to execute his orders and maintain his peace. They were the agents of the new monarchy, and the effect of their activities was to establish uniformity of law and tax throughout the king's domain.

From the combination of Frankish tribes and provincial Gauls was being created something neither Frank nor Gaul had ever known—a nation, France. To mark this change, Clovis moved his capital again, to Paris. This move is a perfect illustration of his sense of geography and of his political genius. Located on an island in the Seine, Paris was easy to defend. At the commercial crossroads and natural center of his greatly expanded territories, it was the logical seat of the royal power. From Paris, Clovis could conveniently watch and control the activities of his subjects. Rumors reached him there of rebellion among the Franks in the original homeland to the east. Many of these were still pagan; they had not been bred up like the Gauls to obey the orders of a central government. Surely, thought Clovis, in a kingdom there is room enough for only one king. So orders went from Paris, and the petty kings of Cambrai and Cologne disappeared from the world. Even the historian most partial to Clovis cannot excuse the means he employed to rid himself of his rivals. Remorselessly he scoured the land for members of the Merovingian family, so that by having them murdered he might have no competitors for possession of his new kingdom, stretching from the Pyrenees to the Weser River. Unity he achieved, at a high cost in atrocities.

In government we have seen little change in Gaul as a result of the Frankish conquest. The same was true in the normal life of the average citizen, in the so-called "culture" of the country. In a meeting between the rough Frank and cultivated Gaul, it was natural that the more sophisticated civilization would tend to impart some of its polish to the more crude. In language, for instance, although there might exist dozens of dialects, there could be only one possible choice for the business of the Church and State. So the Franks must learn Latin. As with language, so with literature, law, education. The haphazard methods of the Franks gave way before the more highly-organized Roman system. But into that system the vigorous Franks would infuse a new vitality. The same land which had fallen as an overripe fruit into the hands of Clovis would become the seed-bed of a new European civilization.

In that civilization, the Church was central. It was obvious to Clovis from his own experience that the Christian God was greater than the native Frankish gods. In Gaul the Church was already rich and efficient. As Clovis widened his kingdom, the expansion of the Church kept pace with him. His conversion assured the triumph of orthodoxy over Arianism. The new kingdom was a Catholic kingdom. The king himself was the foremost defender of the Church, and its bishops were his most able and most trusted advisers. At Clovis' command, a council of 32 bishops met at Orléans to plan for the suppression of heresy and for the enactment of canon, or church, law. For instance, a resolution was passed that none except the son of a priest could be ordained without the king's order or the permission of the court representing the king. Church and State marched hand in hand.

We must not suppose that the cooperation of Church and State was perfect; that all Clovis' realm was justly and efficiently governed; that his kingdom bears much relation to modern France or indeed to any modern nation. Although a new law code gave Clovis increased authority in bringing common sense and orderliness into the daily affairs of his subjects, there were many things in the early Frankish kingdom of which we today would highly disapprove. Moral standards were barbaric; women were deprived of their reasonable rights. The favorite method of settling a legal case was by a duel between the opposing parties, and it was highly honorable to seek revenge without bothering with any legal formalities. The Frankish warriors were treated as though their physical prowess made them a class of superior beings. Murder was a crime which could be atoned for by a simple money payment: 200 gold pieces if you killed a common Frank; only 50 to 100 if your victim was an ordinary Roman. You paid more, of course, if you murdered a member of the privileged warrior caste.

Certain other commonplaces of Clovis' time we would call hopelessly old-fashioned. In point of fact, they served not as the bases of the nation-state system of modern Europe, but rather of the system of feudalism, which we shall see postponing the formation of nation-states for hundreds of years. For instance, the king rewarded the outstanding services of his chief lieutenants with outright gifts of lands that were part of the royal estate. These cessions of land were necessitated by the exhaustion of plundered treasure and the inadequate supply of precious metals for coined money. But the lands involved became free from royal overlordship and taxation, and this made it difficult for the king to enforce his decrees. Payment for ordinary service to the state was also most often made by a grant of land. These grants were intended to allow only the temporary use of the land, which continued to belong to the king, but his right to resume possession was not always peacefully conceded.

We see Clovis, then, compelled to adopt some measures which tended to undermine the national unity and uniformity he had striven to establish. Although his kingship was ultimately accepted as hereditary, the true basis of his authority among the Franks remained always the loyalty of the elite soldiers to a successful military chieftain. They were rewarded with special privileges, such as the exclusive right to hunt game. Some of these "old-fashioned" customs would grow into the worst weaknesses of the European system in later centuries.

5. Personality of Clovis

About Clovis himself it is difficult to form a clear judgment. The historical materials concerning him and his times are scarce and unreliable. In personal characteristics he seems to have been a mixture of strange opposites. Utterly unable himself to understand the Christian ideal, he became the foremost champion of the orthodox Church. A composed and courageous leader in war, his policy in peace more often than not was sly and double-faced. Untrained in statecraft, he was capable of sound reasoning and of accurate weighing of the merits of contrary courses. Suspicious and vengeful in private relations, he yet had the knack of pleasing the majority of his people. Firm of purpose, unyielding in pursuit of his goal, he stooped to foul measures without compunction or remorse. He was shrewd and calculating. On the whole he seems to have been more willing to exterminate than to persuade any who might oppose him. The finality of extermination appealed to him.

Widely differing opinions of Clovis have been formed by various writers, the opinion in each case reflecting the viewpoint of the particular writer. The 6th century church historian, Bishop Gregory of Tours, mindful of the great debt of the Church to Clovis, was able to write: "The Lord cast his enemies under his power day after day, and increased his kingdom, because he walked with a right heart before him, and did that which was pleasing in his sight." Gibbon, rational historian of the rather irreligious 18th century, made more of Clovis' criminal hypocrisy : "His ambitious reign was a perpetual violation of moral and Christian duties; his hands were stained with blood, in peace as well as in war; and as soon as Clovis had dismissed a synod of the Gallican Church, he calmly assassinated all the princes of the Merovingian race." From the vantage point of high Victorian morality, Sir Charles Oman described Clovis as a "ruffian, murderer, traitor . . . morally far worst of all the Teutonic founders of kingdoms."

Somewhere between the black and white estimates is the truth, if we take into consideration Clovis' barbaric background and the ruthlessness and disorder of the times in which he lived. Clovis' deeds were aimed at a goal which he had envisioned — a goal which benefited both him and his world. In achieving his worthy ends, he was guilty of employing means — cruelty, perfidy, outright criminality — which we cannot defend. And good luck frequently played a part in Clovis' success. We may recall the strategic location of the Franks, the weakness of Syagrius, the marriage to Clotilde, the conversion to Catholicism, the cowardice of Alaric. But these do not discredit the alertness of mind and the determination of spirit with which Clovis capitalized on each stroke of good fortune. In a way, he was a supreme opportunist.

Clovis made one mistake which had nearly fatal results. Having worked to create a single nation, he chose in his will to divide his lands among his four sons. The process of unification had thus to be repeated over and over again in the years to come, and France was not permanently unified with roughly its present borders until the 15th century. Amid the fraternal strife, the civil wars, the bloodshed and devastation, which ensued from the precedent foolishly set by Clovis, the civilization of Rome was almost extinguished. But not quite. Clovis, and his alliance of Church and State, had laid the foundations of something stronger than he imagined. The other barbarian kingdoms soon declined. The Ostrogoths were reconquered by the eastern emperor Justinian; the Vandals and the Visigoths were overwhelmed by the Moors. But despite the ups and downs of its subsequent history, the idea of the French nation, its government as a single kingdom, its attachment to the Catholic faith—these survived the Dark Ages to come. There may well be argument as to the honor and purity of Clovis' character. But there was greatness in his achievement. He set up a model for state-builders of future generations. And he did it "in the worst of times," in the midst of the consternation and the debris left by the fall of Rome.

In 511, at the age of forty-five, Clovis died in Paris, a barbarian become a king. He was buried in the Catholic Church which he and Clotilde had had built.

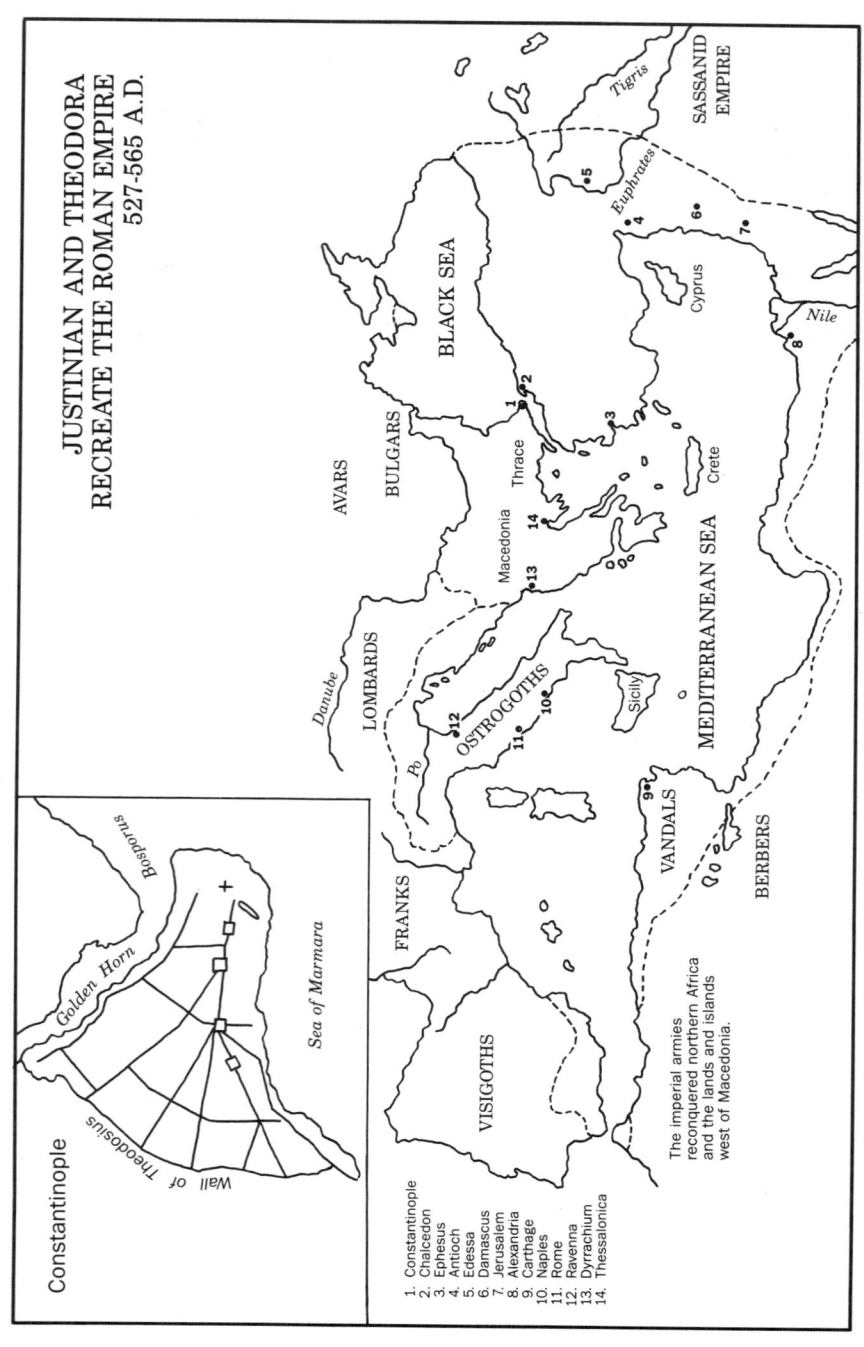

JUSTINIAN AND THEODORA
RECREATE THE ROMAN EMPIRE
527-565 A.D.

SASSANID
EMPIRE

Tigris

Euphrates

Nile

Cyprus

BLACK SEA

AVARS

BULGARS

Thrace

Macedonia

Crete

MEDITERRANEAN SEA

Danube

LOMBARDS

OSTROGOTHS

Po

Sicily

FRANKS

VISIGOTHS

VANDALS

BERBERS

The imperial armies
reconquered northern Africa
and the lands and islands
west of Macedonia.

1. Constantinople
2. Chalcedon
3. Ephesus
4. Antioch
5. Edessa
6. Damascus
7. Jerusalem
8. Alexandria
9. Carthage
10. Naples
11. Rome
12. Ravenna
13. Dyrrachium
14. Thessalonica

Constantinople

Bosporus

Golden Horn

Sea of Marmara

Wall of Theodosius

Chapter Two

RESTORATION:
JUSTINIAN
AND THEODORA
(482-565)

1. The world situation

One day in 537, from Rome where he was closely besieged by
Vitigis the able leader of the Ostrogoths, Belisarius, general-in-chief of
the armies of the Eastern Roman Empire, wrote an urgent letter to
Emperor Justinian in Constantinople:

> It was some fate that saved us, for supernatural deeds should be
> attributed not to human valor but to God. Thus far we have done
> well whether by fate or by our own courage; but as for what is to
> come, I would wish for better things for your cause....Let
> weapons and soldiers be sent to us in sufficient quantities to
> establish us on a basis of equality with our enemies....Think of
> this, my Lord: if the barbarians defeat us now, we shall be driven
> out of your Italy, and lose the army as well, and in addition shall
> bear the great shame of our failure....We should give the impres-
> sion of having abandoned the citizens of Rome, who have thought
> less of their safety than of their loyalty to your Empire....Hunger
> will force the Romans to do many things which they would rather
> not. I know it is my duty to die for your Empire, and for this
> reason no one will be able to remove me from here alive. But con-
> sider what kind of reputation Belisarius' death in such cir-

cumstances would bring to you. [This letter was reported by Procopius, administrative assistant to Belisarius, who became the leading classical historian of his time.]

The brilliant and conscientious commander in the distant battle, one of the greatest soldiers in all history, Belisarius is pleading that the government at home not forget him and that it reinforce him with the warriors, money, and equipment of which there never seemed to be an adequate amount. Belisarius knew Justinian intimately, their wives were devoted to each other. How much he suggests to us about the character of his lord and master. Justinian thought of the realm as his personal possession—*his* Italy, *his* empire. There was an almost magical quality about the idea of the Empire that demanded service of unusual devotion and imparted special dignity to Roman citizenship. His personal reputation was crucial to Justinian; he could not withstand the shame of the loss of Rome.

It may seem surprising that troops of the empire are once again in Rome so soon after its downfall to the barbarians. But we must remember that Clovis, although probably the most far-seeing and effective, was only one among numerous barbarian leaders whose tribes had settled only in Italy and the western provinces of the empire. The barbarian kings were all more or less in awe of the Roman emperor who still reigned in the fabled capital at Constantinople and whose lands around the eastern reaches of the Mediterranean Sea still appeared solid and secure. In other words, the entire empire had not surrendered abjectly and there were those who wondered why Roman wealth should fall uncontested to the avaricious but crude barbarians. Early in the 6th century the emperor Justinian and his consort dreamed that they might reverse the work of the barbarian invaders and reestablish the authority of the empire, in the west as in the east.

When we speak of people as being inspired by a sense of mission, the mission we usually have in mind is something bold, original, and adventurous — like the discovery of nuclear fission or the cure of cancer — or something visionary, idealistic, almost spiritual — like world disarmament or the abolition of famine. The mission which was said to "dazzle" the imaginations of Justinian and Theodora, and to which they devoted their lives with an unrelenting sense of duty, involved religion, Christianity, and political principle, the universal rule of the Roman Empire. But their mission was in no way a new invention; rather it was a task of re-creating what they thought had once existed. Prudentius, a Christian poet of the early 4th century, had described Roman rule as he remembered it:

Only concord knows God; it alone worships the beneficent father aright in peace. The untroubled harmony of human union wins his favor for the world; by division and cruel warfare it drives him away....To curb this frenzy God taught the nations everywhere to bow their heads under the same laws and become Romans. A common law made them equals....Rome without peace finds no favor with God. It is the supremacy of Rome, keeping down disorders by the awe of her sovereignty, that secures the peace so that God has pleasure in it.

This vision of the past — the peace, the law, the unity, the supremacy, the glory of the Christian Roman Empire — Justinian and Theodora might have taken as their plan and their goal for the future. Their mission was to restore and enhance the power and magnificence of the empire. Their opportunity was to build the dignity, prestige, and influence of the occupants of the imperial throne so that the emperor would be both absolute ruler and loving father of all Roman people.

2. Climbing to the throne

Neither Justinian nor Theodora was born to the imperial purple. He was born Petrus Sabbatius, in 482, near Bederiana in the mountains of Macedonia, east of the Adriatic in today's Yugoslavia. His forebears were farmers and herdsmen. Of Thracian origin and speaking Latin, they were part of the old empire. Although their trading was with the east, their outlook was thoroughly western and their attitude enterprising. Some years before his birth, his mother's brother, Justin, a young man of little learning but of strong intelligence and ambition, had gone to Constantinople to make his career in the emperor's army. He prospered and ultimately was to become commander of the bodyguard of Emperor Anastasius. Meanwhile his sense of family loyalty had moved Justin to welcome his nephew, aged ten or twelve, to the capital so that he could receive the best available education in Latin and Greek, under the auspices of the Church. Then, despite his lack of interest in the military, he was enrolled as a junior officer in the palace guards.

Gradually the serious and determined Petrus rose in rank and responsibility. He was made a patrician, the highest social status in the empire, and promoted to be the Count of the Domestics, the emperor's civilian staff, and a member of the consistory, or imperial cabinet. In 518, the aged and beloved Anastasius died, and the empire was faced with the choice of his successor. One of the pervading and most troublesome weaknesses of the Roman Empire was the lack of a generally acceptable procedure for determining the succession. Should the new ruler be chosen by acclaim of the populace or by approval of the Senate? Clearly he must enjoy the favor of the personal bodyguard, and later of the army, or his reign would be cut short. Justin had been the closest adviser of the childless emperor, but several other candidates were proposed.

It may well have been political and financial deals, masterminded by his nephew, that won the consent of the Senate and gained the throne for the rather stolid Justin. In any case, Justin relied more and more for political counsel and administrative efficiency on Petrus, who served as consul for the first time in 521, when he was reputed to have expended 4000 pounds of gold for bread and spectacles for the mob of Constantinople. Before long Petrus was heir apparent to his uncle and came to be known as Justinian. It is perhaps fair to say that, although not born to the throne, Justinian was selected and trained for it.

Meanwhile, so far uninterested in marriage and approaching middle age, Justinian, out for an evening of pleasure, happened to be introduced to Theodora. She came from a far less substantial social class than Justinian. Her father, an animal-keeper at the circus, was an employee of the Greens, one of two popular factions in the capital. When he died young, his destitute wife and three daughters were reduced to begging during the circus performances. The rival faction, the Blues, sponsored the three young sisters as public entertainers. The career of actress at that time was not respectable. Even if we disregard the malicious scandals reported by the aging Procopius in his later *Secret History*, it is clear that Theodora's youth was uncertain and disreputable. As an entertainer she was known for her good looks, quick wit, talented mimicry, and seductive behavior. It is probable that Theodora spent some time in Libya in the company of the provincial governor. Returning home alone, she reached Alexandria, where the patriarch Timothy took pity on her and gave her religious instruction. Back in Constantinople when she was introduced to Justinian, she was living modestly and apparently working as a weaver. Experienced with men and the world, she had gained self-confidence.

The attraction between Justinian and Theodora seems to have been instantaneous, mutual, and deep. To some extent, it was the proverbial attraction of opposites. In appearance, he was of medium height, tending to heaviness, with a plump face, grey eyes, and ruddy complexion. Small of stature, lithe and graceful in movement, she was somewhat pale but charming, with an oval face and large, expressive eyes. Still young and vivacious, she enjoyed social occasions; considerably older and more sedate, he was at heart unsociable. With a clever and practical turn of mind, she had learned to grasp problems in bold outline and to reach quick decisions. More the scholar, he elaborated theoretical schemes and allowed their intricacies and possible pitfalls to render him indecisive. While he was "a demon for work," Spartan in habit and abstemious in taste, she came to love ease and elegance. Remembering her years of wretchedness, she lived for the present and her own good fortunes; always mindful of his position in the state, he lived for the future and the effects of his actions on others. Attentive to his desires for quiet repose and thoughtful conversation, Theodora showed her appreciation of his friendly and generous care. Justinian delighted in her responsiveness to him, her fearless spirit, her penetrating view of human nature.

Promptly, Justinian made Theodora his mistress; henceforth, each was totally faithful to the other. He established her in the House of Hormisdas, with its view that she loved over the Sea of Marmara. Happy in her constant companionship, impressed by the intelligence with which she listened to all his ideas, inspired by her courage and optimism, Justinian called Theodora "a gift from God." It was his wish to marry her without delay, but several obstacles needed to be overcome. First, there was the adamant opposition of Empress Euphemia, who refused to countenance a marriage between the heir and an actress. Conveniently, she died in 524. Then there was the matter of class distinction. To be eligible for such an exalted marriage, Theodora must be a patrician, and this was decreed by a compliant Justin. And finally, a legal problem. The Senate was persuaded to make a special exception to the law that prohibited senators from marrying actresses. In 525, in the old Church of S. Sophia, Justinian and Theodora were married by the patriarch of Constantinople.

Within months, Justinian was declared co-emperor with his uncle. From Anastasius, Justin had inherited a powerful government with a sound system of taxation, a new defensive wall constructed across Thrace, and a surplus of 320,000 pounds of gold. As Justin grew older, he had given his nephew more and more authority in the setting and execution of policy. During what we can call this apprenticeship, Justinian had gained in patience and firmness of judgment, learned to work with a host of assistants and to identify those in whom to have confidence, and informed himself about all details of administration. Already, with we can presume the steady advice and encouragement of Theodora, Justinian was directing the use of the surplus in aid of citizens ravaged by earthquakes and in reconstruction and beautification of half a dozen of the most notable churches in the capital. He was contemplating revision and simplification of the legal code. He was laying plans for the repulse of the Sassanian rulers of Persia, who blocked eastern trade routes, threatened cities such as Antioch and Damascus, and sought to expand their influence in the northern lands between the Black and Caspian Seas.

The succession of Justinian was anticipated with general satisfaction. When his uncle died early in 527, his selection as emperor was uncontested. He was anointed by the patriarch in S. Sophia on 4 April. Then Justinian and Theodora were jointly crowned and acclaimed by the multitude in the vast Hippodrome, where Theodora had appeared twenty years earlier as a desperate suppliant. Emperor and empress then retired to the adjoining Sacred Palace, a splendid city within a city, insulated from the cares of the everyday world, where their every wish would be fulfilled and their every movement arranged by the Chief of Protocol, the Master of Offices, and thousands of retainers.

3. Plans of the new rulers

It is difficult to think of an historical figure who labored more constantly under a more profound sense of duty than Justinian. "It is the natural desire of a noble-minded Emperor," he wrote, "to enlarge the empire and render it more glorious." His authority was unquestioned. He was convinced of his obligation, for the good of his subjects, to uphold the truth of the Christian faith and the just rule of the Roman Empire. "A happy concord" between a pure Church and a benevolent State "will bring forth all good things for mankind." He envisioned his realm as a world-state which he would rule as God's unchallengeable vicegerent, directing policies himself to maintain the integrity and faith and culture of the Roman Empire. His power must be used wisely; his undertakings must be crowned with success.

Now Justinian had Theodora to wear a second pair of the purple shoes that were the exclusive symbol of majesty. First she brought a fresh elegance and vitality to the palace. It was clear that she wished to play a responsible part in the business of government and Justinian acceded to her desire. Devoted to her happiness, he was pleased to have her share his vision and he found her practical judgment and deft handling of people helpful. Although 6th-century Constantinople gave girls an excellent education and treated women as socially and intellectually equal with men, it came as a surprise to Theodora's associates to find her wielding imperial authority. There was no provision in the plan of government for the empress to share power with the emperor. But Theodora was determined and energetic, and she created her own court with a routine of public duties and audiences. She received reports and gave orders to government officials, attended meetings with her husband, appeared at his side in the frequent festivals that were a colorful part of life in Constantinople, greeted ambassadors from abroad and fascinated barbarian rulers with her beauty and extravagant entertainment. Her name was included with Justinian's in virtually all official pronouncements.

In numerous ways Theodora's style and talent complemented her husband's. Where he became known as the emperor "who never slept" and indeed seldom ate or drank, she was self-indulgent and made a ceremonial of royal meals. Her gorgeous raiment and glittering jewels contrasted with his drab attire. He was easily accessible to anyone requesting an audience, but she insisted on respect for royal dignity and rigid adherence to court etiquette. He was gentle and pliable with people, too good a listener; but she was hard to please or convince and trusted no one but Justinian. Her tenacity and will-power brought decision to his juggling of pros and cons. One could say that hers was the vital spirit that activated his theorizing mind.

To every observer Theodora exemplified both Justinian's power and her own genius. Her biographer, Charles Diehl, wrote: "At Justinian's side she held a significant place and often played a decisive role in the government, as a woman of unusual wit, rare intelligence, energetic will, a person despotic and haughty, willful and passionate, complex and often disconcerting, but always infinitely attractive." Chosroes of Persia is said to have inquired in consternation, "What sort of state is this Rome, that is governed by a woman?"

The plans of Justinian and Theodora were as sweeping as their view of the empire. To help put their plans into operation, Justinian was particularly skilled in finding men, often of undistinguished background, who had extraordinary talent. He hastened to enlist them in his service. Despite awareness of his suspicious and jealous nature, they worked for him with unusual fidelity, excited by their opportunity for notable achievement. There was Tribonian, the unscrupulous but learned jurist, who undertook the new coding of the laws. In Belisarius, Justinian found a general who could defeat the Persians and lay the groundwork for an enduring peace. He encouraged Anthemius to make expansive plans for the reconstruction of public works in the cities that had suffered severe earthquake damage.

Some of the imperial projects aroused fear or opposition by their novelty; all, added together, required a continuous outpouring of imperial funds. John of Cappadocia, as treasurer, collected taxes with ruthless disregard for honesty or individual tales of hardship. When farmers who had lost their fields in Thrace flocked to swell the ranks of the unemployed in Constantinople, and the distribution of free bread was reduced, cries of distress multiplied. It is not surprising that many of the protests centered on Theodora. She had risen like a rocket to a place of unprecedented and extra-constitutional prominence. Senators and others from the higher ranks of society were scornful of her mean origins and resentful of her power and haughtiness, the splendor of her wardrobe, and the obsequiousness she demanded from all. People from the lower ranks complained that vast amounts of wealth were expended for her personal comfort and adornment. Criticism of rulers easily grows into opposition to government.

4. The Nika Revolt

From the viewpoint of the empire as a whole, the excessive concentration in the capital of population, wealth, commerce, and authority produced an unbalanced and unrealistic political situation. The local politics of Constantinople could dominate the formulation and execution of policy throughout the realm; and local politics were directed by the rivalries of the Greens, who had abandoned Theodora in her youth, and the Blues, whom she and Justinian now obviously favored. The Greens are said to have represented land and the farming interest, the Blues, business and the trading interest. But their main occupation appears to have been going to the races at the Hippodrome, the open-air arena which accommodated over 30,000 spectators. At bottom, the Greens and the Blues were athletic clubs, whose fiercely loyal adherents gave unbridled vent to their emotions and to the tendency to rowdyism that athletic contests always seem to foment. In the evenings marauding bands of boisterous members in garish costumes roamed the streets and terrorized law-abiding citizens.

Because emperor and empress literally lived and worked in the midst of their capital city, they were never far from public view and always exposed to the fickleness and force of popular opinion. They made a habit of attending the games. Indeed, the Sacred Palace was connected to the Hippodrome by a covered passage and the Kathisma, or royal box, was located between the boxes occupied by the Green and Blue leadership. Rulers, therefore, could not fail to take note of the taunts and arguments that the factions exchanged. Indeed, they were permitted to address their protests or proposals to the royal box and to expect a response from a herald speaking on behalf of the government.

A gathering of the crowd in the Hippodrome was really a town meeting on a tremendous scale. So there was a distinct difference between Justinian's position in theory and in fact. Apparently absolute, isolated, impregnable, behind an array of functionaries and bodyguards, he was actually visible and vulnerable to unrest on an almost daily basis. The forces of potential revolution were always near at hand. Were a crisis to arise, could the reflective, mild, peace-loving Justinian, even with the aid of his capable but unpopular officials, act with prompt determination to resolve the conflict?

The answer to that question is "No" — at least without the assistance of Theodora. Early in January 532, personal insults were directed at Justinian in the Hippodrome as the crowd expressed the discontent engendered by hard times and heavy taxes. Later, anarchy broke out in the streets. Officials arrested the ringleaders but foolishly condemned only those who were Greens. When Justinian made the mistake of not granting a reprieve to the condemned men, the Blues made common cause with the Greens and rioted against the government. Probably their combination was directed in part by senators mistrustful of Justinian and disgruntled by his disregard of their traditional role in government. Fearful of this union of the factions and the Senate, Justinian acceded to the demand that he purge his administration of its most hated members, including the tax-collector, John of Cappadocia, and the lawyer, Tribonian.

Strengthened by this concession, the mobs shouted "Nika" — "Victory" and continued their street demonstrations against the government. Troops were ordered to attack, then to retreat. Fires broke out, and a cloud of smoke obscured the city for several days as churches, baths, and public buildings were destroyed. On 18 January, Justinian met a great concourse in the Hippodrome. He carried the Bible and admitted that his errors were the cause of all the trouble. But the crowd reviled him and he retreated. Popular leaders sought out Hypatius, a nephew of former Emperor Anastasius, crowned him in the Forum of Constantine, and led him to the Hippodrome, to be acclaimed in the Kathisma as their new emperor.

In the Palace the autocrat, irresolute, seemed on "the verge of downfall." What should be done? Could his government be saved? A ship was being secretly prepared for his departure, and he was counseled to escape with his treasure while there was yet time. Theodora, who had remained aloof from the discussion, at last spoke:

> We have no time to argue whether a woman's place is in the home or whether she ought to be meek and modest in the presence of the lords of creation. We must act without delay. My opinion is that this is no time for flight, not even if it is the safest course. Everyone who has been born has to die; but it does not follow that everyone who has been made an emperor has to get off his throne. If you want to make yourself safe, my Emperor, nothing hinders you. There lies the sea, and ships on it and money to pay your way. But if you go you may presently feel that you would have preferred death to safety. As for me, I stand by the old saying that the best shroud is a purple one. May I not live to see the day when people no longer call me Augusta.

After these words of practical wisdom from Theodora, with their interesting undertones of feminist conviction and proud determination, "there was no further word of flight." His courage renewed, Justinian ordered his generals Belisarius and Mundus into action. They led their special troops into opposite entrances of the Hippodrome and slaughtered most of the 30,000 surprised rioters. Hypatius was carried into the Palace, a prisoner rather than a ruler.

The gentle Justinian might well have pardoned Hypatius, who protested that he had been acting only to forestall an attack on the emperor, but Theodora insisted on the death penalty. Hypatius and his brothers were thrown into the Bosporus, other rebel leaders put to death, and the property of disloyal senators confiscated.

Theodora may have acted from selfish ambitions, but she had saved the throne. As Diehl wrote:

> On the day of crisis she had revealed herself a statesman superior in coolness and assertiveness to her husband. [She had] a profound faith, an admirable spirit, rare intelligence, resolute and strong will, despotic and impassioned, a fierce energy, manly strength, calm courage, which showed themselves at the very apex of most difficult circumstances. . . . She had a grasp of important affairs and the spirit to resolve them, a sharp awareness of the necessities of government and a clear view of the realities that were possible.

These events of January 532 were the most decisive in the lives of Justinian and Theodora. They guaranteed her authority and vividly defined the relationship of husband and wife. They established the supremacy of the imperial government over the city populace and the tradition-bound Senate. They laid the foundation of a wall of ceremonial that would separate and protect the rulers from the uncertain waves of popular feeling.

5. Achievements

Buttressed in power and prestige by the outcome of the Nika Revolt, Justinian and Theodora directed their energies to bold ventures.

a.) *Building*. We know a great deal about this because, near the end of the reign, Procopius wrote a detailed report "On the Buildings of the Emperor Justinian." The raging fires of the Revolt had left much in ruins. Some new construction was utilitarian in purpose: repairs to the defensive works of the emperor Theodosius, protective breakwaters for the harbor, vast cisterns underground to guarantee the water supply year-round. Some had immediate beneficial effect on the citizenry: hospitals, homes for the poor or aged, public baths, a public guest house.

To represent the greatness of an empire, what better than the splendor of its capital? There should be wide colonnaded avenues like Middle

Street, for the shops of thousands of skilled artisans who plied their crafts in cloth, metal, and jewelry. There should be spacious forums and court yards, adorned with statuary, for the people, as was their wont, to conduct their commercial, social, and recreational activities in the open air. There should be impressive buildings for institutions like the Library and Archives, the Senate, and the Law Courts, overlooking the Augusteum and providing a proper setting for the conduct of all public affairs. There should be statues of Justinian and Theodora and a magnificent Bronze Gate for the Palace. There should be dozens of churches in which the faithful citizenry could join their rulers in the proper worship of their true God, the Holy Trinity. Much of the construction was in a new style, and of generous proportions, and had a profound effect on the popular imagination. One building stood out above all.

Fire had destroyed the old imperial church of S. Sophia. Now there must be a new church of Holy Wisdom, on a hilltop toward the eastern end of the city, visible to all, a beacon to mariners far at sea. Justinian and Theodora challenged Anthemius and his fellow engineer and mathematician, Isidore of Miletus, to create a church unique in plan and dimensions, in richness of detail and decoration, in impact on the hearts and minds of people. Theodora pushed the project forward even when cracks appeared in a major structural element, and later a new roof had to be installed after the first collapsed because of defective materials. The new Sancta Sophia was a miracle of design and engineering, unequaled before or afterwards.

The new style was a daring departure from the dignified but heavy Roman basilica. The central space was an open 100-foot square, with conventional aisles on one pair of opposite sides but with semi-circular spaces extending 50 feet further on the other sides. Over the square, springing from the great corner piers, was a dome, 107 feet in diameter, soaring to a height of 170 feet above the floor. Circling the base of the dome were 42 arched windows, admitting an abundance of light, and giving the dome the appearance, as Downey says, "of being suspended from heaven." Unadorned on the exterior which exposes its geometrical shapes, S. Sophia was ornamented on the interior with an unparalleled array of materials from throughout the Empire, marbles and mosaics on the walls, elaborately wrought metal lamps, a golden table and jewels and cloth of gold in the sanctuary.

When he first realized the size and light and magnificence of the completed church, Justinian is reputed to have exclaimed, "Solomon, I have surpassed you!" At the dedication at Christmas 537, he proclaimed: "Glory be to God for thinking me worthy of such a work as this." The official historians were comparably impressed. Paul the Silentiary wrote: "Through the spaces of the great church come rays of light, expelling clouds of care and filling the mind with joy." Procopius, more reflective, explained: "Anyone who comes to pray realizes at once that it is not by human power or skill but by divine influence that this church has been wonderfully built. His mind is lifted up on high to God, feeling that he cannot be far away but must love to dwell in this place he has chosen. . . .When they are present in the building, men rejoice in what they see, and when they are away from it, they take delight in talking of it." For the imperial couple and for their subjects the startling impression was space and light, and the prevailing emotions wonder, pride, and joy. Byzantine architecture had created its masterpiece.

b.) *Law.* The body of civil law was a link with almost a thousand years of the Roman past and a symbol of the civilized order which the barbarian states lacked. Tribonian and his committee of legal scholars had been at work reviewing Roman laws in order to eliminate the complexities and contradictions that were producing delay and unfairness in the execution of justice. Already in 529, a *Code* had been published of all the laws currently in force. Viewing himself as the guardian of legal traditions, Justinian had too much regard for the past and too little awareness of changing times. We criticize this *Code* for disproportionate attention to ecclesiastical procedures and emphasis on the rights of the propertied classes.

But Tribonian's task was continuing. Next published, at the end of 533, was the *Digest*, which summarized and codified the decisions made by judges in the centuries past, and the *Institutes*, a textbook to be used in the schools for the study of the law. A year later, a revised Code of Justinian was produced, including recently-made laws. Further additions to the law, during the balance of the reign, were known as *Novels*. Justinian himself was a serious student of the law, with an exalted sense of the emperor's role in law-making. "What is there greater," he asked, "what more sacred than imperial majesty? Who so arrogant as to scorn the judgment of the Prince, when lawgivers have precisely laid down that imperial decisions have the force of law. . . .Who should be capable of solving the riddles of the law and revealing them to men if not he who alone has the right to make the law?" But he was earnestly committed to good government on the basis of fair and clear laws. Theodora's ambition was that he would prove to be "greater than Moses."

The *Novels* deal with civil matters such as local trial, prompt settlement of small suits, fair treatment of foreigners in trouble in Constantinople. They deal with ecclesiastical matters such as election and proper behavior of churchmen, tax-exemptions and legacies for poor churches. They deal with family matters and property such as marriage and divorce, wills and inheritance, the rights of children, punishment for swearing and blasphemy. The *Novels* were published in Greek, the everyday language of the capital, and show Greek influence in modifying the rigid Roman insistence on the authority of the *pater familias*. A number of them show the specific influence of Theodora, protecting the rights of dancers and actresses, providing benefits for divorced women, closing brothels with recompense to the managers and "a sober dress and a gold coin" for each occupant. Concern for the social problems of men and women runs through the *Novels*. Justinian wrote: "Since we are bound to have regard for the frailties of the human race, we mitigate corporal punishment and hereby forbid the cutting off of both hands or feet." He forbade building within 100 feet of the sea lest the views of others be obstructed. He prohibited the sale of arms to private individuals.

In his Preface to the *Digest*, Justinian described the two vital duties of any government as safeguarding the community from external enemies by arms and protecting people from internal maltreatment by laws. He often used the preface to a new law for public relations purposes, calling attention to a notable achievement or to the excellence of the legislation. He explained that a citizen should pay his taxes fully and punctually, so that a healthy treasury may promote "fair and harmonious concord between governors and governed." With extraordinary candor he admitted that all his laws were not perfect. "If we discover better solutions not merely than those enacted by others but even those previously enacted by ourselves, we are not ashamed to legislate afresh rather than wait for the law to be subsequently rectified by others."

The essential purpose of the *Novels*, and of the personal *Edicts* he issued to supplement them, was to provide orderly government, "without deceit or fraud" and without inflicting any hardship on the citizenry. Administrative reforms, for instance, halted the sale of political office and simplified the administration of the provinces. But the hand of the government was everywhere, controlling the daily lives of the people with troublesome regulations. The emperor put too much confidence in good laws as a means of correcting evil conditions. There was a large gap between what he aspired to do by rewriting the laws and what actual improvement of conditions he achieved.

Theodora realized that the corrupt tax-collecting of John of Cappadocia hurt both the public interest and the reputation of the government and so she schemed, with ultimate success, for his dismissal. Meanwhile, Justinian complained that only one-third of the taxes levied actually reached the treasury. The financial demands of the government for defense, for public works, for the elaborate bureaucracy and the magnificence of the court, could never be met. The desperate need for money prevented the exposure of corruption and prolonged the exploitation of the people.

c.) *Expansion*. Now a new element had to be included in the budget. In 535, Justinian pleaded for the faithful payment of taxes, "inasmuch as our military preparations and offensive measures against the enemy are urgent . . . for we cannot allow Roman territory to be diminished, and having recovered Africa from the Vandals, we have greater acquisitions in view."

Justinian, visionary and opportunist, was by then embarked on his plan to recover the empire of the west. Diplomacy — financial subsidies and regal hospitality, backed by territorial troops and border fortifications — was holding the barbarians at bay. Diplomacy, backed by an annual grant of 11,000 pounds of gold, was maintaining the Endless Peace with the Persians. Secure to the north and east, Justinian could look westward. Dissension in the Vandal kingdom in Africa gave him the first opportunity to pursue his most daring ambition. In June 533, Belisarius had set sail from Constantinople with 15,000 men carried on 500 transports. Landing unopposed, he occupied Carthage and then defeated the weak king Gelimer. Returned within a year, Belisarius led a procession like an ancient Roman triumph to the Hippodrome, where he presented to Justinian the captive monarch and his family and the treasure the Vandals had long ago seized from Rome. Africa was restored to imperial rule and Justinian had a medal struck to symbolize the reuniting of west and east.

The murder of the friendly Queen Amalasuntha precipitated Justinian's move against the Ostrogoths in Italy. Belisarius, again in command, occupied Sicily and captured Naples. He entered Rome late in 536 to the joy of its inhabitants, who had been unhappy under Gothic rule. But the skill and persistence of the new king Vitigis, plus breakdowns in the imperial pay and supplies system, prevented Belisarius from achieving the decisive victory. He did gain possession of Ravenna on the east coast, and the Gothic treasure, only to be recalled to Constantinople by a Justinian apparently resentful of his independent successes. Belisarius then campaigned inconclusively against the Persians, who had broken the Peace. Returned to Italy, where the Goths were again on the offensive, Belisarius reoccupied Rome but asked to be relieved of his command. The war in Italy dragged on for nearly 30 years. Although never given enough men and equipment, Belisarius and Narses, the later commander, held Rome, took Ravenna, expelled the Goths, repelled invasion by Franks and Burgundians, and reincorporated Italy in the empire. In thanksgiving, Justinian ordered mosaics of himself and Theodora to be installed in the Church of S. Vitale in Ravenna to honor their universal rule.

Justinian and his people saw reconquests in the west as his greatest glory. The Mediterranian, once again, was a Roman lake, where the merchant marine could trade freely, distributing the golden besants that became the universal currency. Possession of northern Africa guaranteed the food supply in Constantinople and new efforts could be made to import silk from the Orient, via Egypt and the Red Sea. Silk was then a product of great importance for its luxurious quality and, even more, as a mark of the wealth and prestige of its owners. Efforts to import it, circumventing the middlemen of unfriendly Persia, failed, but the silk-worm was smuggled in, about 555, to establish a local supply.

The costs of reconquest, however, were stupendous. The population of Italy was drastically reduced, cities ruined, and fields ravaged. John Lydas wrote: "The tax-gatherers could find no more money to take to the Emperor because there were no people left to pay the taxes."

d.) *Religion*. Justinian and Theodora together presented a rich gift to the Church at the high altar of S. Sophia. They said a prayer: "We Thy servants, O Christ, bring to Thee of Thine Own. . . . Strengthen us in the true faith; increase and guard this state which thou hast entrusted to us." To them the Church and the empire were two sides of the same coin. One guarded the beliefs and morality of their people, the other, the security and wealth. They, absolute rulers, directed both; in turn, they were responsible to God. "It is not in arms that we trust, nor in soldiers, nor in generals, nor in our own genius. We set all our hopes in the providence of the Holy Trinity." Unity in the Church, everyone thought in those days, was just as important as the unity of the state. S. Sophia was built as the awe-inspiring place in which all citizens could worship and, hearing the familiar liturgy, be filled with faith in the heavenly God and with pride in his earthly empire.

A creed held in common, a ceremonial followed in common, would bind together the diverse peoples and distant parts of the empire. Correct beliefs would win God's favor and produce both military victories and internal prosperity and happiness. Incorrect beliefs, or heresy, would cause divisions of sentiment and material disasters. So Justinian, said Bury, was "trying to identify Church and State more intimately, to blend them into a single organism." Procopius described his effort "to close all the roads which lead to error and to place religion on the firm foundations of a single faith." But religious unity proved harder to attain than military conquest or political centralization. Part of the explanation lies in the fact that in religious affairs, Justinian and Theodora were working at what often seemed to be cross purposes.

What was the "true faith?" Late in life Procopius wrote: "I hold it as a sort of mad folly to research into the nature of God. Even human nature cannot be precisely understood: still less can the nature of God. So. . . I will say nothing whatever about God save that he is altogether good and holds all things in his power." Not many achieved this dispassionate stance. Justinian was sure that peace and concord depended on a clear definition of God's nature. To his distress he found that his definition was not universally acceptable. Religious convictions dwell deep within people and are fiercely defended. Justinian found this helpful when as the leader of the regular Christians who believed in the Trinity he liberated Italy from Arian Goths who denied the Trinity. When he tried to send missionaries into the area where Africa and Asia meet, on the other hand, Justinian faced strong opposition.

The question was, how are the human and divine elements combined in the person of Christ who is at once the Son of God and man in the flesh? In 451, the council at Chalcedon had decreed that Christ is always one and the same but is recognized in two natures. But most Christians in Syria and Egypt, called Monophysites, maintained that the human nature was swallowed up in the divine. Fortunately, we do not have to join in this intricate argument, but only note that it plagued Justinian and Theodora throughout their reign. He supported the orthodox or official doctrine, not content that the peoples of the world be united as Christians but insisting that they be uniform in specific creed and daily practice. She, Syrian in origin and more tolerant in outlook, sympathized with the Monophysites and offered protection to their leaders.

The controversy, bound up also with the rivalry of Constantinople and Rome as the capital of Christianity, gave rise to much complex intrigue. For instance, Theodora prevailed on Justinian to appoint a monophysite as patriarch of Constantinople. When he was removed by order of the pope in Rome, Theodora secured the removal of the hateful pope and the selection in his stead of Vigilius, who then disappointed her hopes by turning into a staunch proponent of orthodoxy. She retaliated by securing the appointment of a monophysite bishop of Edessa who for 35 years spread his doctrines throughout Syria. Beliefs and personalities and politics were all entangled in this issue.

It was important to Justinian, as a devout theologian, to ascertain the essential tenets of Christian doctrine. So he held conferences of learned Church leaders in the attempt to find a happy compromise between the orthodox west and the monophysite east. He played an increasingly large role in these conferences, trusting in his personal ability to settle all disputes, not realizing that most people were not as concerned with doctrinal intricacies as in maintaining the beliefs of their homeland.

It was equally important to Justinian, as emperor, to consolidate his realm. So he decreed that all must accept the beliefs and abide by the sacraments as the emperor defined them. He knew that non-believers were in error; he viewed them, also, as potential menaces to social and political stability. One day, encouraged by Theodora, he made concessions to them. The next day he persecuted them, excluding them from office or from civil rights or even sending them into exile. He felt it "right that those who do not worship God correctly should be de-prived of worldly advantages too."

Although his reforms could assure that worthy men held clerical office and that Church property be secure, he could not legislate a creed. The mystery of faith does not yield to the hair-splitting logic of the theologian, nor does the fervor of a national creed long held yield to a doctrine imposed by a foreigner. Although he embellished the Church and increased its power, Justinian failed in his effort to bring all the sheep into one fold. Theodora, less visionary and more broad-minded, provided a sanctuary for discredited Monophysites and sup-ported the charitable work of the Church through its monasteries, hospitals, and houses for the poor.

6. Final years of Theodora and Justinian

The 540's were a turbulent decade. The new Persian king, jealous of the Empire, renewed the war, sacked Antioch, and threatened Edessa. Moors rebelled in Africa, Visigoths stirred in Spain, Ostrogoths under Totila created unrest in Italy. Barbarians were a constant menace on the northern frontier and had to be bought off with the usual gifts and state visits. The bubonic plague developed in Egypt and Syria and spread to Constantinople in 543. Five thousand victims are said to have died each day in the capital. Trying to sustain morale the rulers made countless public appearances, until Justinian fell desperately ill. With the succes-sion in question, the court officials took to quarreling in mutual mistrust and jealousy. Theodora nursed her husband and for months directed the government, following his policies. For instance, she persuaded the Per-sian commander Zabergan to halt his offensive by promising him a rich bribe and reminding him that "the Emperor never decides anything without consulting me." Unfortunately, Peter Barsymes, her choice as treasurer, had proved to be more honest than John of Cappadocia but equally exacting and therefore unpopular. Sometimes Theodora let her personal animosities cloud her judgment and resorted to shameless scheming to effect her wishes. Even Belisarius was temporarily in disgrace, falsely accused of plotting to overthrow the emperor.

As Justinian slowly regained his strength and resumed his respon-sibilities, it became obvious that Theodora was in failing health. She was away from the capital more and more, resting on the luxurious estates Justinian had built for her on the Asiatic side of the Bosporus. In 548, wasted by what modern doctors identify as throat cancer, she died.

Unconstitutionally perhaps, the imperial government had been a joint enterprise for Justinian and Theodora. Much of its direction and success had been owing to her bravery and tenacity, her wit and intelligence, her grace and sensibility, her creativity. Despite her excessive love of power, money, pomp, and display, despite her secret and sometimes vengeful manipulations, she was a clear-eyed observer of state affairs and an astute maker of public policy. Her hand was everywhere, strong and influential. As Diehl writes:

> Having come from the lowest depths, she learned to be, despite her faults and vices, a masterful Empress; from her stormy youth, by a strange and unexpected reversal, she developed a deep concern for serious affairs and care for public sentiment.

He sees her as a wiser judge than her husband of the resources and importance of the eastern provinces, of the dangers to the government of religious differences based on nationality, and of the need to curtail the expenses of western campaigning. Although aloof in personality, she urged a policy of compromise and concession rather than inflexibility.

Some were relieved at Theodora's death; others mourned deeply; Justinian was devastated. Ure comments: "Justinian lost his masterful wife, and with her he seems to have lost much of his hold on both men and situations." Alone, with narrowing vision and declining energy, he gave way to harmful habits: fond of intellectual discussion, he hesitated to make decisions; concentrating on details, he lost sight of his main objectives; without the accurate information Theodora's agents had collected, he became suspicious of virtually everyone.

In the remaining seventeen years of Justinian's reign, there was little fresh achievement. The task of uniting all citizens in a single Christian faith proved impossible. Fewer new buildings were planned; fewer new laws enacted. Not all was lost by any means. The government operated without the slightest relaxation of its impressive ceremonial; the emperor, officially, was almost a god. Commerce flourished, and the empire controlled the Mediterranean and the crossroads of Europe and Asia. Behind the Danube, defenses were constructed in depth against the Avars, Bulgars, and Slavs, and, with the genius again of Belisarius, an occasional victory was won. But the drain on manpower and resources was severe, and taxation so crushing that the provincials came to fear the tax-gatherers more than the enemy. Some barbarians were made allies, some assimilated into the imperial army. Although Menander said that Justinian destroyed barbarians without fighting them, Procopius complained that "Justinian wasted the riches of the Empire in extravagant gifts to the barbarians," who returned annually to ravage the land and the people and demand an ever-larger ransom.

Church and State were maintained, Christianity taken to the pagans, and the welfare of the people protected as much as possible. But the spark of vitality, inventiveness, and excitement had died with Theodora. Thenceforward Justinian seems to have been acting almost mechanically. The Macedonian peasant risen to the zenith of authority, he insisted at all costs on performing the emperor's essential duties of expanding and preserving the empire, glorifying and enriching the Church. He was the patron of the national heritage, Greek as well as Roman. His statue towering above the Forum showed him in the armor of Achilles, defending his vast realm against all barbarian assaults. In his hand he held the globe, surmounted by the cross.

It is easy to criticize Justinian. He was too authoritarian, not receptive to change or diversity, not sympathetic to local needs or desires. His reach far exceeded his grasp; his ambitions were too sweeping for the empire's resources. Diehl even called him "mediocre" in character — too fussy about details, vain, jealous, untrusting. But his accomplishments, we have seen, were significant. His greatest success was as a conservator of the prestige and traditions of the Roman past, which he believed represented the best that humanity could achieve. As an innovator, however, he improved the legal system with his *Novels* and inspired the new architecture of S. Sophia. Given his character and training, the goals he set himself, and the limitations of his means, it seems unfair to ask that Justinian accomplish more, that he have the foresight and vigor of an Old Testament prophet. But we may regret that he did not share more of Theodora's perceptiveness and tolerance, which might have liberated his rule from the constraints of the past.

In November 565, Justinian died, old and unpopular, but still conscientiously performing the tasks of ruling. Within a few years, the empire that Justinian and Theodora with ambition, labor, and good will had made so massive and splendid, began to give way to barbarian and Moslem attacks on the west and east. Even though the old Roman Empire could not be restored as Justinian had pictured it, we should remember that the core of the new empire would last until 1453 and Constantinople stand as the wondrous city of the Middle Ages.

Justinian and Theodora, then, had a long impact on history. As Barker summed them up, "Whatever their several faults, together they made one of the most extraordinarily gifted pairs of rulers the world has ever seen."

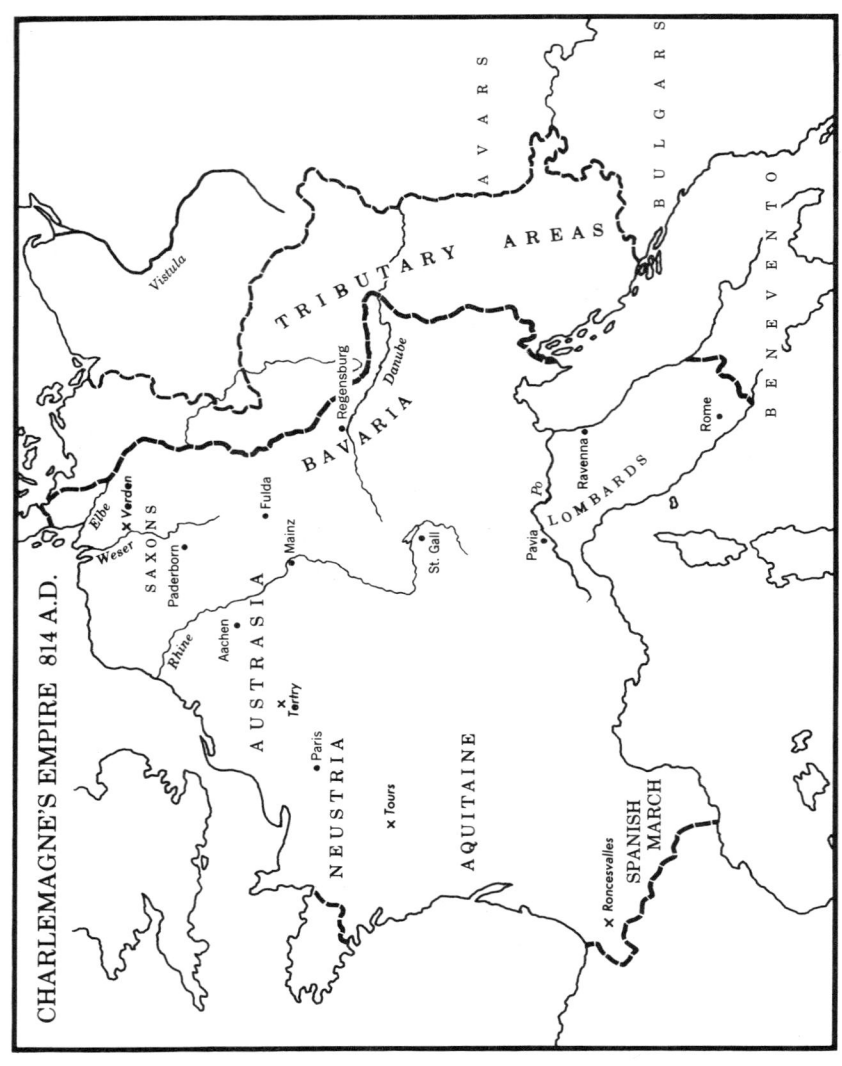

CHARLEMAGNE'S EMPIRE 814 A.D.

Vistula

AVARS

BULGARS

TRIBUTARY AREAS

Elbe

Weser
x Verden

SAXONS

Paderborn

Regensburg

Danube

BAVARIA

BENEVENTO

Rome

Ravenna

Po

LOMBARDS

Pavia

St. Gall

Fulda

Mainz

Rhine

Aachen

AUSTRASIA

x Tertry

Paris

NEUSTRIA

x Tours

AQUITAINE

x Roncesvalles

SPANISH
MARCH

Chapter Three

RENEWAL:
CHARLEMAGNE
(742-814)

Romancers of the 12th century made of Charlemagne a legendary hero, who could cut asunder a horseman and his horse with a single stroke, and eat in one meal a goose, two chickens, and a quarter of mutton. But Charlemagne did not need their fanciful exaggerations to spread his fame. Myths accumulate only around the greatest individuals. His actual achievement places him among the most impressive figures of European history in the Middle Ages.

Sometimes it is a great handicap to be born into a famous family. You inherit broad obligations, you are judged by the highest standards, and much is expected of you. Sometimes on the other hand, illustrious ancestors may be a great help to you, for they will have established a position in the world for you and will have done the preliminary work that sets the stage for your outstanding accomplishment. This was the case with Charlemagne. His family, which historians call Carolingian, was ancient and noble and rich. His was the fourth consecutive generation to produce a man of remarkable ability and vigor.

1. History of the Franks after Clovis

After the death of Clovis, it was only rarely and for short periods that the Frankish kingdom could be held together as one state. Parceling out the realm among a ruler's sons became the custom and, ultimately, the law. Many individual Merovingian kings were short-lived, necessitating regencies during the long minorities of their sons. Family strife was the rule, and the recurring plots and assassinations of civil war left the nation more and more disordered and weak. The realm was divided into two states, Austrasia to the east and Neustria to the west. In each, lawlessness spread as the royal power decayed. The Merovingian stock suffered progressive deterioration and the long-haired kings themselves grew more and more helpless. Gibbon says that they "ascended the throne without power and sunk into the grave without a name." Their authority slipped into the hands of the mayors of the palace, who combined the positions of major domo of the king's household and prime minister of his government. In theory executors of the king's will, they were in fact the king's master, and their office became hereditary.

In Austrasia the Carolingian family provided the mayor of the palace. Charlemagne's great-grandfather, Pippin, defeated the Neustrians in the decisive battle of Tertry in 687, which made him in effect, though not in name, the ruler of the Frankish nation. He consolidated his power and handed it on to Charlemagne's grandfather, Charles the Hammer. He it was who met the advancing Moors, fresh from their sack of southern Gaul. The Frankish footmen "stood immovable as a wall, or as if frozen to their places by the rigorous breath of winter, but hewing Arabs with their swords." Charles' victory at Tours in 732 ended the Moorish invasion and the possibility that western Europe would become Mohammedan in religion. Charles had three sons but, fortunately, one was caught in rebellion and killed and another entered a monastery, so that a unified state passed into the control of Charlemagne's father, Pippin the Short.

By this time the Merovingian king was only a shadow-man. Einhard says he "held only one manor bringing in a modest revenue . . . with a pension for his support, hardly assured and regulated by the mayor of the palace. . . . If there was need for him to travel anywhere, he went as the peasants did, seated in a wagon drawn by oxen and driven by a cowherd. It was thus that the king came to the general assembly of the nation." Everyone recognized this state of affairs as illogical, and the ambitious Pippin found it highly irritating. He who does the work of the ruler should enjoy his rights and prerogatives. And the Carolingians had unified the realm and protected it against the Mohammedans. Law and order existed by their efforts. Like Clovis, they were the champions of the Church and of the elements who desired political stability. The Frankish nobles were ready to obey Pippin as their king. The pope was consulted, lest anyone feel conscience-stricken, and he gave his consent. The last Merovingian was placed in a monastery, and Pippin was anointed at Soissons by the great missionary and legate of the Church, Boniface. Thus the *de facto* change from the rule of the Merovingians to the rule of the Carolingians was given a cloak of legitimacy. The change did not affect the ordinary person, and all those who mattered were pleased to have appearances brought into line with reality. Pope Stephen II visited Paris in 754 to mark his approval of what had been done. Charlemagne, aged twelve, escorted him from the Swiss border, and the pope anointed the boy as a royal prince in the Church of St. Denis.

When Pippin died in 768, Charlemagne might well have been grateful for his inheritance from the great Carolingians who had preceded him: their name and example as heroes, their well-organized and invincible army, their unified and obedient nation stretching from the Pyrenees Mountains to the Rhine River, their close alliance with the Church, their strong physique, firm will, and political experience. This rich inheritance represented work Charlemagne himself would not have to do; it would be the springboard for his own career. A single flaw marred the inheritance. Pippin's will divided his authority between his two sons, Charlemagne and Carloman. The young men were not friendly, but prospects of fatal division disappeared with Carloman's death three years later. Charlemagne alone carried the destiny of the Carolingian race; in him all their powers and all their virtues came to fullest maturity.

2. Expansion of Charlemagne's power and pacification of Europe

The first and obvious task of the new king was to maintain peace and order in his realm. Nor was this an easy task, for Charlemagne had to keep watch over four frontiers. To the southwest he was protected by the Pyrenees, but beyond them were the Moors filled with Mohammedan missionary fervor. To the southeast he was protected by the Alps, but beyond them were the barbarian Lombards, burning with ambition for dominance over all Italy, including the pope at Rome. To the east the frontier was long and natural barriers were few. Across the Rhine lay Frisia and Bavaria—territories nominally tributary to and dependent on the Franks but exposed to the disruptive pressures of the barbarians beyond. The most immediate threat to border security came on the northeast from the Saxons, whose paganism and loose tribal organization were contrary to the religious and political ideals of the Frankish regime.

Peace might be desirable, but in the 8th century war was the normal order of events and spring the season "when kings go out to battle." In the spring of 772, after Carloman's death had removed the danger of a schism in the kingdom, Charlemagne decided to take the initiative and attack the Saxons. Tribal levies could not stand up to trained soldiers, and the Franks drove deep into Saxon territory. They reached the holy place of the Saxons, the Irminsul, and destroyed the great tree which, tradition said, held up the roof of the world. But the independent spirit of the Saxons could not so easily be destroyed, and the work of subjugating them was not to be accomplished in a summer. As soon as Charlemagne himself departed, the Saxons began guerilla warfare in reprisal for the sacrilege at Irminsul, and against isolated armies in rough country guerilla warfare proved most effective.

Charlemagne would have liked to "mop up" the Saxons, but their fate was far from being his only concern. We know already that for the purpose of its own protection the Church desired the civil government to be strong and unified. For this reason it had accepted Clovis and had viewed with satisfaction the rise of the Carolingian mayors of the palace. After his own conversion, the first Pippin aided the work of English and Irish missionaries like Willibrod. Charles the Hammer, to be sure, boldly appropriated church lands and offices to his own uses, but his military might was indispensable to the safety and growth of Christianity. Boniface, whose zeal in "carrying the word of God to unbelievers" and in organizing new bishoprics made him the effective founder of the Church east of the Rhine and led to his martyrdom in Frisia, said, "Without the aid of the Prince of the Franks, I should not be able to rule my church, nor defend the lives of my priests and nuns, nor keep my converts from lapsing into pagan rites." The truth was that in those times the Christian Church would not flourish save under the protection of a strong Christian state. The only such state was the Frankish kingdom.

Pope Stephen recognized that he must rely on the Franks to preserve him from the rapacious Lombards. We have found him willing, therefore, to approve Pippin's seizure of the royal dignities. By begging for Stephen's approval, Pippin recognized the pope's importance and put himself under obligation to him. Stephen received his compensation when Pippin led a Frankish force into Italy and defeated the Lombards, saving the old Roman province of Ravenna from their grasp. Pippin went further by declining to recognize the rights of the Eastern Empire to Ravenna and by presenting it instead to the pope. "For the love of St. Peter" Pippin thus founded the States of the Church and the power of the pope as a temporal ruler. Some authorities have declared this "Donation of Pippin" to have been ultimately fatal both to the Franks, who were distracted from their real function in northern Europe by ambitions in Italy, and to the papacy, which was corrupted by its concern for worldly matters. In the short run, nevertheless, Pippin's action gained him much prestige and made the Frankish king the sword and shield of the papacy.

Now, in 773, a new king ruled in Lombardy. Desiderius had no love for Charlemagne, who had married his daughter and then callously put her aside. Again the Lombards sought to overthrow the papal power in Italy. And the new pope, Adrian, sent messengers to Charlemagne, beseeching his assistance. With a twofold motive, loyalty to the Church and ambition for widening his dominions, Charlemagne halted his campaign against the Saxons and moved an army in two columns across the Alps against the Lombards. He drove Desiderius back and bottled up his forces in his capital of Pavia.

While the siege was in progress, Charlemagne took the opportunity to make his first visit to Rome, at Easter 774. Adrian came out of the city to meet him, declaring, "Blessed is he that cometh in the name of the Lord." No mortal ruler could fail to be impressed by such a greeting. And even the warlike Lombards must have trembled when they saw the array of Charlemagne's armed might. The Monk of St. Gall, whose narrative was one of the earliest contributions to the Charlemagne legend, describes the effect of his approach: "When you see an iron harvest bristling in the fields, and the Po and the Ticino pouring against the walls of the city like the waves of the sea, gleaming black with glint of iron, then know that Charles is at hand." After ten months, Pavia fell. Charlemagne assumed the iron crown of the Lombards and confirmed Adrian in possession of the papal states. Charlemagne stood forth as the arbiter of the fate of Italy and the champion of the Church.

It was thus with new zeal and vigor that Charlemagne returned to the problem of the Saxons. Against them he considered he was fighting for himself as king and for the Church as its great, and indeed unique, secular agent. He saw his double duty: first, to pacify the land even beyond the Elbe River, to divide it into counties and to found in it cities obedient to the Frankish king; second, to incorporate this vast land and its population in the kingdom of Christ. Charlemagne decreed "Christianity or death" for the Saxons. In 782 he enacted a law of uniformity for them. All were ordered to conform to the Christian faith; the tithe, or church tax, was to be universally collected; the death penalty was imposed on those who continued their pagan practices. Charlemagne's inflexible resolve to conquer and convert the Saxons brought forth this harsh law. It also brought forth maximum counterefforts by the enemy, under their skillful leader Widukind. This opposition to his will aroused Charlemagne's temper and moved him to a rare act of inhumanity. As the result of a fierce battle at Verden, near the River Weser, 4500 of Widukind's foremost followers were his prisoners. He ordered them to be massacred. This slaughter incited still further rebellion, and Charlemagne felt obliged to spend a winter among the Saxons ravaging their lands. At last Widukind submitted to Charlemagne's superiority in numbers and organization and accepted conversion to Christianity. The desperate struggle of the Saxons to preserve their independence failed.

Even so, the Saxons were not wholly subdued. From 792 on, there were a number of Saxon uprisings in which they enlisted the aid of the Frisians. Of the total of over fifty campaigns in which Charlemagne engaged, more than one-third had to be devoted to checking the Saxons. Their final submission did not come until 803. To ensure the hard-won peace, which included the Saxon acceptance of Christianity, Charlemagne adopted harsh but effective measures. Many young Saxon men, taken from their homes as hostages, were trained for the clergy in Frankish church schools. Something over 10,000 of the wildest Saxons from east of the Elbe were forcibly displaced to distant Flanders.

Charlemagne announced, "We have reduced the country into a province." And well might he boast, for this pacification of the lands beyond the Rhine was a task the Roman Empire at its strongest had failed to effect. In rendering the Saxon lands a province, the armies of Charlemagne by their depredations had almost rendered them a desert. Nevertheless, they had advanced the frontiers of civilization at the expense of barbarism. With the establishment of bishoprics, towns like Bremen, Munster, and Paderborn began to grow around their cathedrals. From the Elbe, the Franks could take quick measures against the tribes stretching along the Baltic as far as the Vistula River. Yet Charlemagne's success was not complete. He tried to legislate conformity and to enforce it with the death penalty. Human history teaches the folly of such measures. Resentment smoulders and the law will be broken. The Saxons were never transformed into a willing and peaceful component of the Frankish dominion.

Long before the quelling of the Saxons Charlemagne had met other threats to the internal and border security of his kingdom. Some local lord chafing under the Frankish supremacy could always stir up trouble. At the very outset of his reign Charlemagne had had to wrest the province of Aquitaine from its independent-spirited duke and subject it to the supervision of Frankish officials. Later, in 778, to take part in the quarrels of the two Arab families seeking domination in Spain, Charlemagne marched his army over the Pyrenees. His Franks proved their fighting mettle, but the expedition produced little concrete gain save for the establishment of military posts in Barcelona and Pamplona to serve as Frankish footholds across the mountains.

One other result of this campaign should be noted. Returning through the mountains, the rearguard was set upon by the Basques, who cut it to pieces with the slaughter of many Frankish notables. This event is narrated in probably the most celebrated of all medieval romances, the "Song of Roland." Thus Charlemagne's sharpest reverse is given an immortality denied to most of his victories.

The area subject to Charlemagne's control was vast, and the bonds connecting its diverse inhabitants were weak or nonexistent. They had no common loyalty, no spirit of nationalism nourished by centuries of traditions. Even in language they were many people, not one. Communication between distant parts of the realm was painfully slow, and large land-owners had tremendous local power and influence. Gauls, Lombards, Saxons, Romans, Franks could not be expected to think and feel alike. But each individual group, and often an individual province, had its own fierce pride and local tradition. Without submitting to such separatist tendencies, Charlemagne recognized them and even attempted to cater to them. He would not divide his authority in fact; he did divide it in name. Spending Easter of 780 in Rome, his younger sons were baptized by the pope, Pippin was named king of Italy and Louis, king of Aquitaine, in the hope that the populations would be pleased with the semblance of separate governments.

The doubtful loyalty of Bavaria created another trouble spot. Its Duke, Tassilo, had acknowledged the overlordship of the king of the Franks, but his actions repeatedly denied his words. He failed to provide the support he promised his overlord in battle, and he was conspicuously friendly toward the deposed Desiderius of Lombardy, one of whose daughters he had married. Overawed by Charlemagne's power, Tassilo renewed his vows of submission, but he could not keep his word. Finally in 788 he was brought to trial for treason, removed from his position, and forced into a monastery. Bavaria then fell under the effective administration of Charlemagne, who made Regensburg a great trading center.

Meanwhile, 787 had been a busy year. A Moorish invasion aimed at Toulouse had been repulsed. And a campaign in southern Italy had been required to chastize the Duke of Benevento. This noble saw the Franks protecting the papacy and blocking his plan to expand his power northward. The defeat of his army, however, forced him to pay tribute and to abandon his schemes for a private kingdom in Italy.

Even within Charlemagne's own family disruptive tendencies were at work. His oldest son, Pippin, perhaps illegitimate, obviously a cripple and therefore scorned in a world of warriors, had suffered from the slights of his stepmother Fastruda. This lady has been accused of "diverting her husband from the kindness and accustomed gentleness of his nature." Her cruelty to Pippin drove him to conspiracy, but his plot was discovered and he was sentenced to a monastery, where he died before his father.

Charlemagne now undertook a major political and religious

effort—a crusade against the heathen Slavs of southeast Europe. Of these, the Avars in modern Hungary were the most dangerous and warlike. From their distant strongholds they, like the Huns or the Mongols, could launch devastating raids in force on the civilized lands to the west. Several campaigns were made against them before Charlemagne's son, the younger Pippin (not the Hunchback) gained the decisive victory in 796. He captured their central stronghold, the Hring, surrounded by many concentric circles of fortifications, and brought back as spoils the plunder the Avars had collected. Charlemagne had made civilization and Christianity safe to the Danube River.

This list of military activities may give an inaccurate impression of Charlemagne. We may wonder how he earned the title "pacific," especially when we note the year 790 singled out by the chroniclers as that extraordinary thing, a year of peace! But we must remember that Charlemagne did not go to war lightly, for pleasure or pillage. He fought only for reasons of state — to round out his realm to defensible frontiers, to stabilize his government, to protect and spread Christianity. By 796, his military career was largely over. The net results of his campaigns were the general pacification of Europe, the expansion of Christianity, the consolidation of the realm under his peaceful sway. Europe might well benefit from the unified rule of Church and State which Charlemagne imposed on it.

3. Personality and purpose of Charlemagne

Meanwhile, what of Charlemagne himself, this new master of all Christian Europe? For one who lived so long ago in an age when little history was written, we know a great deal about Charlemagne, even to the intimate details of his life. His long reign and great influence have induced much study about him. More important, the dwarf Einhard who was continuously at his master's side, wrote his biography. Here is part of the portrait which Einhard painted for us:

> He was tall and strongly built . . . his head was round, his eyes large and lively, his nose somewhat above the common size, his expression bright and cheerful. Whether he stood or sat his form was full of dignity; for the good proportion and grace of his body prevented the observer from noting that his neck was rather short and his person rather too fleshy. His tread was firm, his aspect manly; his voice was clear but rather high-pitched for so splendid a body. His health was excellent . . . to the very last he consulted his own goodwill rather than the orders of his doctors, whom he almost hated because they tried to persuade him to give up roast meats. . . .

This is a handsome, alert, friendly man, slightly self-indulgent or at least scornful of the quavering warnings of physicians. Most people would like him. As a Frank, Charlemagne naturally had a strong and active physique, trained by outdoor exercise. He rode and hunted diligently, and Einhard mentions his uncommon ability in swimming, of which sport he was especially fond. Charlemagne's vigor of body was matched by his vigor of mind, which is the characteristic that sets him apart from his contemporaries. Charlemagne was interested in everything and everbody. Einhard says that he welcomed so many foreigners to his court "that their number often seemed a real burden . . . to the realm." Gibbon mentions his "familiar connection with the subjects and strangers whom he invited to his court to educate both the prince and people." His mind was always open to ideas, both old and new.

This was the Charlemagne whose mind formed the concept of a united Europe, whose will drove him forward to the dozens of tasks necessary to bring his concept to reality. He organized Europe according to his own vision and by means of his own incessant activity. He seemed to be everywhere at once, so that according to Gibbon, "his subjects and enemies were astonished at his sudden presence, at the moment when they believed him at the most distant extremity of the realm." Everywhere he acted with firm decision and maintained his dignity as a ruler. Withal there was no false ostentation about him. "Temperate in food and drink," he lived simply, scornful of superfluous luxuries. He dressed like the Frankish nobles, in linen shirt, long trousers, and coat with a silk border. It was not display, it was strong character and effective action that won Charlemagne the respect of the world.

What role did this architect of Europe plan for himself to play? It is impossible to give a conclusive answer to this question, for here we confront the historical axiom that the individual, however great, is not completely the master of his or her own destiny. The state of the world, the character of the times, the mind of the mass of people, modify the intentions of the great individual. And history is shaped by the interaction of the person and the situation.

In western Europe life had been growing increasingly hard for the last several hundred years. The old Roman roads fell into disrepair, commerce stagnated, and cities decayed, lands were wasted, ignorance and disease spread, and the population declined. Crime and private war multiplied, and all went to sleep trembling lest their fields, their homes, and their very lives be ravaged before they woke. These were the Dark Ages, when the light of Roman culture had been almost extinguished and most could find no relief from poverty and misery. There was little difference then between the life of humans and the life of animals, except that the former had the power to recognize their wretchedness, and a few of them had the will to refuse to accept it. In their insecurity, these few dreamed of a time of peace and order. Such a time had been known only in the days when Rome ruled the world. Barbarian kings had since acquired some of Rome's authority, but their rule had always been limited, tentative, partial, a matter of expediency rather than of right. These local Germanic kings had fought amongst themselves, and Europe had relapsed into chaos.

So far no one had been able to reproduce the Roman Empire, but no one could forget it. As Bryce describes it: "The idea of a Roman Empire as a necessary part of the world's order had not vanished; it had been admitted by those who seemed to be destroying it; it had been cherished by the Church; it was still recalled by laws and customs; it was dear to the subject populations who fondly looked back to the days when despotism was at least mitigated by peace and order. . . . The False Prophet [Mohammed] had left one religion, one empire, one commander of the faithful: the Christian Commonwealth needed more than ever an efficient head and center." What city but Rome could serve?

4. The imperial idea

Charlemagne was at Paderborn. Pope Leo III came to him there in 799 to request his intervention in the turbulent politics of Rome. The pope's independence, even his personal security, was menaced. There was a numerous faction which was conspiring to dethrone him. He had been set upon in the streets, beaten, and left for dead. Barely had he made his escape, and now he came for succor to Charlemagne, the only ruler strong enough to defend the Church from the power of ambitious Italian lords. Already Charlemagne had been called, in official documents, "Lord and Father, King and Priest, the leader and guide of all Christians." Now he responded quickly to Leo's appeal. Both from personal conviction and for reasons of policy, Charlemagne was sincerely interested in the welfare of the Church. He believed in the closest possible alliance of Church and State. Earlier he had written to Leo, explaining his policy: "It is ours with the help of the divine piety to defend the Holy Church of Christ by our arms from all pagan inroads and infidel devastation, and internally to fortify it by the recognition of the Catholic faith. It is yours . . . to help our warfare." This very spring, Charlemagne's old friend Alcuin, now abbot of the Monastery of St. Martin at Tours, had written: "Now on you alone the salvation of the churches of Christ falls and rests." Clearly the troubles at Rome called for action by Charlemagne. Bolstering up the orthodox Church and the legitimate pope would be for him congenial work.

In November 800, Charlemagne made a royal entry into Rome, to be present when Leo should answer his accusers in open court. In December, an emissary came from Jerusalem bearing to Charlemagne the keys of the Holy Sepulchre. This mission seemed prophetic. The atmosphere of the city was one of anticipation. Charlemagne cannot have failed to be aware of an impending great event and to suspect what that event would be.

On Christmas Day, Charlemagne knelt in prayer at the altar of the Church of St. Peter. Suddenly the pope took from the altar the Roman crown and placed it on Charlemagne's head. "To Charles, most pious and august, crowned by God, the great and peace-bringing Emperor of the Romans, be life and victory," prayed the pope. The congregation roared its acclamation.

Thus, the successor of St. Peter gave the imperial crown to the ruler of Europe. Rome, the ancient imperial city and the center of the Catholic Church, was now the coronation city of the revived empire. The crown bestowed in Rome carried with it the accumulated prestige of Rome's majestic past. The true Roman Empire was alive again; the Dark Ages since 476 were simply an intermission between its former glories and the greater glories yet to come. Both temporal and spiritual power would be exercised by Rome, once again the capital of the western world.

This crowning of a Roman emperor by a Catholic pope was a brand new phenomenon. No law permitted it, nor can we explain in any other way precisely how it came about. Charlemagne did not conquer the imperial throne, for no emperor existed from whom he could seize it. The pope did not grant him the crown out of gratitude for his services, for the crown was not the pope's to give. The people did not choose Charlemagne for their emperor, for no election was held. And yet all three — king, pope, and people — favored the crowning. There might exist no right or principle by which to justify it, but Leo's action expressed the spontaneous desire of the populace that their ruler should be clothed with the traditional authority of Rome. The crowning might not be legitimate, but it developed inevitably from the existing state of affairs. It was supremely reasonable. As Bryce says, the "possessor of the real power should be clothed with the outward dignity also. . . . Charlemagne [was] the hero who united under one sceptre so many races, whose religious spirit made him appear to rule all as the vicegerent of God." He should have the highest title imaginable. It was only commonsense to call him emperor, to acknowledge his "overwhelming greatness." More perhaps than any other human event, the crowning of Charlemagne by the pope was done by "the will of God." At least, so people felt in 800 A.D.

The chief effect of the elevation of Charlemagne to the imperial throne was symbolic. It did not add one acre to his dominions. In no way did it increase his practical power. Yet it had a profound and lasting significance. To the authority of Charlemagne the Emperor it gave a legitimacy, almost a sanctity, which Charles the Warrior had not possessed. As nearly as any mortal can, Charlemagne became omnipotent. To break his laws would be heresy, the denial of God's moral commandments. Charlemagne was now the lord of Europe, the protector not only of cities and frontiers but also of God's plan for the future of the world. To Europeans, he was the symbol of their common destiny, the God-given master of Christendom. The revival of the Roman Empire marked the victory of faith over paganism, of unity over localism, of order over chaos. History, after centuries of uncertainty, might now resume its forward progress.

Charlemagne had succored the pope, and the pope had crowned him emperor. The State had upheld the Church by physical action; the Church had upheld the State by moral influence. Church and State should be fused together, so that their laws would be one law, controlling the lives of the people united in a Christian Europe. The duty of the Church was to pray for the salvation of the people. The duty of the emperor was to rule the people, to protect both State and Church, and to guide the Church in the path of true doctrine.

There was this very high idealism in Charlemagne's conception of his empire. In 802 he directed that all men over twelve should swear a new oath to him. This oath was to be "not merely a promise to be true to the emperor and to serve him against his enemies, but a promise to live in obedience to God and His law . . . a vow to abstain from theft and oppression and injustice, no less than from heathen practices and witchcraft . . . a vow to do no wrong to the Churches of God, nor to injure widows and orphans, of whom the Emperor is the chosen protector and guardian."

This all-inclusive oath indicated the broad field in which Charlemagne thought his empire should function. It would concern itself with sins against morality no less than with crimes against society. A citizen must obey the emperor not only as the head of the State but as the guardian and defender of the Church. The emperor assumed control over the religious and moral and social life of his subjects, as well as over their political life. His personal role in the empire was one of unquestioned supremacy. Charlemagne's plan was magnificent: the efficient, unified political system of Rome was to operate under the direction of the Christian spirit. Could he carry out his plan? It was similar in many respects to Justinian's, but it had a different geographical focus and it was to face different kinds of opposition.

5. Political organization of Charlemagne's empire

We must examine now the structure of Charlemagne's empire, by which Europe was to be ruled. Essentially, the emperor was no different from the Frankish king, save that the area of his authority had been expanded and he had been given a more impressive title. By conquest, Clovis had made Gaul his private domain, in which the king's word was law. Theoretically, then, the emperor was an absolute ruler and the empire would be governed in accordance with his decrees. In practice, Charlemagne issued a steady stream of orders. These were of two kinds: laws, to be obeyed by the various peoples in the empire; and capitularies, or regulations prescribing the ways and means of imperial administration. Most of these laws were executed by the local officials we shall mention, but certain of them came under the immediate supervision of the emperor. Desertion from the army, sacrilege, wronging the poor or widows or orphans, were considered offenses against the king's peace and came directly under crown jurisdiction.

Charlemagne himself, the lawmaker, was the supreme judge, who sometimes administered justice personally and, on occasion, most informally. Einhard tells us: "While he was putting on his shoes or his cloak, he not only admitted his friends, but if the Count Palatine stated a case which could not be determined without his order, he bade the litigants be brought in at once, heard the case, and delivered judgment, just as though he were sitting in court." In this personal role of the emperor in the making and the execution of the law are the signs of despotism, but Charlemagne did not abuse his vast power. His autocracy was tempered by his own respect for the law and adherence to Christian morality and by his sense of responsibility for the welfare of his people.

Furthermore, of course, the job of governing the empire was far too large for one man. The extent of his personal control would depend on his success in enlisting exact and loyal agents of his will. To this end, Charlemagne attempted to create a hierarchy, or organized group, of administrators, each one assigned to a particular job and rewarded and respected according to its importance. Immediately surrounding the emperor were the palace officials. Of these, the most important was the count of the palace, or Count Palatine, who might serve as chief justice in the emperor's place. To handle the normal business of the government — letters, orders, and records — there were two officers: the archchaplain for religious affairs and the chancellor, or secretary who guarded the royal seal, for non-religious affairs. These two were in intimate relation to each other, for it was the Church alone that could provide the chancellor with the necessary education for his duties. Usually the government's records were preserved in the vaults of the royal chapel. Financial affairs were in the hands of the chamberlain, who was also charged with guarding the ruler's personal treasure.

These officials, with others less important such as the seneschal and constable, were experienced in the routine business of government, and administration could normally be carried on without the necessity of any extraordinary decisions of state. Occasionally, however, these officials met, with certain other invited dignitaries, as a council to advise the emperor. They formed what we might call a permanent cabinet. Relying on them, the emperor only rarely needed to call for the opinion, advice, or assistance of the local leaders scattered throughout the realm. Therefore, the popular assemblies by which the Franks had once been ruled declined in frequency and in significance. The only essential assembly was that of the warriors, preparatory to the summer's campaign.

The laws decreed at the imperial court had to be enforced in the far outlying districts of the empire. For this purpose, the basic administrative division of the realm was the county. Border counties, exposed to invasion, were known as marches and were governed by margraves who were virtually military dictators. The more peaceful counties of the interior were in the hands of counts. The count was most often a noble of wealth and influence in his district. He was selected by the emperor as the chief local representative of the royal government. He was responsible for law-enforcement, he held courts, he saw to the collection of taxes; he was charged with the maintenance of peace and order. He had the assistance of one or more viscounts and of a number of secretaries, investigators, tax-collectors. Originally these had composed a sort of traveling government. In Charlemagne's time, some of the subordinate officials were established in the various towns of the county as permanent municipal magistrates. But all the reins of local government were ultimately in the hands of the count.

For the conduct of church business there was a parallel organization. The realm was divided into provinces and dioceses, under the supervision of archbishops and bishops, who ruled from their cathedral cities. There were also monastic foundations, ruled by abbots and independent of the bishops. It was the emperor who selected the bishops, as he did the counts, and without his approval the abbots could not be elected. It was his authority that sanctioned the regular collection of the tithe, for the support of the Church. So it may be seen that the religious officials formed another hierarchy, dependent on Charlemagne and prepared to give effect to his wishes.

In the vast authority exercised by counts and bishops, there was a strong tendency to decentralization. Charlemagne perceived the danger that the decisions of the imperial government might be thwarted or ignored in the local administrative districts. Therefore, he appointed from time to time a number of *missi dominici*, or crown inspectors. These traveled about the country in pairs, one for secular affairs, one for religious. Together they made a commission of investigation and a court of appeals. Acting as the direct representatives of the emperor, they questioned the local administrators. They made sure that the proper percentage of the revenues was being transmitted to the imperial treasury. They administered crown justice and heard appeals from the local courts. They listened to any complaints of the population against the government. Owing their authority solely to the emperor, and not at all to local favor or prestige, they could enforce the equal and fair execution of imperial laws in the various districts.

By means of these inspectors, Charlemagne checked up on his counts and bishops. At the same time, the inspectors could exercise on individual subjects "the needful care and discipline" which he himself could never hope to exercise. A capitulary of 802 announces that he has chosen as inspectors "the wisest and most prudent men ... and has sent them throughout his kingdom.... Moreover, where anything established by law seems to be other than right and just, he has ordered them to seek this out most zealously and let him know about it; he desires, God willing, to reform it." The inspectors were the strongest links in the chain binding the empire into a unified whole.

Despite the institution of the inspectors, efficient control over county governors and equitable enforcement of imperial decrees remained problems which Charlemagne, and the Middle Ages, could never solve. The empire's population was composed of many groups diverse in custom and stage of civilization. Traditional enemies might find themselves neighbors. The language of the count might well not be that of the emperor. His ambitions, and those of his district, might well seem obstructed by the supreme power of Charlemagne. The county was more interested in itself than in the empire.

Under such conditions centralized rule was impossible; effective government of any kind was most difficult. Charlemagne, for instance, might have the laws of the several nations written down and might work to eliminate differences between them. But he could not produce a single legal code for the whole empire. It would have been neither understood nor obeyed. His laws had to allow for tribal or provincial customs, traditional rights, and local institutions. For their enforcement he had to rely on the personal justice of the great men of the local scene. The unity provided by the inspectors was unity brought from outside, from a court often considered foreign; when the inspectors moved on, the count might ignore their instructions with the heartfelt approval of his people.

The oath which Charlemagne required all his subjects to swear to him was a long forward step toward unity, but it was a unity imposed from above, not spontaneously felt. In ancient days the Roman's proudest boast had been the simple statement, "I am a Roman citizen." This had served to identify, to protect from local injustice, and to give a superior status. In Charlemagne's time, people were not attracted by this idea of citizenship in a super-state. Instead, each important individual desired to carve out a private domain. The statement he or she would like to make was, "I am lord of all I survey." Rather than serve Charlemagne's Empire, the subjects wanted to gain independence from it.

There were other difficulties in the way of the imperial government. The first of these was the matter of money. To carry on the government, and especially to finance the continuous military campaigns, was expensive. Paper money which we use today was, of course, not even thought of in 800. Gold and silver coin was extremely scarce. Private and institutional wealth, such as it was, consisted entirely of jewelry or the gold and silver vessels of the churches, and was, consequently, not easily "negotiable" — that is, it could not be used for daily business transactions. How then were the expenses of the government to be met? Whenever feasible, taxes and court fees were imposed and collected in coin, but the income from these was small and irregular. The counts were only required to send two-thirds of what they collected to Charlemagne, the other third they retained for the expenses of their local administration. After a successful war, indemnity might be levied on the vanquished, and certain tribes were required to pay tribute to the Empire. In time of special need, voluntary gifts might be requested, or even demanded, of the churches or wealthy landowners.

On the whole, however, ready money was extremely hard to come by. The economy was, of necessity, a barter economy—that is, you traded your excess grain for a pair of shoes. And it was an economy of scarcity—that is, each landowner produced what was needed for personal support and laborers, and no more, for excess could not be sold. From the general rule that "a lord should live of his own" the emperor was no exception. The produce of Charlemagne's private domain was the major support of his government; because the government was large and elaborate, the produce must be large. And it was never large enough. It was impossible for Charlemagne either to maintain his officials from his own estates or to pay them in money. But the services of the counts, particularly, could not be dispensed with; without them, the sway of the central government would not exist.

The solution is obvious, when we remember that the chief wealth of an agricultural civilization is land and that Charlemagne, by conquest, owned a great deal of land. He planned, therefore, to pay for the services of his officials by granting them benefices—certain tracts of crown land, of which they were to have the use and the income. In this way Charlemagne hoped to build up his hierarchy of administrative officials. He would repay their service with land; when their service ceased, the land would return to him. A new and capable servant of the State would be rewarded with the lands formerly enjoyed by the disloyal or incapable or deceased servant replaced. Charlemagne would thus have immediate and effective control over his subordinates, in that he could take away their source of income. The administrators must do his will because they would be dependent on his favor.

As Bainville puts it, Charlemagne "wished to dominate what he could not destroy." The economy of the times saddled him with the necessity of paying for service with land, as was the universal practice. He must make sure that final control over the land did not slip from his grasp. The benefices must be revocable, when the duties for which they were granted were no longer being performed. As soon as the holder of a benefice felt personal ownership of the land, able to defend it by force of arms and to pass it on to future generations, so soon would Charlemagne's authority be disregarded and the central government would shatter into many pieces. And this, even Charlemagne, occupied as he was all over Europe, could not wholly prevent.

A second difficulty was the matter of the army. The Middle Ages knew no professional or standing army. Each spring there was a fresh mobilization, in which all citizens might be called. "Every free man was a soldier, bound to equip himself according to his means and to set out, under the severest penalties, at the king's command." This was all well and good for local warfare, but Charlemagne needed a force for the protection of distant frontiers and for fast-moving expeditions into the territories of troublesome barbarians who would not easily be brought to book. For such purposes independent foot soldiers were not adequate; the prime requisite was cavalry. But the average free man could not afford a war-horse, nor had the emperor the means to mount an army himself. There was only one source from which cavalry might be drawn. The holders of the various benefices could be required to provide bands of trained horsemen, the numbers determined by the size of their holdings. But the horsemen might not be forthcoming if the holder of the particular benefice felt unduly restrained by Charlemagne's government. Thus, even the military force on which the empire's existence was based came to depend on the loyalty and good will of the local notables whose services Charlemagne could not do without.

Then there was a third difficulty, common to all rulers of the Middle Ages. They never succeeded in separating the affairs of their households from the business of their government. The chief royal officials, we have already seen, had a dual function. The chancellor, for example, was the king's private secretary and at the same time responsible for the issuance of all state documents. Charlemagne's laws and capitularies give us evidence of the confusion which existed between private and public business. Some of them dealt with national problems and political abuses. Each subject of the realm must promise personal fidelity to Charlemagne as emperor. Others dealt with social problems, with the purpose of improving manners and morals. Bishops and priests should live according to the church canons and should teach others to do likewise. Although it has been said that Christianity did not exert a significant influence on Charlemagne's personal life, one capitulary called for the abandonment and prevention of willful murder—unusual enlightenment for the 9th century. Another prohibited the stealing of game from the royal forests. Still others dealt with the management of the king's farms and went into such minute detail as to prescribe the number of eggs which were to be sold and at what price. The ruler could never be rid of the task of making a living, lest the ruler become dependent on the charity of the subjects, and so powerless. The character of the times restricted Charlemagne's freedom. He had to "live of his own." He had, perforce, to use his lands as a medium of exchange by which he might pay for the services, private and public, done him. He had, finally, to live by the rules of feudalism, the system which was based on the holding of land in return for services promised. Even a Charlemagne could not prevent the growth of a developing feudalism, although the spirit of feudalism was the exact opposite of the imperial unity which it was his chief aim to establish.

6. The Carolingian Renaissance

Were we to end our consideration of Charlemagne here, we would write him down as a persistent general, an able ruler, and a loyal Christian. His campaigns, though not brilliant, were uniformly victorious. His organization of a new Roman empire was the supreme political achievement of the Dark Ages. He devoted his power and prestige to protecting and expanding the Catholic Church. But we would be underestimating Charlemagne. For he was not satisfied even with a combination of military and political exploits. Charlemagne was what 15th-century Italians were going to call a "universal man"—a man whose own talents were varied and whose interests covered every field of human activity. We cannot leave Charlemagne until we suggest how his reign affected all aspects of western civilization.

The fall of Rome itself, the inroads of the barbarians cutting off the Eastern Empire, and the advance of the Mohammedans around the shores of the Mediterranean, had been steps in the break-up of the old Roman Empire. These had isolated the province of Gaul as the sole remaining center of Roman Christian civilization. In the brief and bloody reigns of the feeble successors of Clovis, this civilization was barely preserved. Decline set in, buildings fell down, the arts were neglected, fewer people were educated. Then, under Charlemagne, the process was reversed. There began suddenly what historians have named the Carolingian Renaissance. The French word *renaissance* means literally "rebirth." Basically a renaissance is the rebirth of the creative desire in people. They cease to be content with life alone—the mere succession of growing up, marrying, earning their bread, dying. They begin to want pleasure and beauty in their lives, leisure and luxuries to enjoy, scope for the exercise of their minds and imaginations. They realize that life can be more agreeable and more productive than it has been before, and thus more satisfactory both to themselves and to God. They see that institutions as they exist—schools, churches, ways of business—are far from perfect. And then it becomes clear that people by their own efforts can improve these institutions, giving them a more effective interior organization and a more graceful exterior appearance. Such a revival of ambition and the capacity to create occurred in the time of Charlemagne. His own spirit inspired it and his peace made it possible.

Unlike many important people in history, Charlemagne is as distinguished for his thoughts as for his deeds. He had a widely curious mind. He wanted to know everything there was to know, he perceived the possibility of preserving Roman culture and the contribution that art and learning might make to his empire, and he attracted to his court the best educated men of all Europe. Charlemagne's original interest in scholars like the grammarians Peter of Pisa and Paul of Lombardy was not that of a patron but that of a student. He was himself learning to be proficient in Latin and to understand Greek. He put all available time on his own studies. Einhard tells that "during supper he listened to music or to the reading of some book, generally histories." He "delighted in the writings of St. Augustine." After the Englishman Alcuin, who was the most learned man of the age, came to his court in 786, Charlemagne studied with him the "liberal arts," so that he became "full even to overflowing in his eloquence." But he had little success in learning to write; he was already too old when he started and he never did produce much more than an illegible scribble.

The presence of scholars was not for the benefit of the emperor alone or for the splendor of his court. There was practical service for them to perform, spreading their knowledge throughout the empire, training the officials both lay and cleric who would help to rule it. Charlemagne hoped that under the direction of Alcuin the capital at

Aachen (Aix-la-Chapelle) might be made into a new center of learning, like ancient Athens. Alcuin founded a palace academy. Charlemagne went into the classes himself and criticized the laziness of the sons of the nobility. They would get no reward from him, he told them. On the other hand, he praised the attentiveness of the sons of those of smaller estate. To them he promised a bright future; he hoped to employ them in administrative positions and break the stranglehold of the great nobles on the imperial government.

Other schools were established in the principal cities and monasteries, and teachers were brought from all of Europe—from England and Ireland and Visigothic Spain as well as from Italy—to train the rough Franks. Charlemagne himself was the driving force behind this flowering of education, and few could resist his urgings. He was shocked to find that the letters of most of his bishops were "very correct in sentiment but very incorrect in grammar." Individual piety or intelligence would not ensure the progress which Charlemagne expected his Empire to foster. Education must be spread widely. Every monastery should have a school because "it is useful that men of God should not only live by the rule . . . but should devote themselves to literary meditations . . . that they may be able to give themselves to the duty of teaching others." Charlemagne's bold and estimable purpose is clear in a reprimand he wrote to the archbishop of Mainz: "You are striving by God's help to conquer souls, and yet you are not anxious to instruct your clergy in letters, at which I cannot be too astonished. You see on all sides those who have submitted to your rule plunged in the darkness of ignorance, and you leave them in their blindness." Charlemagne desired such darkness dispelled.

To all the arts and crafts Charlemagne gave encouragement. Architects were challenged by the task of beautifying the capital city with a new palace and cathedral. When local stone was found not sufficiently handsome, they imported marble columns from Italy. Einhard thought the Chapel at Aachen, modeled after San Vitale in Ravenna, was "a marvel of workmanship." Charlemagne's bath house, in which a hundred people could bathe at once in the warm water, was one of the wonders of the time. A remarkable feat of engineering was the bridge built across the Rhine at Mainz, five hundred yards long. Another project was the digging of a canal to connect the Rhine and the Danube Rivers in a continuous waterway. Charlemagne ordered this in 793 as a military measure, but it proved too difficult.

Throughout the empire Charlemagne proposed the use of a single scale of weights and measures, which would facilitate business and trade. In the field of literature, the emperor was instrumental in the collection of old texts, whether Christian, Roman, or Frankish. With Alcuin's help, he directed the copying of many old books, "almost worn out by the carelessness of our ancestors." At his court Theodulph of Orleans wrote new hymns for the Church, including the well-known "All glory, laud, and honor to Thee, Redeemer, King."

In Charlemagne's desire that learning flourish and that life once again be beautiful, a religious motive played a prominent part. "No object was dearer to his heart," reports Einhard, "than that the city of Rome by his care and toil should enjoy its old preeminence, and that the Church of St. Peter should not only by his aid be safely guarded, but also by his resources should be adorned and enriched beyond all other churches." Where Charlemagne lived, church services were held twice a day, and he "took great pains that all rites should be performed with the greatest decorum." Not only did Charlemagne give most generously to the poor, but he insisted on the observance of the monastic rules and worried over the growing worldliness of the clergy. He did not hesitate to admonish Leo III to live strictly and set an example of humility. Sensing the superiority of Italian church music, he imported choirmasters to teach the Gregorian chants in the Frankish churches. In a capitulary of 807 he ordered that "all interior surfaces of churches should be painted for the instruction of the faithful." His own battles were depicted, beside the founding of Constantinople and the story of David and Solomon, and we may imagine that priests and parishioners, historians and painters, all rejoiced.

For the improvement of religious practice, Charlemagne directed the writing of a new standard text of the Benedictine Rule, which was the basis of all monastic life. To Alcuin he entrusted the revision of the Vulgate, St. Jerome's famous version of the Bible in Latin. These important writings were done in a new type of script, which Charlemagne approved because of its simplicity, dignity, and legibility. This "Caroline minuscule" was standard in Europe for 400 years, and must be counted as one of the foremost gifts of the Carolingian Renaissance.

Not all the accomplishments of this fertile period were destined long to survive. Fire destroyed the great bridge at Mainz in Charlemagne's lifetime, and his successor ordered the destruction of his collection of Teutonic ballads because they were too pagan. But it remains clear that Charlemagne's reign was a period of splendid achievement. Churches were reformed and decorated, schools were established, the arts and sciences flourished. Creative faculties were stimulated at the same time that classical models and ideas were preserved. The vitality which Charlemagne's inspiration injected into Christian civilization kept it alive until the next great revitalization in the 13th century. This we may well consider a more glorious and permanent achievement then the conquest of the Saxons or the establishment of a new Roman empire.

7. The achievement of Charlemagne

Despite Charlemagne's genius, the empire he put together could not endure. The plan of it was magnificent—a unified government inspired with the Christian ideals of peace, charity, and brotherhood. But history had already gone too far for such an empire to exist. Subjects were willing to think of it as utopia, but as a practical matter they were unwilling to live under it. They were too narrowminded to understand Charlemagne's plan, too illiterate to serve effectively the state he built or to carry it on without him. The wisdom and the energy of Charlemagne himself were the only sure supports of his empire. In politics, in war, Charlemagne was supreme; no part of life escaped his influence. His rule was universal, but it was never firmly established. In theory he should have governed from Rome; in fact he had to live in the center of his realms—in Aachen, which Bainville calls "a post of surveillance," from where he might more easily suppress disorder and rebellion.

Too many practical difficulties stood in the way of the perpetuation of the empire that was Charlemagne's dream. For example, there were his sons to be provided for by the customary division of the realm. In 806 the father made plans for a three-fold division. Charles, the oldest son, was to inherit the old homelands of the Franks, the northern territory on both sides of the Rhine, including the capital, along with supervision over the tributary area north of the Danube. Pippin, king of Italy, was to retain that peninsula and the southeastern countries of the empire. Louis, king of Aquitaine, was to hold the territory roughly comparable to modern France. What would have happened had these plans been carried out we cannot tell, for fate took a hand to postpone the division. Pippin died in 810 after an unsuccessful campaign to conquer Venice; Charles died in 811. Louis alone was left and was declared Charlemagne's sole heir in 813. The empire would be handed on intact. But it was unfortunate that it should go to the least vigorous of Charlemagne's sons, the one least fitted to handle the complex and testing job of ruling it.

Looking at the intended dividing lines of the empire, we should notice how they correspond in general to the boundaries of modern European states. Italy, France, and Germany may be clearly discerned. These lines were, of course, not hit upon by chance. They represent the emergence of the feeling of nationality even under Charlemagne's unified rule and the compulsion the emperor was under to make concessions to that feeling. The differences of language and custom and temperament that keep Europe divided to this day were beginning to bulk large in the minds and hearts of the people. The differences were to grow more and more important until they completely overshadowed the idea of a single empire and a single Church.

Already in Charlemagne's time local and personal loyalties competed with loyalty to the emperor. The central government was distant and largely unknown. Many people never got so much as a glimpse of Charlemagne. But the local lord was near-at-hand and familiar. It was safer to rely on his strong right arm. He would provide the necessary security. He had the needs of his locality at heart, in a way that the emperor or his inspectors never could have. The local lord thus found himself with a following. He remembered his own personal ambitions—to hold his benefice independent of the Emperor, to increase its size, to hand it down to his sons. If these selfish ambitions could not be fulfilled without disrupting the king's peace, then the king's peace must be sacrificed.

The empire had done everything that could be expected of it in the way of border protection and territorial expansion. It had established peace and security, and so there was no further need for it. Now that danger from the Lombard, the Moor, the Saxon, the Avar, no longer threatened, there was no reason for patriotism to the empire. Even Charlemagne's own Franks began to object to being required to serve in his army and to pay taxes to a central government. It was time now to "feather one's own nest," to play local politics and to carve out for one's own exclusive possession a secure and prosperous domain. As individuals increasingly sought local gains from local wars based on local animosities, imperial unity was undermined.

Had Charlemagne been able to build up the efficient corps of trained and paid civil officials which he wanted to balance the hereditary aristocracy, the disintegration of the empire might have been prevented. It might even have been more profitable for the local magnate to serve the state than to fight for himself. But the time and the treasure necessary for the organization of such an official hierarchy had to be diverted again and again to immediate military needs. And now, at the very end of his reign, a new threat appeared.

The Norsemen from Scandinavia began to raid the long sea coasts of the empire, and in 810 Charlemagne had to order the construction of a navy to repel their attacks. A story is told in the chronicle of the Monk of St. Gall:

> Once Charlemagne arrived by chance at a certain maritime town [near Narbonne]. While he was sitting at dinner, some northern pirates came to carry on their depredations in that very port.... The wise king, knowing from the shape and swiftness of the vessels what sort of crews they carried, said to those about him, "These ships bear no merchandise but cruel foes." At these

words all the Franks rivaled each other in the speed with which they rushed to attack the boats. But it was useless [because the Northmen, scared of Charlemagne's reputation, fled precipitately]. Charles, seized by a holy fear, looked out of the window his face bathed in tears.... "Know ye why I weep? Truly I fear not that these will injure *me*. But I am deeply grieved that in my lifetime they should have been so near landing on these shores, and I am overwhelmed with sorrow as I look forward and see what evils they will bring upon my offspring and their people."

So we see that Charlemagne's talents included those of a prophet. The story, though surely fanciful, is nevertheless instructive.

A final difficulty to confront the empire was the very power of the Church which Charlemagne had helped to establish. We must remember that he was crowned by the pope. This was not exactly what Charlemagne had expected or desired. He did not feel beholden to anyone for the crown which his own efforts had won. Indeed, according to Einhard, "if he could have known beforehand the intention of the pope, he would never have entered the church on that day." Charlemagne, of course, acknowledged no inferiority to the pope, whom he had preserved from street ruffians. The pope had nothing to do with the choice, or the coronation, of Charlemagne's successor. Gibbon writes: "The royal youth was commanded to take the crown from the altar and with his own hands to place it on his head, as a gift which he held from God, his father, and the nation."

From the original event of 800, however, a different implication could be drawn. The pope had given the crown to the emperor; therefore, his authority was superior to the emperor's. The empire was, in fact, the creation of the papacy, and the pope would retain a final right to dictate imperial policy. While Charlemagne lived, such a possibility did not exist. He had protected the pope and raised him high in public esteem, without ever a thought of accepting him as an overlord. But Charlemagne had given the pope, with temporal estates, the independence necessary for him to assume such a high-handed attitude in years to come. If he did assume it, the close alliance of Church and State would break. And Europe would be convulsed by the fierce struggles between the forces of the super-State and the super-Church, both of which owed their foundation to Charlemagne.

All these discords and difficulties, happily for Charlemagne, were in the future, and no one can surely foretell the future. When the great emperor died in Aachen, in 814, he had every reason to be proud of his unique career. He had made Europe one, he had kept it safe from all external pressures, he had fortified the Church and widened the boundaries of Christianity.

One measure of Charlemagne's greatness is provided by the troubles into which Europe again plunged after his guiding hand was removed. The Dark Ages returned, to extinguish most of the bright lights of the Carolingian Renaissance. The empire crumbled before the onslaughts of new barbarians and the blind selfishness of its own aristocracy. The Church devoted itself to temporal rather than spiritual affairs, until it deserved people's scorn, not love. The union and stability and optimistic faith which Charlemagne's empire had brought to Europe were dependent on one man. He had had the vision to conceive, the will to fight for, and the ability to create a united and enlightened Christendom.

To the strength and vigor and pride of the Franks, Charlemagne had added the appreciation of classical learning and the zeal of the Christian missionary. He had not relied on the chance opportunities thrown in his path. From the earliest he had had a master-plan in mind and he had followed it systematically. His constancy of purpose matched his courage in the face of danger. As Einhard wrote, he willed "not to be conquered . . . nor forced by weariness to desist from his undertakings." That he had brought his plan to life was the result of the outstanding trait in his personality, which Bryce calls his "vivid and unresting energy." With it Charlemagne tackled and solved every problem that came to him. "Under his vigorous hand, Europe came nearer than ever before or since to the ideal of unity."

History could never forget him or disregard his work. By his unique combination of physical and mental vigor and by his ability to inspire others to unexpected effort and unimagined achievement, he made an "indelible impression" on their minds. Resilient and resourceful, Charlemagne had preserved the idea of the Roman Empire and infused it with a new vigor and purpose. Thereby, he had drawn the lines along which Europe and the Christian civilization of the Middle Ages must develop. His reign has been described as a period of "radiant accomplishment."

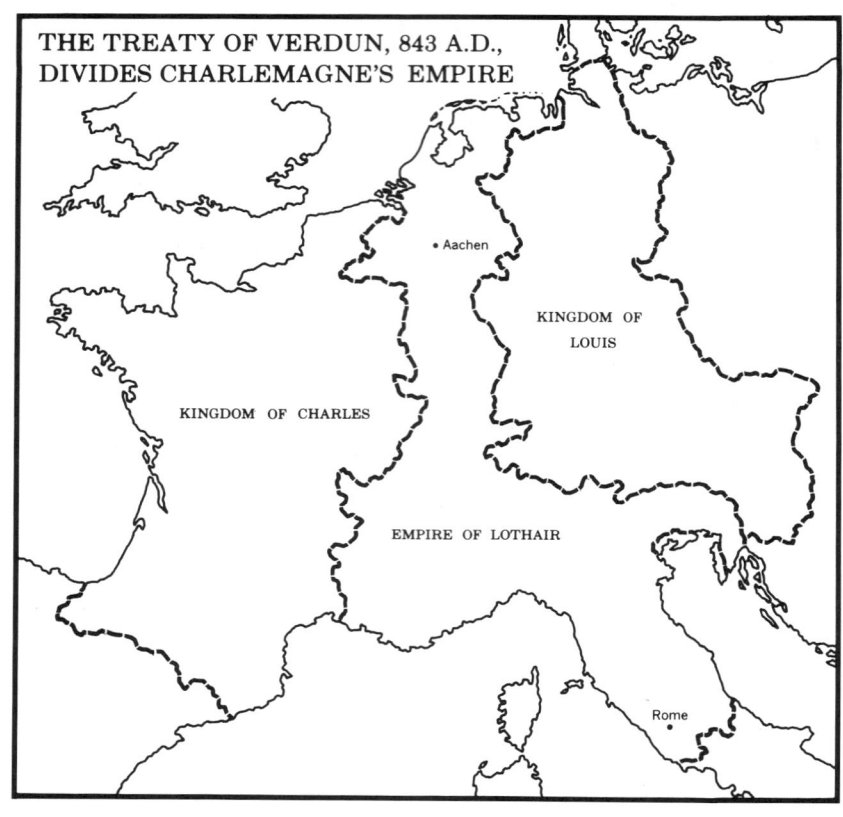

THE TREATY OF VERDUN, 843 A.D.,
DIVIDES CHARLEMAGNE'S EMPIRE

Aachen

KINGDOM OF
LOUIS

KINGDOM OF CHARLES

EMPIRE OF LOTHAIR

Rome

Chapter Four

A NEW SYSTEM: WILLIAM THE CONQUEROR (1027-1087)

The impact of Charlemagne on people and history was more durable than his material achievement, and the European Empire he established did not long outlive its founder. His son Louis the Pious, although sore pressed, did manage to preserve it until his death in 840, when he divided it among his three sons, specifying that Lothair should be called emperor and should exercise final authority over his brothers. This division provoked quarreling, the two younger brothers uniting against the emperor and defeating him in civil war. In 843, as a result of this fighting, there was signed the treaty of Verdun. This fateful agreement divided Europe into two main parts—France to the west, Germany to the east—with a narrow and totally indefensible "no man's land" in between. Ancient and natural boundaries, like the Rhine, were ignored in this division. The two capitals, Rome and Aachen, were included in the narrow central strip of territory, which was called the empire and presented to Lothair. But geography and nationality combined to keep this realm from ever being a "going concern." It was further partitioned in 870, and the more powerful sections on either side have fought for possession of it ever since.

1. Europe in 1000 A.D.; feudalism

After 843 imperial unity no longer existed, although as an ideal it might still be recalled and even revered. The crumbling of Charlemagne's empire laid Europe open to attacks from abroad. Before effective governments could be established in the various sections of Europe, they were assaulted by a new wave of invasions. In the south it was the Moors who once again seized the offensive. In the east it was the Magyars of Hungary who swept the Christian forces before them until they were checked by Otto of Germany at Lechfeld in 955. On all the maritime frontiers—the English Channel, the North Sea, the Mediterranean—it was the roving and adventurous Northmen who established bridgeheads from which they might expand inland.

There was no imperial authority to direct the repelling of these scattered invaders. The new national governments (as they would have liked to have been) had not the resources, the prestige, or the strength of leadership to put an effective counter-force in the field. Consequently, to meet the invaders there was only the greatest landlord of the vicinity, his retinue, and the lesser lords he could rally to his banner. Such a force was usually insufficient. The invader carved out a province to be his private preserve. His opponent, abandoned by his royal overlord, scorned the so-called king, from whom he, too, might declare and maintain his independence.

The history of Normandy is a case in point. Early in the 10th century the warlike Norsemen effected landings on the northwest coast of France, in territory subject to the king. Meeting little opposition, they pushed inland, advancing up the Seine River to Paris itself. Charles the Simple was utterly unable to raise an army to meet the fierce invaders and was compelled to bargain with them. Gold alone would not buy them off. By a treaty of 912 the large area which came to be known as Normandy was handed over to the Norsemen for their occupation and control. One condition was imposed. Rolf the Norseman must acknowledge Charles as his overlord. Rolf demurred and sent a substitute to the ceremony. This substitute knelt to kiss the king's hand and then promptly overturned the royal throne. It was obvious that the Norsemen would pay little attention to the wishes of their overlord. The king of France had been forced to give away much of his richest land. The sole outlet from Paris to the sea was in the hands of pagan enemies.

Looking back to the Europe of the opening of the 11th century, we can easily see what did *not* exist. There were no national states such as we would recognize today. The king of France, the king of England, the Emperor (for the title survived) were figureheads who might be more or less respected according to their personal characteristics, but they were not "heads of state." There was no political unity even in the sections of the old empire. No king received taxes paid uniformly by the subjects in all parts of his "realm." There was no national army to enforce the king's orders. The king might issue decrees but they would not everywhere be obeyed. He had no organized corps of officials to execute his will, and there were parts of the country which such agents as he did have would not dare to enter. There were wide areas which were not subject to the operation of crown justice. In short, no European nation had what we would call a functioning central government.

What then *did* exist in the Europe of 1000? The answer in one word is anarchy—the word we use for lack of power, lack of government— in short, for disorder and lawlessness. Murder, arson, brigandage, war were the commonplaces of life. European civilization was in the process of committing suicide.

Even though nations and civilizations collapse, individuals do not choose to die before their time. In the midst of distress and desolation and disaster, people seek security. In the face of danger, they seek protection. In a time of anarchy, when law and order have no practical value, individuals must rely on their own strong arms.

In the absence of government, there developed a substitute for it which we call feudalism, or the feudal system. The basis of this system was extremely simple. It was an agreement between two men. One man, who owned a tiny cottage and an acre or two of tilled land, lived in constant fear of losing his possessions to a band of armed marauders. So he went to another man in the neighborhood, who owned a much larger house with a courtyard surrounded by a high fence and who owned so many acres of land that he was organizing a sort of private army to guard his possessions from the marauders.

Said the man of small property to the man of large property, "I need protection. The government does nothing for me. Will you protect me?"

"Yes," said the man of large property, "I will protect you, but naturally you must pay me for my protection. Here are my terms: I will become the owner of your land. But you will live on it. In fact, you will not be allowed to leave it. You may cultivate the land for your own support, but you must give some of the annual produce to me. I will provide the armed force to keep you safe, but you from time to time must perform certain tasks in my house."

These terms were hard. The man of small property realized that, if he accepted them, he would lose his property, his independence, his chance to make something of himself by hard work and to improve his family's prospects for the future. On the other hand, his own livelihood and the immediate safety of his family were at stake. The sacrifice seemed worthwhile; he accepted the terms. The bargain was struck.

Said the large man: "I will nourish and defend you; you will serve and obey me." The small man descended to being a serf, with his exact status determined by the particular services he agreed to perform. The large man ascended to the role of a lord of a manor.

Higher up the social scale, substantially the same bargains were made. Let us consider three men of property, of education (such as it was), and of military skill. Their lands adjoin, and the lands of the man in the middle are of considerably less extent than those of the other two. The man in the middle fears that his avaricious neighbor to the east is planning to snatch his lands away from him. He turns, therefore, to his other large neighbor to the west. He may say: "I commend myself to you. My lands are yours and I will serve as an officer in your private army if you will ensure me a decent living according to my rank in society." But he is much more likely to say: "I commend myself to you. You may take title to (legal possession of) my lands. But obviously your holdings will then be too extensive for you properly to manage them yourself. Therefore, you will entrust a part of them to me. I will live off them and control my own workers as before. But in time of need, for a period of up to forty days each year, I will come on horseback to fight in your army and will bring with me twenty fully-equipped soldiers."

"All right," replies the large neighbor to the west. "But this is a rather complicated agreement, and, as befits men of our noble rank, we must bind ourselves to it by means of an oath." So it transpired. The lesser man swore an oath of fealty, or personal loyalty, to the greater. He also performed an act of homage, kneeling before the greater and promising to be his man. In return for this promise, for the required military service, and for certain special aids (at times like the wedding of the greater man's daughter), the lesser man retained his lands, which he held as a fief of the greater man.

So the aristocracy bound themselves by oath to the essential feudal contract. The greater man became the lord, the lesser man the vassal. Between them there was mutual obligation, which their personal honor urged them to respect. And from the obligation came mutual benefits. The vassal received the use, enjoyment, and (within specified limits) the disposition of valuable lands and a strong house. The lord gained in prestige and influence; his army grew stronger; he could call on his vassal for assistance and advice.

We have heard of the beginnings of this feudal system before; but, by 1000, the original system had changed in the very ways which Clovis and Charlemagne had feared. We remember that feudalism grew from the necessity of repaying services with land. Basically it was an economic transaction, for the convenience of the king in administering his government. Charlemagne had insisted that the system should be kept flexible—the lands to be granted for a limited time and the king to retain the right to revoke the grant if he deemed it advisable. But what had started as a custom came to operate with the force of law. What had been a convenience for the king became a hindrance, preventing the uniform execution of his laws throughout the realm. What had been an economic agreement developed into a contract binding people, and their descendants, to a certain way of life and a fixed social position.

Because governments failed, feudalism imposed itself. It became a permanent principle, instead of a temporary expedient. It spread throughout Europe and included in its mold every class in society. Above all, it became the subject of hereditary right. Fiefs, with their services and benefits, were handed on from generation to generation. The son of a vassal became himself a vassal; the daughter of a serf became herself a serf.

The personal contract of feudalism was more important than the public law of the nation. This had a decisive effect on the organization of society. Serfs were required to obey their lords. These lords must be the loyal vassals of other greater lords, who were in turn the vassals of the great dukes, who were supposedly the chief vassals of the king. But the feudal contract held good only between the two adjacent social classes. That is, the serf was bound to the vassal, or the vassal to the lord. No oath of loyalty, however, bound the serf of the subvassal to the king. A person looked for protection and justice from his or her immediate lord. He or she never had to think of the distant overlord, the king.

Indeed, if the occasion should arise, serfs and vassals were obliged to follow their lord even in rebellion against the king. The king, although he remained at the apex of the social system, exercised no direct rule over his subjects. He had lost the powers Charlemagne had possessed. The feudal system did not rest on his authority. Many feudal contracts were made without his consent and without his knowledge. Two vassals might swear fealty to the same king. But they swore no oath to each other, and no feeling of common nationality made them hesitate to wage war on each other. Such wars the king was powerless to prevent. His own position was precarious, for it depended on the personal loyalty of his vassals who, by right, had the armed strength with which they might oppose him. He must be careful to placate them; they could often coerce him.

It was not only the king who declined in importance. Small, independent farmers had no place in the feudal system. It was they who had once been required to provide the king with the soldiers of his army.

It was they who, meeting in public assembly in early Frankish times, had swayed the policy of the nation. Without them the king had no force with which to oppose his great nobles. The disappearance of the free individual and the weakening of the king, then, go hand-in-hand. Two classes, only, retained their vitality in feudal society: the lords and the peasants. To these two we must add the churchmen. The clergy were indispensable as the saviors of souls. But, as a practical matter, they must fit into the economic framework of society. So we find archbishops and bishops holding and ruling vast tracts of land, binding themselves in feudal contracts as either lords or vassals.

In summary, the society of 1000 was divided into three classes, or estates. The first two were privileged, the lords and the churchmen who owned the land; the third was not privileged, the peasants who worked the land. And the map of Europe in 1000 did not show a few nations with clearly drawn boundaries. Charlemagne's empire had disintegrated into a hodge-podge of feudal holdings—dukedoms, baronies, bishoprics. Of these the royal domain was one, and nothing ensured that it would be the greatest. "Feudalism," writes the great English historian G. M. Trevelyan, "is the opposite of despotism. It may often be tyranny and it may sometimes be anarchy, but it is never despotism, for it is an elaborate balance of defined rights and duties as shared by the king and the various holders of land."

2. Feudalism in England, France, Normandy

We have been considering the feudal system in general terms. We must notice that in the several countries of Europe there were differences in the extent and the operation of feudalism.

England, for instance, had not been part of Charlemagne's Empire and was isolated from the currents of continental civilization. For some three hundred years the still-barbarian Anglo-Saxons had been competing with the more barbarian Danes for supremacy in the island. We shall not be surprised then to find that many tribal customs, similar to those of the Franks, survived in England. The warrior class was still dominant in society. Its position depended on its military skill and maintenance of professional standards rather than on land-ownership. Its leaders, or thegns, were those who could command the personal loyalty of other warriors.

The monarchy was still elective, not hereditary. When a king died, his successor was chosen by the Witan, a meeting of the most important lay and clerical men in the realm. The Witan could choose whom it pleased, and its choice alone made a man legally king, regardless of his other qualifications, or lack of them. The king was guarded by a military elite, known as the housecarls, whose royal service was a badge of honor. These housecarls were heavily-armed; they might go to battle on horseback, but they still fought on foot, in the barbaric tradition. In the absence of cavalry, each free warrior could still equip himself for war.

Only recently had the numerous kings in England been merged into one, and he had never enjoyed real control over the whole country. Rather than an active ruler, he was the head of a confederation. The old kingdoms were recalled in the division of the country into six great earldoms and there was no *national* sentiment. Government was carried on not by royal officials in the counties, but by the earls and their thegns. No great number of counts, therefore, had asserted their independence and built castles from which to dominate the surrounding countryside. On the other hand, the king's power, even from a theoretical standpoint, was limited by his elective status. He maintained himself not so much by making contracts with numerous vassals as by relying on the friendship of one or two of the great earls.

We find, in sum, that feudalism was comparatively undeveloped in England. Much land was held quite apart from any feudal contract. Many villages and individuals had managed to maintain their independence of feudal lords. Many of those who had become vassals were still able, in a simple society, to change their allegiance at will to another chieftain. The great earls, Godwin of Wessex, Edwin of Mercia, Morcar of Northumbria, stood in feudal relationship to the king; but each was, by popular support, virtually a king in his own district, and none was prevented from aspiring to be selected king of England.

In France, on the other hand, feudalism existed in its most virulent form, and the consequent decentralization of authority left the national state hopelessly weak. Royal power decreased to the vanishing point; no one could rely on the king, and so no one obeyed him. Defense for the common person could only be provided locally, and the country was split up into countless petty principalities. Inhabitants gladly gave up their liberty to escape ruin and death. Commoners rushed to construct, as their refuge, the fortified castle which the feudal lord might afterwards use as their prison.

The king inherited the Carolingian titles, but his real power was overshadowed by that of his chief vassals—the counts and dukes of Burgundy, Gascony, Toulouse, Guyenne, and Flanders. When Hugh Capet, who had replaced the Carolingians on the throne in 987, objected to the seizure of his city of Tours by the count of Perigord, he demanded: "Who made you count?" "Who made you king?" came the insulting reply. The king was overlord in name only, and his great vassals felt strong enough to disregard him. So much of the royal land had been granted away that the king was truly less than one among equals.

In the Europe of 1000, Normandy was a unique state. After 912, there had taken place what has come to be recognized as a frequent and predictable phenomenon in history. The conquering minority was assimilated by the conquered majority. The Norse invaders established themselves as a ruling class, composed of sea-captains, traders, and landowners, but they adapted themselves to the typical ways of life of the land they had seized. The Norse intermarried with the French, learned their language, accepted their Christian religion, imitated their arts, and absorbed their culture. As warlike conquerors they paid the French the high compliment of learning from them a new method of warfare. They recognized the advantages of fighting on horseback rather than on foot and of relying on the thrusting spear and cutting sword in preference to the bludgeoning battle-axe. Most important for our immediate discussion, the Norse adopted from the French the feudal organization of society and also had a chance to study such vestiges of Charlemagne's unified government as survived in France.

To their task of ruling, the Norse conquerors brought a discipline, an energy, a sense of unity, a hard-headed practicality—the very characteristics that in 10th-century France were in the process of eclipse. The Norse took over from the French the framework of the feudal system and the machinery of the central government. Then they performed the surprising feat of making them both operate effectively. Rolf and his successors—dukes of Normandy as they chose to be called—were thus able to establish a dual supremacy over their lands, both as feudal overlord and as sovereign ruler. In form, Norman society became thoroughly feudalized, but at the same time the dukes retained firm, direct control over their subject population. One thing had been of great advantage to the dukes in achieving this happy result. Normandy had fallen to them "in one package." They had not acquired the land piecemeal, by defeating or bargaining with its feudal holders. By the single stroke of conquest the land was theirs, subservient to their authority, ready to be organized according to their will and their native genius for firm administration.

First, Norman feudalism. By comparison with it, the elaborate complex of interdependent lords, chief vassals, and sub-vassals in French feudalism was haphazard and inefficient. In Normandy, feudalism was really systematized: land tenure was based on military service, according to a rigid formula. The land was assessed and divided into units judged capable of sustaining five mounted knights in the field for forty days. Vassals were then granted fiefs of a size proportioned to the rendering of their prescribed military service. Furthermore, rules limited their enjoyment of feudal rights and privileges. They had to obtain a license before building a private castle; they could not transfer their allegiance from one lord to another without permission of the overlord, who was ultimately, of course, the duke. Private wars were frowned upon, and a limit was placed on the amount of plunder one lord could take. By these measures the dukes made their overlordship felt and averted the danger of any one vassal becoming over-great and challenging their supremacy. Normandy itself was a great barony in France, nominally subordinate but actually independent. Within Normandy, however, there were no such great baronies.

Meanwhile, the Norman dukes spread the network of their own government, to parallel and to check the feudal authorities. For administration, viscounts were the agents, directly responsible to the duke. They held court, commanded his armed forces, collected his revenue. Each county was required to yield a certain sum, acquired by farming the taxes to the rich men of the neighborhood. Since the Normans were the masters of sea-borne commerce, a considerable part of the duke's income was in money, with which he could pay his officials. No baron shared in the duke's privilege of coining money. Certain parts of the dukedom were reserved for the legal jurisdiction of the duke; and certain crimes, wherever committed, could only be tried in his courts.

In addition, the Christianized dukes made themselves the masters and champions of the Norman Church. They used their power of appointment to church offices to build up a feudal hierarchy beholden, and therefore loyal, to them. To acquire and retain a bishopric, a man need not have had a religious education. He must be strong and he must do the will of the duke. The greatest Norman warrior of 1066 was Odo, a relative of the duke, who appointed him Bishop of Bayeux because of his powers with the mace, which he used because the Church disapproved of fighting with a sword. The duke of Normandy, then, was more of a king than any of those who called themselves king. His state was the most stable, the most firmly-governed, in Europe. In Normandy there was little individual freedom for any citizen, even for the barons. The duke's will prevailed and law and order were enforced.

In the final analysis, the basis of government in the Middle Ages was the use, or the threatened use, of armed force. In the rather formalized fighting of feudal contests the decisive factor was often the personal one: that is, the superiority of one leader in strength, courage, military ability, or diplomatic skill. In any system or organization in which the personality of an individual counts for so much, there come periodically times of crisis—when the leader is incapacitated or dies, when the choice of a successor must be made, when this successor is young and untested. A feudal holding was gravely menaced when its lord was a weakling, when it passed into the hands of a woman, when its inheritor was a child. The danger was proportionately greater when the stakes were higher and the future of a whole country or kingdom was involved.

3. The young duke of Normandy

It was at such a critical time in the affairs of Normandy that we must introduce William, the subject of this chapter. William was in the direct line of the rulers of Normandy, being the only son of Robert, the 5th duke. Unfortunately, he was also an illegitimate son, his mother being the daughter of a mere craftsman. Bastardy, to be sure, was not a deleterious stigma in medieval times. Illegitimate children were usually freely acknowledged and often, especially in the absence of legitimate offspring, endowed with all the rights of succession. Nevertheless, it was something of a handicap to emerge on the world's stage saddled with the name of "William the Bastard," as the youthful William was identified by his contemporaries. It put on him an added burden of proving himself; it suggested that he had his own way to make in the world. It would be comparatively easy to argue that William the Bastard should not legally be duke of Normandy and to stir up active opposition to him.

More unfortunate for William than his illegitimacy was the early death of his father. Robert died as he was returning from a pilgrimage to the Holy Land in 1035. At the age of eight William inherited the task of maintaining the efficient government of Normandy.

There can have been little opportunity for William to enjoy his childhood or to receive an education in anything but political plotting and the arts of war. All the dangers and problems of a minority beset the realm. At first, his title was not seriously threatened, apparently because the barons felt that, with a child ruler, they could break the ducal regulations with impunity and build up a power which William could never overthrow. They built private castles without permission and indulged at will in private warfare. Not until William had grown into young manhood and had shown the desire to assert his will and some potentiality of forceful leadership did the barons break into open revolt. Their rising in 1047 took William by surprise. He was on a hunting expedition near Valognes in lower Normandy when he received warning of a plot to seize his person. He fled by night, half-dressed, with no escort. He was lucky to reach the security of Falaise, having come by roundabout ways across the territories of his enemies. But he quickly proved himself more than a match for them. He secured the aid of his overlord, the king of France; he met and defeated the rebels at the battle of Val-des-Dunes; he sent their leaders into exile and destroyed the strongholds they had illegally constructed. William was henceforward master in his dukedom.

The next challenge to William was an even more serious one; it came from his overlord. The king of France, Henry I, could not be content to see the Seine River dominated by anyone but himself. William's control over this critical waterway was both an affront to the dignity of France and a serious economic burden for the merchants of Paris. Henry, therefore, engaged the assistance of his other chief vassals— Aquitaine, Burgundy, Anjou, Champagne, and Auvergne—and invaded Normandy, first in 1053, again in 1058. William had the military craft not to engage his enemy on the frontier but to draw him into the interior, tiring him. Further, William did not scruple to order the scorching of Norman lands, so that his enemy would be faced with the difficulty of supplying himself. Then at the decisive battles of Mortemer and Varaville, he checked the invasions, sent his enemy in full retreat, and seized his baggage. William did not follow up his advantage over the king. Nothing was to be gained from a direct attack on France save the wasting of prolonged campaigns and the united enmity of all the other great vassals of the king, who would fear Norman dominance far more than the weak overlordship of France. William himself was perfectly willing to remain Henry's vassal in name, as long as he was, in fact, the more powerful of the two. So the feudal contract was reinstated between them, with a parade of the fullest mutual guarantees and satisfaction. But it was a contradiction of reality, and either contractor was likely to break it any day that he saw a clear advantage to be gained.

There was no feudal bond between Normandy and Anjou. Both had powerful and able leaders, William, and Geoffrey the Hammer, and both had long coveted the county of Maine, which lay between them. War was inevitable. In 1063 the Normans captured the capital of Maine, Le Mans. The Angevins were evicted and Maine was incorporated in the ducal territories.

William had made his reputation. He was, says his biographer Freeman, "the model prince of Europe, the valiant soldier, the wise ruler, the pious son of the Church, and the prince, who, among unparalleled difficulties, had raised his paternal duchy to a state of prosperity and good government which made it the wonder and envy of continental lands." William had faced many obstacles: the misfortune of his birth, the long minority, revolt at home, attack from his feudal superior, war with a bold and capable peer. He had surmounted them all. Normandy was secure and strong. William could look around for wider opportunity.

4. The situation in England

William had always been interested in England, which lay just across the Channel from the Norman domain. He had a family connection with English royalty, being the great-nephew of a former king, Ethelred, and a cousin of Edward the Confessor, the reigning king. This Edward had spent most of his early years in exile on the continent while the Danish Canute ruled England, and he had been thoroughly educated in Norman ways. Himself the son of a Norman mother, he found the Normans far less crude than the Anglo-Saxons, and after he became king in 1042, he invited many Normans to his court. There they were honored and rewarded with gifts and positions of responsibility. They became the confidants of the king, and people began to protest with some reason against the foreign influence in the government. Edward was a particular admirer of his cousin William, with whom he was on the friendliest terms. It seems probable that at one time, Edward, who was childless, promised the English throne to William after his death, or at least expressed the wish that William might succeed him. The English king being the choice of the Witan, Edward had no right to make any such promise, but the suggestion was planted in William's mind; and the Norman remembered, of course, his blood-connection with English kings.

Now we must tell a story of events about which no certainty exists, but which determined the course of English history. In 1064, probably, an Anglo-Saxon ship was wrecked on the Norman coast and a young Englishman named Harold was taken prisoner by Guy of Ponthieu, who planned to hold him for ransom. This Harold was Earl of Wessex, son of the great Earl Godwin and brother-in-law of King Edward. Godwin, for his own purposes, had opposed the Norman element in Edward's government and had thus become a popular champion. He so far succeeded in dominating Edward that he made himself the most influential nobleman in England, and his power was the indispensable foundation-stone of the government in Edward's later years. Harold had inherited Godwin's power and popularity. When news of the capture of Harold reached the crafty William, he recognized the opportunity presented to him and compelled his vassal to release the captive to the ducal court.

Apparently William and Harold quickly grew congenial and enjoyed each other's company. They hunted together, and Harold even accompanied William on a minor military expedition, after which William dubbed him knight. He was naturally grateful for such polite and friendly treatment. On the eve of his departure, therefore, he was willing to accede to William's request that he should swear an oath. Exactly what the oath was we are not sure. It may have been that Harold would marry

William's daughter. It was said to have been that Harold would hold the English throne for William, when Edward died; but it seems improbable that Harold could have been induced to make such a statement which, in any case, he had no shadow of right to effect. It is most likely that the oath was simply that of homage, of being William's man, made lightly by Harold in the thought that it was courteous but not binding. We are told that after Harold had sworn on the Bible, William tore away a cloth, disclosing under the book a pile of the most sacred relics of the Church. Whatever the true story of the oath may be, Harold attached no great importance to his action. William, on the other hand, considered the oath to be a vital event in the construction of his foreign policy and planned to capitalize on it in the future.

The time for action was not long delayed. Edward died at the opening of 1066, less than a week after the consecration of the abbey at Westminster to which he had devoted his thoughts and his treasure. He murmured that the country should have Harold as his successor—which meant nothing more than his earlier choice of William. The Witan met to exercise its power of selecting the new king. Not unnaturally, although perhaps unwisely, the members chose the man of the hour, Harold. By blood, Harold had less claim to be king than William, and the elevation of a great feudal earl to the throne would not meet with universal approbation. The Norman knights, churchmen, and merchants whom Edward had welcomed to England would all oppose Harold.

William let on that he felt slighted, and easily assumed the attitude that he had been cheated out of an inheritance. In truth, as a matter of practical policy, he saw a golden opportunity slipping from his anxious grasp. If he could not gain his ends in peace, nothing prevented his going to war. Once his rear was secure—and he had shown former enemies that he was not casually to be interfered with—he had the military force and organization necessary for an invasion of England. Furthermore, he could make a good show of self-justification. There was Edward's promise. Far more significant, there was Harold's oath. We must try to understand the medieval mind. There was nothing more important than an oath. It was made in the sight of God and received a sort of divine sanction. To break it was to transgress God's will. By contrast, taking from others what was legally theirs or plunging a country into civil war were minor offenses, for they involved injustice to humans only, not to God. The Middle Ages could see much formal right on William's side, whereas we moderns concentrate on the wrong he did by deciding to overthrow forcibly the legally chosen king of England. Nor was William the only one to challenge Harold's succession. Far to the north, Harold Hardrada, the king of Norway, determined to press his own claims, and he gained the support of Harold's own brother, Tostig.

NORMANDY AND THE CONQUEST
OF ENGLAND
LATE 11TH CENTURY

NORTH SEA

Durham

Stamford Bridge

York ×

Chester

Shrewsbury

E N G L A N D

Wallingford
London
Thames
Salisbury
Canterbury
Hastings
Pevensey

FLANDERS

ENGLISH CHANNEL
St. Valery

Rouen
Beauvais
Bayeux • Caen
Seine
Falaise
Mantes
Paris
N O R M A N D Y

Le Mans

F R A N C E

5. 1066—The Conquest

An amphibious operation was not lightly to be undertaken in 1066. And William's preparations had to include the political and diplomatic, as well as the naval and military. In the care with which William prepared for his transmarine expedition we see clearly illustrated what Freeman called his "combination of vision, patience, and masterfull will." Politically, Normandy was so efficiently administered that William had no hesitation in leaving the government in the hands of Lanfranc, the capable and learned archbishop of Rouen. From the standpoint of diplomacy, William may well have counted on France and Anjou being pleased to see him occupied elsewhere than on their borders, but he was determined to have on his side the public opinion of Europe, and especially of the Church. Accordingly, while Harold was exclusively engaged in efforts to put England into a proper posture for defense against the twofold invasion which threatened, William sent embassies to Rome to explain his right to the English crown and to condemn Harold for having broken a sacred oath. Pope Alexander II was impressed, and William used his skill in negotiations to paint his invasion of England in the hues of a crusade for the Roman Church.

Truth to tell, the condition of English society and the English Church was not good. William of Malmesbury, writing his Chronicle early in the next century, speaks of the "nobility given up to luxury and wantonness ... the commonalty, left unprotected, a prey to the most powerful." Furthermore, the English churchmen were too easy-going. "The clergy could scarcely stammer out the words of the sacraments ... the monks mocked the rule of their order." The archbishop of Canterbury himself led the opposition to papal authority in England. Stigand even permitted his clergy to marry. What a chance, said William's propaganda, for the pope to purify the English Church at the same time that he could establish his own control over it more securely. The pope should supervise the national churches more closely and thus be sure to obtain from them the revenues that were his due. When Alexander II gave his blessing to William's enterprise, he conferred on him a tremendous moral advantage. The pope's desires were known throughout Christendom; Europe condemned the usurper Harold and prayed for William's success.

The strictly military preparations had obviously to be far more extensive than those for a conventional feudal expedition. In the first place, since the campaign must inevitably be protracted for more than forty days, their feudal contracts did not bind William's knights to accompany him. But, in spirit, they were ready and willing to go. Their loyalty to William, their expectation of victory under his banner, their anticipation of rewards in the shape of plunder and feudal fiefs, brought them to his summons. Also came many non-Norman knights, for adventure and for spoils, until the expedition took on the appearance of what has been called a "joint-stock enterprise" for the exploitation of England. All who participated assumed a share in the risks, but their investment gave promise of a rich return.

Despite all the interest and enthusiasm, William's host was tiny by modern standards. A generous estimate has numbered his entire army at 12,000, of which almost half were cavalry. Even so, transportation was a problem, especially shipping the trained war horses. William directed the construction of 700 boats according to a simple plan. There would be no room for oarsmen, and so propelling power would come from a single large sail. When all was in readiness in August, the winds were perverse and blew steadily toward the Norman shore. Sailors of that era could not compete with head winds, and for six weeks William's army was harbor-bound. The men-at-arms muttered in discontent. But the delay may have been intentional and it proved beneficial. As September wore on, the local Saxon militia charged with defense of the English coasts dispersed to collect the harvest. In any case, William, who had conceived the whole plan, had the patience to wait for the chance to execute it and the inflexible determination that bent his men to his will. He transferred his fleet down the coast to the mouth of the Somme, nearer to his objective. Finally, with a favoring breeze, they set sail from St. Valéry.

Like the earlier Norse forays, the invasion of England was essentially a large-scale pirate venture. Plotted with cunning to meet certain feudal standards of right, it was carried through with a ruthless disregard for injustice or injury to friend or foe. From the first, fortune favored the invader. Navigating by the stars, he lost only two boats on the hazardous 60-mile crossing of the Channel. His landing at Pevensey on 28 September was unopposed, Harold having had to hasten northward to repel an attack from Norway.

As he leaped from his boat, William fell to his knees and his hands grabbed the soil. A good omen, thought a quick-witted Norman, who said, "You hold England, my lord, its future king." William was anxious to bring Harold speedily to battle before he should have a chance to recruit greater forces. To provide a defensible base of operations, William moved east to Hastings, where he erected what we would call a prefabricated fort that had been transported with the fleet. Then he began to ravage the towns and country of Sussex, doing extensive damage.

Harold had to hurry down to oppose him. In the north, Harold had managed to destroy his enemies at Stamford Bridge, killing both Tostig and Harold Hardrada and reducing their army to a scattered remnant. But the battle had cost him many of his best-trained men. Now the forced march to the south wearied his army. William's policy of destruction, however, compelled Harold to fight or to abdicate his role of defender of the English people against the foreign tyrant.

Nor was Harold averse to fighting. He hastened back from York to London and then marched southeast, twenty miles a day, to confront the invader. His army of about 10,000 was roughly the equal of his opponent's in numbers. His men had proved their worth in the North. He chose a strong defensive position on a hill near Hastings. Around him, to meet the onslaught of the Normans, would stand the picked body of the housecarls. These well-disciplined, professional soldiers, wearing protective armor of leather and iron and wielding battle-axes, would form a solid wall of shields.

William, on his side, was confident of victory. On the morning of October 14, he put on his helmet backwards, remarking, "My dukedom shall be turned into a kingdom." Then he gave orders for the attack to begin.

William's army was more flexible than Harold's. The Anglo-Saxon strength was in heavy infantry alone. For these, William's footmen were no match. But William could send out archers whose clouds of arrows, falling at a sharp angle, did heavy damage behind Harold's wall of shields. To the archers, Harold could make no effective answer unless he attempted to come to close combat. This would require breaking his chosen formation and descending the hill. To provoke such a disorganized response, William's armored horsemen — the gift of the French to the Norse line of battle — skirmished in front of the enemy line. Their efforts unsuccessful, they withdrew to wait another opportunity. Then the Norman infantry advanced in force, only to be heavily repulsed.

Late in the day, when the Anglo-Saxons seemed on the point of making good their defensive stand, the moment for the horsemen arrived. Perhaps the Normans adopted the tactical ruse of pretended flight; perhaps the poorly-disciplined mass of Harold's army suddenly broke under the constant galling of the Norman arrows; perhaps William in desperation resorted to a full-scale cavalry charge and, after the charge was broken, the Saxons could not resist the chance to loot the bodies of many fallen knights. Whatever the cause, the solid wall of shields disintegrated at last, and the Norman horsemen could ride down the scattering Anglo-Saxon foot soldiers. Just then Harold fell, mortally wounded — whether by arrow or sword we may never know. The hard-fought contest turned into a rout. From the military standpoint, the combination of archers and cavalry proved superior to infantry. From the larger historical standpoint, "a single battle settled the fate of England."

After the "melancholy havoc" of that "fatal day," as the Chronicle tells us, "the French had possession of that place of slaughter, as God granted them because of our nation's sins."

Hastings was a conclusive battle. There was no further organized, national resistance to William's army. Harold had not had time to make himself a real king. He had remained the great earl; his cause was personal, not national. It collapsed with his death and that of all his remaining brothers at Hastings, and there was no other leader of sufficient stature to construct a national front against William. Indeed, many of the great men in England were as willing to have William as Harold for their overlord. They hastened in, as individuals, to make their private peace with William and to establish a feudal relationship with him. They admitted his claims to the throne and, of course, hoped their own positions might thus be secured, even though the kingdom changed hands. Even the intensely anti-Norman Stigand of Canterbury made his submission.

Despite the absence of effective opposition, William was not yet king. He must penetrate to the center of the realm, win popular acceptance, and, above all, be legally crowned. Until these things happened, he was a usurper in hostile territory and there would remain the possibility that the Anglo-Saxons might fix upon another candidate for the throne behind whom they could all rally. This the Witan tried to do, selecting as king Edgar the Atheling, but this pale young man was unequal to the task wished upon him. William moved fast but not rashly. He took the ancient religious and royal city of Canterbury and advanced on the capital, London, hoping for its surrender.

London prepared to resist his entrance and William did not deem himself strong enough to capture it. But London was indispensable to him. He could not be a true king until the seat of government, the royal treasury, and Edward's new church at Westminster were in his hands. Whether he could or not, he did not want to seize the crown; he was maintaining that he was the rightful successor to the Confessor. Strategy must substitute for overwhelming force, and we have already seen that William was a master-strategist. He chose what the modern military historian Liddell Hart called the "indirect approach." Circling around London, he would come up from the rear, where he was least expected. Meanwhile, the capital must be isolated, in the midst of a country terrorized and devastated by the Norman army, until normal life in the city became impossible. The people must be led to realize that the sole way out of their miseries and sufferings lay in accepting William as their legitimate king.

To accomplish this end, William marched westward to cross the Thames at Wallingford. From there he swept around to the north and east of London, ruthlessly desolating the country. His plan worked to perfection. Unable to oppose William in the field, the great men of England realized that it was costly as well as fruitless to oppose his political pretensions. A sort of rump Witan met in London and sent to William at Berkhamstead praying him "to accept the vacant crown." William had won his point: he had not simply imposed himself as a feudal overlord, his accession to the throne came via the traditional elective method. The Witan had selected William; the people would look upon him now as their rightful king.

It remained to be crowned and to consolidate his hold over the whole of England. Neither was achieved without incident. William came to London at Christmastime for his coronation. Clearly Stigand of Canterbury was disqualified, but it was desirable that an Anglo-Saxon churchman should perform the ceremony. So the second dignitary of the English Church, Alfred, Archbishop of York, officiated at the coronation. A fire in the neighborhood of Westminster, perhaps set by Norman horsemen to avert other disorders, caused the audience to rush out, leaving only the essential actors. William swore to give England good government, and we shall not be surprised to learn that this necessitated imposing a heavy tribute on the people.

In campaigning to gain sure control over all England, William represented a unifying force. By contrast, the opposition he met was scattered, both geographically and chronologically. William fought to make England one, for himself; his opponents fought to divide England by keeping certain parts of it under their rule, independent of the king. By 1068, all southern England was firmly in William's grasp. Northern England was more difficult to subdue, for the great earls, Edwin and Morcar, after having once submitted, raised in 1069 the standard of revolt. William resolved to crush them so completely that no one else would dare make a revolution. He systematically ravaged the northern counties, giving free rein to the ferocity in the Norman character. Not a house was left standing from York to Durham, 100,000 men, women, and children were massacred; the country was made a desert. The north was convincingly subjected to William's rule, although it was not fully to recover from his devastation for seven hundred years. In 1071 a final island of resistance at Ely, ably but futilely commanded by the great baron Hereward, was reduced; and in 1072 King Malcolm of Scotland did homage for his fief of Cumberland. In 1075 there was a revolt in East Anglia, this time raised by a Norman earl, which William quickly suppressed. By then, the conquest was long since complete, and William, Duke of Normandy, had made himself also William, King of England.

6. The Norman pattern transforms English society

The effects of the Norman Conquest on England were both deep and widespread. Let us look first at the matter of government. William might owe the legitimacy of his position to the Witan, but he was determined that his government should be the creature of no powerful group or individual. He intended to rule England alone. In doing so, he gained for the crown an entirely new stature in English history. Where before it had been an elective office, it became a personal possession; where before it had been weak, it became strong. This metamorphosis of the English kingship was made possible by the fact of the conquest. William commanded the victorious army and was master of the land; with the army and the land, all practical power was in the hands of the king, who had never before been permitted thus to monopolize it. William used this practical power to unify a realm that had previously been deeply divided and to make the royal court in London the sole and effective center of an authority that had previously been shared among many.

The legal process by which this change was effected was as sweeping as it was abrupt. Asserting that from the death of Edward he had been the rightful king, William claimed that all those who had joined Harold to oppose his coming were in fact rebels-in-arms against the monarchy. The rebellion having been put down, the persons and possessions of the rebels were forfeit to the king. William confiscated the lands even of those who had made private submissions to him and he canceled all land-titles dated before Hastings. The king became virtually the only landowner in England. All others who wished to own land must go to the king and buy their lands from him. With the loss of their lands, the Anglo-Saxon nobility found that their power was gone too. The break-up of the great earldoms was particularly significant because these had been the main administrative divisions in the kingdom.

William, of course, had no intention of retaining all England as a private estate. It would be unwieldy; and furthermore, there were the 5000 knights who had fought for him who expected their reward in the form of feudal landholdings. So William replaced the Anglo-Saxon tenants-in-chief with Norman tenants-in-chief. One ruling class he displaced; another he imposed on the populace.

The influence even of the greatest nobles was scattered far and wide by the splitting up of the vast holdings of pre-1066 into numerous small fiefs. No centers of power which might one day be disloyal to the king were permitted to exist. Only Chester and Shrewsbury and Durham were entrusted to a single lord, and this was for reasons of border security. As the Normans consolidated their conquest, the chief barons were from time to time granted lands widely separated from each other.

There was, consequently, no section of the realm in which the power of any one individual was comparable to that of the king; William planned to have no overweening vassals who might disregard his orders. Foreign, rapacious, merciless as they in general were, his vassals could muster no popular support for themselves. So the new ruling class in England owed its preferment to William's prosperity; its permanence depended on the permanent supremacy of the Norman kingship. We would expect the vast majority of the aristocracy which William's conquest had created to be amenable to his control.

By his land distribution William had called into being a new group of feudal governors for the Anglo-Saxon population. No landlord could forget that he was ultimately indebted to William for his land: all landlords, bound by their feudal contracts, should thus be at least the indirect servants of the crown. The greatest of these landlords William called to him periodically for consultation on the affairs of the state. The Great Council, as this body of feudal magnates was called, had no independent authority, such as that of the old Witan to select the king. And the king's power was now so extensive that there was little possibility of his being over-awed by the Great Council. It met at his summons and discussed what he proposed. It was the king's privilege to call on his chief vassals for advice; it was their duty to give advice and their privilege thus to exert their proper influence over the policy of the state. Within the Great Council was a smaller committee, the *curia regis*. This was composed of the chancellor, the treasurer, the two archbishops, the justiciar (who exercised the king's prerogatives in his absence) and a few others. These feudal dignitaries were the forerunners of the permanent officialdom by which later kings would govern the country. Already in William's reign they were the chief advisers and chief agents of the royal will, feudal lords become the active instruments of a brand new central government.

From his experiences on the continent William knew that feudal government, no matter how secure in appearance, was in constant danger of deteriorating into anarchy. The Norman feudal regime in England had the added disadvantage of being foreign and, therefore, unpopular. The ruler of a rich and contented people, however, commands praise and popular favor, and so William set himself to fulfilling his coronation vow of good government for England, and of doing so outside of the feudal framework. William had political acumen and, like most rulers, conservative instincts. In the conquered country he found certain national institutions which were full of meaning for the people. Despite the revolutionary effect of his conquest, he saw the wisdom of preserving such of these institutions as he could, so as to cloak his new administration in traditional forms. To gain popular support, William wished to change and to oppress as little as possible. So as we study William's reign we find not only the preservation, but the strengthening, of a national government along side of, but often in competition with, the pyramid of feudal contracts.

Anglo-Saxon freemen had been subject to a military levy, the fyrd. They had paid to the royal treasury a tax, the geld. These institutions were continued under William: the fyrd providing him with a military force with which to check an over-ambitious feudal lord; the geld giving him a money revenue, beyond feudal dues, with which he could govern the realm. For the male citizen, subjection to the fyrd and geld was a badge of his independent status, which he would not willingly surrender. So he paid the land tax of sixpence a hide, which netted William a million dollars a year, and he accepted the tripling of the tax rate to which the Danish occupation had accustomed him. William did not use the taxing power gently. The Saxon Chronicle says that he "extorted immense sums from his subjects, upon every pretext that he could find, whether just or otherwise."

More significant still to the average man was the retention of the ancient local organization of towns, hundreds, and shires. In each of these, a small body of representative citizens sitting as a court had always been responsible for some legal and social regulation. These local courts stayed in operation. Although the town and hundred courts declined in importance, the shire-court increased. Here officiated the Anglo-Saxon sheriff, as did the Norman viscount in his county. The sheriff was a royal officer, appointed by the king as the representative in his shire of the royal authority. In the shire-court the great lords of the neighborhood might be called to account, and the sheriff could limit their pretensions to independence. And within each shire certain towns or abbeys might save themselves from rapacious lords by securing a charter from the king. Overseeing all, came the king's traveling commissioners, similar to Charlemagne's inspectors. So William, by means of the fyrd, the geld, and the sheriff, maintained some control over his subjects. To the national institutions and to the direct exercise of royal power the feudality objected strenuously, for by so much was their authority weakened; but his conquest had made the king strong and rich enough to override all opposition.

Aside from the field of government, we find the conquest bringing many changes to both the form and substance of English life. We have already observed that in all Europe Norman feudalism was the most carefully regulated on a strict territorial basis. It now replaced in England the former very loose organization of land tenures. The personal vassalage of the housecarls ceased to be effective. Land holdings were rigidly balanced against military service, at the rate of 5 hides (600 acres) in return for 40 days service of one fully-armored horseman. Freehold grants were discontinued, in accordance with the motto, "No land without its lord." The number of free men declined tremendously, in Cambridgeshire alone from 900 to 200 in William's reign; all were to be bound by feudal contracts, to feel the "heavy hand" of Norman overlordship. To mark this overlordship, timber fortresses rose on mounds of earth, surrounded by an open courtyard and a fortified wall. Anglo-Saxons were forced to labor on the castles which would dominate their lives.

Many of the fortresses were the king's, and he kept much of the land in his own hands. He was well able "to live of his own" on the royal domain, which became much more extensive than ever before. An estimate of it, for the end of William's reign, includes 1422 manors. In addition, many chartered towns paid tribute to the royal treasury.

Avarice must have combined with political wisdom in William's character. His selfishness exposed him to criticism even in his own day. Very fond of the hunt, he decreed that an area, which we call the New Forest, should be set apart as crown lands for that sport. He was not concerned that sixty parishes must be laid waste and their inhabitants dispersed. To reserve the enjoyment of the hunt for himself, William decreed fierce laws against poaching. Offenders were to be tried in the special Forest Court, in which the king was his own judge. Says the Chronicle: "He made large forests for deer and enacted laws therewith, so that whoever killed a hart or a hind should be blinded. As he forbade killing the deer, so also the boars. And he loved the fall stags as if he were their father. He also appointed concerning the hares that they should go free." The diet of his subjects might need to be changed, but William had his sport. The penalty for poaching was later increased from mutilation to death, and in the next century sixty-nine forests (one third of the whole kingdom) are said to have belonged to the crown. Some maintain that William was punished for his selfishness when two of his sons and one of his grandsons met violent deaths in the New Forest.

We should take note of other effects of William's coming in English history. The doors were closed to further invasions from the North, for if the Normans plundered their subjects they also defended them. At the same time that William excluded Danish influence, he brought England much closer to western Europe and subjected her to French influence. Norman French became the language of the government, the courts, and the schools; and Anglo-Saxon was preserved solely as an oral tongue among the lower classes. The mixture of the two, with the Latin added in the 16th century, made the English spoken today. The scholarship of the continent returned to England. Lanfranc and Anselm, who were successively archbishops of Rouen and of Canterbury, were probably the most learned Europeans of this era. Every important church, except Edward's Westminster, was rebuilt in the Norman style of architecture. It provided for more spacious construction and called for the use of much more stone than had been customary. The Normans, who had learned from the French, carried their culture to England, where it was found more sophisticated than the Anglo-Saxon. Aided by the weight of official support, the Norman aristocracy set new standards for English art and thought.

In the last year but one of William's life came two achievements to crown his career, marking the extent to which William had imposed his system on English life. The first of these achievements was the compilation of the Domesday Book, a census of the inhabitants and the property of the entire nation. Nothing of this sort had been attempted before, and it was a mammoth job. William's investigators went into every hamlet and collected information from a small jury of the citizens concerning every family in the neighborhood. The questioning was thorough. "There was not a single hide nor a rood of land," reports the Chronicle, "nor—it is shameful to relate that which he thought no shame to do—was there an ox or a cow, or a pit passed by." The 11th century was not as accustomed as the 20th to the census-taker and the tax collector.

When the Great Survey was complete, William knew exactly what were the resources of each part of his realm. He had also an historical record of the ownership and the product of the land in Edward's time, in 1066, and in 1086; he knew "how much had been added" during his reign. He knew finally "whether more could be had than was had" from his subjects in taxation. Domesday was the tax book for the nation. Using it as a basis for calculation, William could levy a certain total sum on each shire and on each manor and leave the collection of it to the local authorities. The tax burden would fall equitably. There would be no malingerers. His information of the wealth and power of each one of his people was detailed and accurate. Such information was invaluable for the effective operation of his central government; the collection of it was a unique accomplishment.

The Domesday data was not arranged according to the ancient township divisions. Rather, all the holdings of vassals and sub-vassals were listed under the name of their overlord. The manor, not the town, was to be considered the basic unit of English social organization. Every citizen's property was to be counted as part of a larger feudal holding. Apparently the king was finding Norman feudalism more orderly and manageable than Anglo-Saxon local government as a system for controlling his realm. This would suggest that he was sacrificing the direct royal authority to the indirect influence of feudal contracts. But such was not the case. We must remember that the king was the universal overlord and the feudal contracts must be scrupulously lived up to.

The other great event of 1086 shows the king reminding his aristocracy of his overwhelming might. William called all the feudal dignitaries to a meeting at Salisbury. "All the landholders of substance in England, whose vassals so ever they were, repaired to him there, and they all submitted to him, and became his men, and swore oaths of allegiance, that they would be faithful to him against all others." The king of England was not to be one among many feudal lords of equal power, against whom a disloyal vassal might raise disastrous rebellion. No, the king of England was to be a true sovereign, the one supreme overlord, reaching out a strong arm to control every individual in his realm, for all were the king's men. William accepted feudalism as every medieval monarch was forced to do. But the Salisbury oath makes clear his own dominant position. In France, feudalism might lead to the disintegration of the kingdom into warring dukedoms. In the England of William, the feudal machinery would function under the firm, unifying grasp of the king.

Similarly, William maintained his supremacy over the religious hierarchy. The weak and lax Church of Anglo-Saxon days was much affected by the conquest. A foreign clergy was brought in to occupy all its important positions: not a single Englishman did William appoint to be a bishop, and only a few to be abbots. This clergy introduced higher standards into the Church. The Normans were already infected by the reforming zeal of Hildebrand, who became Pope Gregory VII, and rules such as the celibacy of the clergy were henceforth enforced. The moral influence of the pope over the English Church was increased. We have already noted that Lanfranc and Anselm went to England. They had originally come to Normandy from Italy and they had attracted multitudes when they taught at the monastic school of LeBec. There was also established by one of William's supporters, the Earl of Warenne, the first Cluniac monastery in England, where the monks rigidly adhered to the three-fold Benedictine vow.

Any such ecclesiastical improvements William wisely approved and encouraged. But he had no intention of admitting himself inferior to the pope or of permitting the existence of any church power in England not subject to his oversight. As long before as 1053, William had married Mathilda of Flanders against papal opposition and had worked for six years to win approval of his act. He refused to tolerate any spiritual interference in the exercise of his rights or the accomplishment of his purposes.

His royal pride and independent spirit brought William into frequent conflict with the equally domineering Gregory. The papal legate demanded from the king an oath of fealty and a money tribute. In 1076 William wrote to the pope: "I refuse to do fealty, nor will I; because neither have I promised it, nor do I find that my predecessors did it to your predecessors." He was unwilling to be in any sense another's man. Money he was willing to send in the reasonable and traditional form of church taxes, known as Peter's Pence, but most of the income from fiefs granted to the Church William used to meet the expenses of his civil government. He was glad to see church courts established to handle cases concerning "the rule of souls," which secular courts were not competent to try. He was ready to use his power, exercised by his sheriffs, to enforce penalties church courts decreed. But he insisted on the strict independence of the royal courts from church influence or Roman legal practices.

William resisted all efforts to extend papal authority at the expense of royal. Gregory desired to control the English Church directly from Rome, independent of the king. This William flatly refused to allow, and a compromise agreement was worked out, called the Triple Concordat. (Concordat is the name used for a treaty between a religious and a secular power.) Letters from Rome to English churchmen might be sent but must be seen by the king. The Church might hold its own exclusive meetings, but only with William's permission; church laws might be decreed, but only with William's approval. Barons and ministers of the king might be condemned for a religious offense, but could be punished only at William's command. None could be excommunicated. In sum, the king was not to be excluded from the English Church. His will was not to be disregarded in its practical control over the lives of the people. William championed a strong Church, but it must be a national Church, allied to his royal power. Archbishop Lanfranc began the custom of convoking the leading ecclesiastics to assemble at the same time as the Great Council. With them, as with his feudal advisers, William had "very deep speech." Lords and bishops would in years to come meet together in Parliament.

7. William's character and role in history

The Norman Conquest, then, resulted in a vast transformation in England — in its government, its church, its social and economic organization, its culture. We might ordinarily expect such changes to have occurred in the course of perhaps a hundred years, during the successive reigns of several strong kings. The changes take on a truly remarkable aspect when we realize that they were the work of a single man. They were planned in William's brain and driven to completion by his energy within a reign of twenty years. Furthermore, William had to impose his system on a hostile country. Anglo-Saxon England had not yearned for his coming—most of the population had never heard of him. One chronicler described the Norman invaders as "ignorant upstarts, wondering how they had arrived at such a pitch of power and thinking how they might do whatever they liked with it." England was not forced to submit to them because of internal weakness; the Anglo-Saxons might have long continued to do quite well in their own ways. But William, as conqueror, reorganized their land and society according to his conception of what a well-ordered realm should be. Despite the extent of his transformation, we cannot say that William wielded despotic powers to achieve it. He was restricted by the feudal system into which he was born and by the old Saxon customs into which he moved.

Never was he able to devote all his attention to his new kingdom. England's productivity and manpower were valuable additions to William's strength. But time and time again he was called back to the continent to look after his affairs as duke of Normandy, and his absences from England stretched from months to years. Normandy did not have the English Channel as a defensive moat, and its feudal neighbors were troublesome. In all his later years, William could never put aside warlike preparations; he was never free from fear of internal revolt or external attack. And his ambition made him unwilling to rest with what he had won. Here was a border to secure; there a feudal holding to annex. In 1076 the Normans invaded Brittany but were repulsed by the Bretons, with the aid of the king of France, who was distressed to find the power of his nominal vassal so far superior to his own. In 1079 there was a revolt in Normandy, led by William's own son Robert, who found his father's control—even from England—too stringent. At the seige of Gerberoi William suffered his first personal military setback.

Finally, in 1087, war between Normandy and France broke out again over disputed border territory, called the Vexin. Philip's defense was strong, but late in the summer the Normans captured his city of Mantes and set fire to it. William, now sixty years old, rode through the streets of the burning city. His horse stumbled. The king, his tough, muscular frame turned somewhat to fat, fell heavily to the ground. On 7 September he was dead. Times were bad and manners were harsh. No respect was shown for the dead monarch. His body was stripped of its clothes and jewels. Only the concern of a private knight saved it from disappearing; he carried William to the Norman capital at Caen for burial. The interment service was interrupted, and William's body was hurriedly pushed into a vault too small for it. The king's commanding presence was gone; and there were many, no doubt, who breathed more easily for its departure.

What estimate should be made of William the Conqueror? His temperate private life and devotion to his wife, the tiny Mathilda of Flanders, can be contrasted with his heartless treatment of his opponents. His ability as a governor must be weighed against his greed, his skill as a diplomat against his unscrupulousness. Zealous in the destruction of his enemies at Hastings, he ordered the construction of famous Battle Abbey to commemorate his victory. Scornful of individual churchmen like Stigand, he built another monastery at Canterbury. He rewarded freely the services of faithful followers, but he was a demanding master, who did not hesitate to punish bishops and sheriffs and even his half-brother Odo for opposition to his wishes. William has been described as a "stark" man. He required unquestioning obedience; there was no trifling with the king. He loved power and brushed aside any obstacles that stood in his way. Although he appreciated the virtues of life according to Christian principles, he was often inhumane. Pity and mercy were sentiments he did not feel. But his industry, the breadth of his mind, the commanding strength of his personality, are impressive traits.

The author of the Anglo-Saxon Chronicle describes William fully and fairly:

> This King William was a very wise and a great man, and more honored and more powerful than any of his predecessors. He was mild to those good men who loved God but severe beyond measure towards those who withstood his will. This land was filled with monks who lived after the rule of St. Benedict.... He wore his crown three times every year when he was in England: Easter at Winchester, Pentecost at Westminster, Christmas at Gloucester. And at these times all the men of England were with him.... A very stern and wrathful man, so that none durst do anything against his will, he kept in prison those Earls who acted against his pleasure.... The very good order that William established is not to be forgotten, such that any man, who was himself aught, might travel over the kingdom with a bosomfull of gold unmolested, and no man durst kill another.... Being sharpsighted to his own interest, he surveyed the kingdom so thoroughly that there was not a single hide of land throughout the whole, of which he did not know the possessor, and how much it was worth, and this he afterwards entered in his register.... Truly there was much trouble in these times, and very great distress; he caused castles to be built and oppressed the poor, and he took from his subjects many marks of gold, and many hundred pounds of silver, and this either with or without right, and with little need.... He was

given to avarice and greedily loved gain. The rich complained and the poor murmured, but he was so sturdy that he recked nought of them; they must will all that the King willed, if they would live; or would keep their lands; or would hold their possessions; or would be maintained in their right.

The chronicler found many faults in William's character but admired his power and justice. He thought of the king as the greatest ruler of 11th century Europe—a man who would long be remembered. This ancient judgment is repeated in the modern judgment of Freeman: "No man ever did his work more thoroughly at the moment; no man ever left his work behind him as more truly an abiding possession for all time."

The defeat of Harold's army at Hastings gave the deathblow to old Anglo-Saxon England. The Conqueror took the loose collection of Anglo-Saxon earldoms and welded them into a solid nation. William's genius was the central organizing force of the new England. To the whole kingdom he gave uniformity of government—one law, one system of taxation, one Church, one loyalty. He made feudalism universal in England, but he bent all his feudal inferiors to the royal will. Instead of exerting their normal divisive tendencies, therefore, the feudal energies of the medieval English were made to serve the national state. To the people William allowed much of their traditional freedom and a measure of self-government. At the same time, with his sheriffs and *curia regis*, he began to build up the officialdom which would govern the country as a centralized monarchy.

The England William left was nothing like the England he had found. Churches, great houses, and roads had begun to appear on what had been a largely pathless expanse of forests. But William's realm foreshadowed the England which was to come. For a time the Norman conquest had the direct effect of bringing England too close to the continent, of involving her in continental wars, especially with France. Eventually, however, England and Normandy were separated for good and all. Then was to be seen the permanent effect of William's work. The England he created was a unified state—the first in Europe. The royal power was everywhere equally effective; all the citizens owed a common loyalty to the same ruler. William showed the way to create a national monarchy, based on a common law and order stronger than any feudal contracts. His own power was so great that he could give his people some local liberty at the same time that he could force the barons to treat the people with respect and could prevent the formation of any independent feudal powers.

William was more than a feudal overlord; he was a statemaker. Among his vassals he had no would-be equals; his subjects, great and small, obeyed the royal laws. His true descendants were not the kings who fought with France for the possession of Normandy; they were the great Edward's and Henry's of the Middle Ages, and even the 16th-century Tudors. For William's England was the earliest and became the strongest of Europe's medieval monarchies.

Historic Figures in Art
and Sculpture

The Bettmann Archive

CLOVIS and CLOTILDE - *Statues mounted near the entrance of the Church of Notre Dame at Corbeil. Because they were not contemporary, but done in the 12th century, with stylized clothing, one cannot rely on them as accurate likenesses. The fact that Clotilde was represented beside her husband attests to her importance in national affairs and to the love and respect she had inspired.*

HAROLD.

Second Son of Godwin Earl of Kent, in 1065, seized the Crown Sep.3.1066. Willm Duke of Normandy made a descent upon the Coast of Sussex, with a great Army, to obtain the Crown of England; came to an Engagement with Harold, 14. Oct. who was killed on the Spot, and his Army entirely defeated. He was bur.^d at Waltham Abbey in Essex.

this Portrait is taken from one of his Coins. NB. the Drapery is added.

HAROLD - *This likeness taken from one of his coins. The son of Earl Godwin of Wessex, Harold was accused by some of seizing the crown from William, the rightful claimant. After his death at Hastings, he was buried at Waltham Abbey.*

The Bettmann Archive

MATILDA of TUSCANY - *From a 12th-century manuscript account of her life. Matilda and Hugh, Abbot of Cluny, listen to Henry IV plead for their intercession on his behalf with Pope Gregory VII, before Canossa.*

The Bettmann Archive

GREGORY I - *From an illustrated manuscript. Pope Gregory I, the Great, dictates to two scribes working on the Gregorian Chants. The dove symbolizes the voice of the Holy Spirit.*

The Bettmann Archive

LOUIS VII - *From a 13th-century statue. Like Clovis and Clotilde, Louis was sculpted wearing stylized diadem and raiment, carrying a sceptre, to be placed on the front of a cathedral, like Notre Dame in Paris.*

MOHAMMED - *From a miniature in the Royal Asiatic Society. The prophet is welcomed by civilian and military leaders as he arrived at Mecca from Medina.*

JOHN - *A modern engraving of the Great Seal of King John. The seal bore portraits of the king as a warrior and holding his regalia. It was used at the signing of Magna Carta, a part of which is shown in facsimile.*

THOMAS BECKET - *From the manuscript of a Latin Psalter, c. 1200. At the altar of Canterbury Cathedral the archbishop is murdered by four knights of King Henry II. Although the drawing might appear unskilled, the action is detailed and graphic.*

The Bettmann Archive

The Bettmann Archive

HENRY III AND ELEANOR OF PRO-VENCE - *Unlettered worshipers appreciated the painted and stained-glass windows in great cathedrals and small churches that depicted personages of the day as well as incidents from the Bible. These windows suggest the character of the in-decisive king and his beautiful queen.*

Part Two

The Universal Church

FRANCE, ITALY, AND THE
HOLY ROMAN EMPIRE
1050-1150 A.D.

H O L Y

R O M A N

E M P I R E

FRANCE

Frankfort
Tribur
Worms
Speyer

Augsburg

Paris

Sens
Clairvaux
Vezeley · Dijon
Citeaux
Cluny

Clermont

ALPS

Milan · Brescia

Canossa

Ravenna

PAPAL

Toulouse

STATES

Rome · Monte Cassino
Capua · Benevento
· Salerno

Chapter Five

GREGORY VII AND THE RISE OF THE PAPACY (1025-1085)

The date was 22 April 1073. The place was the Church of St. John Lateran in Rome. The occasion was the funeral of Pope Alexander II, with Archdeacon Hildebrand officiating. At the conclusion of the solemn service a tumultuous scene ensued. Murmurs arose among the crowd, then shouts, "Let Hildebrand be our bishop... It is the will of St. Peter ... Hildebrand is Pope!" So it was that Gregory VII found himself elected pope by popular acclaim. "They rushed upon me like madmen," he wrote later, "and with violent hands forced me into the seat of apostolic government." This choice by the crowd was as irregular as it was hurried and unexpected. More than two months passed before Gregory was consecrated, but no princely hand was raised in opposition and the riotous Roman population remained unusually calm. From the day of Alexander's funeral, therefore, Gregory VII was effectively pope.

1. The pope in early European history

Just what does it mean to be pope? Today, we know, the pope is the head of the Roman Catholic Church. He lives in the Vatican and directs the faith of millions of Roman Catholics. Although the pope also rules over the diminutive Vatican states within Rome, his political power is not important. The world respects his profound influence in theology, morality, and international affairs. But it has not always been thus. The position and importance of the pope have changed with the times. Three questions raised in the early days of the Church have recurred time and time again throughout its history, Shall there be one Church or many? Who shall govern or control the Church? Can the religious and spiritual leader be at the same time a temporal or political ruler?

At the very beginning of Christian history, as the apostles of Jesus went around spreading the good news of his resurrection, the small groups of converts to the new faith formed churches in their own communities. These early churches, although bound together in doctrine by the teaching and letters of men like St. Paul, governed themselves and were entirely independent of each other. The speed of their growth varied, but naturally the Christian brotherhood tended to be larger in the larger cities, and the churches whose origin stemmed directly from the visit of an apostle enjoyed a prestige which the "branch" churches did not have. Thus, the churches at Jerusalem, Alexandria, Antioch, and Rome stood forth above the rest.

We know that Christianity, persecuted for three centuries, gained final toleration under Constantine, who indeed gave it a favored status among the religions of the empire. He employed his imperial power to maintain the unity of the faith, and councils like that at Nicaea determined the official doctrine for all Christians. Despite differences of opinion between churches and churchmen, such as the Donatist heresy, the combination of imperial pressure and the council system ensured that there should be one Christian Church for many centuries to come. This Church grew rapidly in prestige and influence. At the end of the 4th century, Emperor Theodosius made Christianity the official state religion, outlawing paganism.

The emperor himself experienced the power of the Church. In retaliation for the murder of a government official, his soldiers massacred 7000 citizens of Thessalonica, and Theodosius was held responsible. When he went one day soon afterwards to attend services in the church at Milan, Bishop Ambrose met him at the door and physically barred his entrance, insisting that he first do public penance for his crime. The emperor, said Ambrose, was just as much bound by his Christian duties as were his subjects. He did not rule the Church; rather he must protect it and respect its moral laws. The bishop defied the emperor: "If you demand my person, I am ready to submit; carry me to prison or to death, but I will never betray the Church of Christ." And Theodosius admitted the authority of the bishop in spiritual matters by meekly accepting the rebuke of the fearless Ambrose.

Meanwhile, also, the Church had grown rich in land and money since the day when Constantine had legalized its ownership of property. The question of who should control this powerful body, patronized by the State but able to stand on an equal footing with the State, became increasingly important. Might it be the emperor? Should it be any one bishop? If so, which one?

Independent of outside influence, the Christian Church had already organized itself into bishoprics and adopted a standard doctrine. Both were based on the theory of apostolic succession—the recognition of the continuity of Christianity through the ages of history. The apostolic succession meant, first, teaching the traditional faith. What the Church taught in the 4th or 7th or 10th centuries was what the apostles had taught in the 1st century, as interpreted by great churchmen like Ambrose and Augustine. The apostolic succession came also to have another meaning. Bishops of the later centuries were chosen and consecrated by their predecessors in point of time, and this succession of church rulers could be carried backward, generation by generation, to the era of the apostles, themselves selected by Jesus.

Jesus, the Bible told, had turned to the apostle Peter and said: "Thy name is Peter, the Rock, and on this rock shall I found my church." Then Peter had established the church at Rome. The bishop of Rome, therefore, was the direct successor of Peter, the inheritor of his unique position and authority. Here is the justification for the Roman church's early assertion of dominion over the churches in other cities.

Then, in the 5th century, its bishop, Leo the Great, stressed the practical necessity of the principle of authority in managing the affairs of the Church. In each province good order demanded that one church should have the ruling voice, and the churches in the larger cities should have even wider responsibilities, covering several provinces. "Through these," said Leo, carrying his idea to its logical conclusion, "the oversight of the whole Church is concentrated in one see, that of Peter, and from that head there should never be any dissent." Emperor Valentinian III gave his support to this theory of centralized control: "Not only the bishops of Gaul, but those of the other provinces, shall attempt nothing counter to ancient custom without the authority of the venerable father of the Eternal City. Whatever shall be sanctioned by the authority of the Apostolic See shall be law to them and to everyone else."

Aside from rational arguments, imperial decrees, and the principle of apostolic succession, however, there were other factors supporting the claim of the bishop of Rome to be the supreme ruler of all Christians. Geography and politics and tradition were all at work to accomplish what Leo desired. The church at Rome was in several respects unique. It was the only church founded by an apostle in the western part of the Roman Empire; it was located in the time-honored political capital of the world; it owed its founding to not one, but two apostles, Peter and Paul, who had both been martyred at Rome.

And, in addition to these forces, historical events now played their part. The permanent shift of the imperial capital from Rome to Constantinople had created another Christian center of outstanding importance. But the patriarch of Constantinople could always be closely observed and influenced by the emperor. The bishop of Rome, on the other hand, was freed from such control. After the reign of Justinian the authority of the emperor at Constantinople over his western domains grew steadily more shadowy, and in the 8th century the Lombards seized Ravenna, whence his representatives, called "exarchs," had supposedly ruled. What was left in the west? One centralized authority, one organized hierarchy—the Christian Church. The Church fell heir to the dwindled power of the empire and also to its very considerable prestige. In a barbarized and disintegrating world, the Church stood as the one remaining symbol of unity and stability. Theoretically, at least, all owed allegiance to the Church. Loyalty to Rome was, as we have seen, the one common possession binding people together in the Dark Ages. History had worked to give to the one Church, consolidated in the reign of Constantine, one ruler, who was the bishop of Rome, now called the pope. It remained to be seen whether the pope could maintain himself as an international ruler and whether he could assert his authority over the churches in the Eastern Empire.

The great popes of the Dark Ages understood the uniqueness of their position and recognized the opportunities and obligations it imposed on them. Their outlook was international. Their duty was to create the City of God, not in Rome only, but everywhere. Thus Gregory I, at the end of the 6th century, encouraged missionaries to spread Christianity and thought of himself as the guardian of the welfare of all Christendom. Thus Nicholas I, in the decay of the 9th century, issued canon laws for the regulation of the universal church, trying to make the Church's moral teachings effective in the daily life of every Christian, wherever he or she might be. Under such popes there opened the possibility of the Church exerting a real worldwide influence. The papacy was an effective organ of centralization, a nourisher of order and decency.

Centralization of power was contrary, of course, to the prevailing trend of feudalism, by which land was divided and subdivided under the control of individuals. If he wanted all people everywhere to give heed to his admonitions, the pope must be above criticism for selfishness or prejudice or ambition. He must be indebted to no one and to no nation; he must be wholly free from personal influence or control. Here the pope's task was made extremely difficult. Since the days of Constantine, churchmen had become increasingly concerned with the temporal possessions with which they had been endowed by generous or penitent princes and laymen. Bishops were spiritual ministers; they were also, willingly or unwillingly, temporal barons, committed to preserving or augmenting the lands under their control and the worldly prestige to which such control entitled them. Without the income produced by their lands, indeed, how were they to support themselves?

Amid the brutality and the rough turbulence of the 9th and 10th and 11th centuries, Europe was ruled by the power of the sword. To protect its possessions, the Church must resort to the sword, must bind itself to the mutual contracts of service by which all medieval people bound themselves. The pope himself was not immune to this necessity. As a temporal lord, he must mix in local politics or find himself stripped of the Church's property. But insofar as he bound himself with local obligations, he found his international authority endangered. Thus, about 1000, the popes found their influence, universal in theory, to be in fact narrow and often negligible. The power of the Holy Roman Empire, revived in 962 by Otto the Great, was far superior to that of the papacy. Emperors and kings used the educated churchmen as their governing officials and handed over to them vast fiefs. With this imperial patronage, however, went imperial control, and bishops owed their position and advancement to the Emperor rather than to the pope.

Early in the 11th century it appeared probable that the one ruler of the one Church would cease to be Father of all Christians and would degenerate into a petty Italian potentate. The papacy reached the nadir of its history. Popes whose character was far from exemplary ascended the throne for personal or family profit. Their moral influence decreased to zero. Their control over the Church in France, in Spain, in England, in Germany, was all but lost. They were the creatures of the "refuse" of Rome, the quarreling princes who kept the ancient seat of empire in turmoil. Finally the choice of the pope came to be the prerogative of the powerful family of Tusculum. The depths were plumbed when three members of this family were in succession elected pope—Benedict VIII, John XIX, Benedict IX—each one less capable of filling the position with dignity and less concerned with the spiritual welfare of Christendom. The world naturally disregarded the pronouncements of such popes, and even the Roman populace was at last outraged by the viciousness of Benedict IX. Driving him from the city, the people chose a new pope, Sylvester III. Benedict, contemptuous of the action of the citizens, had the effrontery to sell the papal position to a relative, who took the name Gregory VI. This last was an educated and purposeful man who set out on a series of good measures: to recover lands lost by the papacy in Italian wars; to prevent the outrageous plundering of pilgrims on their way to Rome; to halt the custom of buying church offices. Yet he himself had bought the papacy! Meanwhile, the princely supporters of Benedict had reestablished him in Rome, and the Church found itself at one and the same time with three supreme heads.

2. The need for reform and the rise of Hildebrand

Serious-minded churchmen saw the vital need of immediate reform. As their strongest available champion they begged the aid of Henry III, Holy Roman Emperor, a man of upright and pious character and the most powerful ruler in Europe. As Charlemagne had descended into Italy in the 8th century to protect the pope against the Lombards, Henry came down in 1046 to purge the Church of unworthy popes. At the council which Henry convoked, Benedict was permitted to abdicate, Sylvester was ordered to prison as a usurper, and Gregory—convicted of buying his position—was degraded and retired to Germany. With the slate washed clean, Henry dictated the selection as pope of a worthy German bishop who became Clement II. Within a little more than a year he and his successor fell victim to the unhealthy Roman climate. A third German cleric, chosen at the imperial assembly at Worms, mounted the papal throne as Leo IX.

There was an element of grave danger in the selection of these three popes (and of Leo's successor, Victor II) by the Emperor. We remember the accomplishment of Charlemagne in securing the safety of the papacy and in strengthening Christianity throughout his realm. Henry III was not a direct successor of Charlemagne. His empire was the new creation of Otto the Great—the Holy Roman Empire of the German Nation. It was limited in extent to the Germanic states and Italy, and the Emperor was rather the central figure in a loose alliance of princes than an absolute ruler like Charlemagne. But, as patrician of Rome, the Emperor might prohibit the election of anyone as pope without his authority. Even though the Emperor might give his favor to only the best-qualified churchmen, the Church would inevitably be subordinated to the control of a secular ruler and its spiritual independence thereby reduced. Would a French citizen or a Spaniard or an Italian happily obey and revere a pope hand-picked by a German Emperor? Was the papacy any better off under the thumb of Henry III than as the plaything of the Roman aristocracy?

As a matter of fact it was much better off, because of the noble aims of Henry. He gave full support to Leo IX, and under this vibrant and far-seeing leader the papacy initiated an aggressive reform movement to liberate the clergy from worldliness. The church synod of 1049 laid down the two main points of this movement: it condemned simony, the buying of a church office; it ordered the clergy to respect the ancient rule that prohibited their marrying, so as to concentrate their lives on the service of God. Aware of his responsibility as leader of Christendom, Leo progressed through Italy, France, and Germany to ensure that his reforms were being effectively carried out. To localize and simplify his tasks as a temporal prince, he exchanged certain claims to land in Germany for the overlordship of Beneventum in southern Italy. Yet it was a temporal concern that proved fatal to him. The Normans, who had been infiltrating into southern Italy since 1017, were threatening to swallow up some papal territories. Leo led a large but ill-trained army against the Normans and was hopelessly defeated. Although well-treated, the pope remained almost a year in captivity and died soon after his return to Rome.

In 1056 an insurrection headed by the influential Godfrey of Lorraine disturbed the peace of the Empire, and, in October, Henry III died suddenly. He left his realm to his infant son, with the Empress Agnes as regent. The long minority of Henry IV was marked by repeated threats of civil war and by the bickerings of the rival churchmen who tried to dominate the young king. With the strong hand of Henry III removed, the papacy found itself largely freed from imperial control. So it was possible for the Romans without consulting the Empress to choose as pope Stephen X, Godfrey of Lorraine's brother. When Stephen died in 1058, troubles broke out anew regarding the right and the method of electing his successor. The Roman nobles chose Benedict X, but the leading prelates retired to Siena and elected Nicholas II. Godfrey of Lorraine, whose marriage had brought him power over the wide domains of Tuscany in northern Italy, used his strength to secure the recognition of Nicholas. Again the Empire was not consulted.

Clearly it was desirable that a definite procedure for the selection of popes be agreed upon, to eliminate the control of any individual or group and to avert the disgrace of warfare between the papal candidates of rival factions. Nicholas II laid down such a procedure in a decree of 1059. The small group of cardinal-bishops gained the right of nominating the new pope. The larger group of other cardinals was to act on this nomination. If they approved, the choice was unalterable. It was further stated that the nominee should be of the clergy of Rome, unless no qualified member could be found. A vague provision called for the formal approval of the nomination by the Emperor, but it is notable that this electoral procedure envisioned a papacy independent of the Empire.

Unfortunately, the new procedure was not followed when Nicholas

II died. Alexander II was acclaimed pope by the clergy and people (not by the cardinals) and the imperial regency promptly put forward a rival, Honorius II. Civil war followed, complicated by a conflict between the Empress and the nobles for control of the young Henry IV. An appeal for a decision between the two popes was made to the imperial court. The synod was called at Mantua, with the archbishop of Cologne presiding, as representative of the Empire. The decision was reached for Alexander II, but the whole incident was humiliating for the pope and seriously compromised the newly-claimed independence of the papacy. Alexander revived the policies of Leo IX. Meanwhile, in Germany, the headstrong and undisciplined Henry IV reached his majority and asserted his right to rule. When Alexander died in 1073, the problem of papal election would once again have come up, had it not been forestalled as we have seen, by the popular clamor for Gregory VII.

Indeed the choice of Hildebrand was virtually inevitable, and the cardinals quickly echoed the popular sentiment. Said Cardinal Hugh the White: "From the days of Pope Leo, Hildebrand has exalted the Roman Church and has given freedom to this city. . . . We can find no better man, nor one who is his equal for the Roman pontificate." And he was declared to be "a man eminent in piety and learning, a lover of equity and justice, firm in adversity, temperate in prosperity."

Hildebrand's beginnings had been humble. Born at Sorano in Tuscany about 1025, he was the son of a goatherd. But under the influence of an uncle who was abbot of St. Mary's, he was educated in Rome, lived in a Benedictine monastery, and must early have shown signs of marked ability.

His first preferment came when he was chosen chaplain for Gregory VI. When that prelate retired to Germany, Hildebrand loyally accompanied him. There he attracted the attention of Leo IX, who brought him back to Rome. Hildebrand was made cardinal-subdeacon and entrusted with the administration of some of the papal possessions in Rome. More important, Leo appointed him papal legate to France, to investigate the possible heresy of Berengarius, a theologian whose teachings concerning the presence of Christ in the bread and wine of the Holy Communion were suspect by the Church. Hildebrand faced this difficult duty with boldness but refused to render a final decision. Not himself a theological scholar, he has been accused by some of being incapable of deciding the case. Others have praised his suggestion that the whole case be referred to Rome as a move to exalt the power of the pope. His statement at this time –"Invincible are the faith and arms of Rome"– foreshadows his future belief. On this trip to France, he was impressed by his visit to the monastery of Cluny, where the monks led a severely religious life in strictest obedience to their prior.

Under succeeding popes Hildebrand was time and again selected for delicate and important missions. For Victor II he went to France to depose prelates who owed their offices to simony. For Stephen X he urged moderation on the reformers in Milan whose zeal was endangering the lives of both clergy and laity. He went to the imperial court to uphold the election of Stephen and to gain the Empress' approval. Absent from Rome on this mission when Stephen died, he was a leader of the movement to elect Nicholas II and secured the indispensable support of Godfrey of Lorraine. Nicholas elevated Hildebrand to deacon and then archdeacon, and he became papal chancellor, with particular responsibility for political relations. At this time the papacy attained an enviable position in European affairs. In Italy, friendship was made with the Normans, who acknowledged that they held their territories under the overlordship of the pope. The strong Milanese reformers looked to the pope as their patron. Godfrey and his wife made Tuscany a bulwark of support for the papacy. In France, the moral reforms of the Church met with favor, and even Germany made no strong protests against papal pretensions.

Hildebrand favored the election of Alexander II and continued to serve him as chancellor. Their joint aim was to make effective the international influence of the papacy and to make the whole Church realize that ultimate authority was centered in Rome. Two instances deserve note. Hildebrand was delighted when William of Normandy appealed for papal approval of his invasion of England. He respected William as a ruler who was free from the sin of simony. Here was a wonderful chance to spread the influence of Roman Christianity to hitherto independent, even rebellious, England. So William carried a papal banner on his campaign. Again, after desultory warfare against the Normans in Italy, Hildebrand revised papal policy. The Normans proved generous in gifts of land and wealth to the Church. Their opponents in Sicily were the Saracens and in Apulia were the Greeks, subjects of the eastern emperor and loyal to the patriarch of Constantinople. Hildebrand realized that the Normans, conquering southern Italy, were doing the work of unification for the Roman Church, and so the pope gave them his favor.

By 1073, Hildebrand had had twenty-five years of training under six popes. He had served as their "ace diplomat and trouble-shooter." He had been a keen supporter of their reform measures and had taken the lead in determining papal policy. His loyalty to Rome and his long experience qualified him uniquely for the papal throne. In fact, many said that under Alexander II, Hildebrand had been pope in all but name. In any case, he summed up in himself all the purposes and all the strengths of the revived papacy. The choice of the people that April day was as wise as it was inevitable.

3. Gregory's plans; Church vs. State

In the 11th century we see the papacy rescued from the depths of degradation by Henry III, placed in the way of exerting a healthy moral influence by several reforming popes, but constantly threatened with secular interference, both in its particular temporal possessions and in the selection of the pope himself. One Church, one ruler; but how should that ruler be chosen? And how should he handle both spiritual and temporal affairs? We may fairly say that the papacy to which Hildebrand acceded as Gregory VII was in a state of flux, that the lines of its future development were by no means firmly drawn. Could the pope maintain his independence of all political rulers, or must he again submit to the superior physical strength of the Emperor or some other prince? Could the pope's reforming decrees purify the Church, or would it be further subordinated to selfish ambition and secular interests? Could the Church devote itself exclusively to the service of God and the eternal welfare of mankind, or would it be forced to cater to the temporary needs of some powerful state? All these questions pressed for answers, in an age of violence and unrest. What the answers would be, in the years following 1073, depended on the will and the courage and the capacity of the new pope.

Gregory had been so long involved in papal affairs that there could be no doubt of his intentions and purposefulness. His aims were simple but far-reaching: to establish the absolute freedom of the Church and to cleanse it of all corruption and worldly interests so that it might best fulfill its primary function—the service of God. It goes without saying, then, that Gregory was unalterably opposed to simony and to clerical marriage. Simony introduced into church office men wholly unmindful of spiritual duties, who bought their positions in order to profit from the attendant prestige and power and revenues. Simony put "wolves in the place of shepherds." Clerical marriage divided the minds of churchmen and exposed them to worldly ambitions. Further, it threatened, if widespread, to create an hereditary priestly caste, whose aim would be not the service of other men but the preservation of its own privileges.

In the sphere of principles, Gregory—like Nicholas I two hundred years earlier—asserted the absolute supremacy of the pope over all Christian churches. The clergy were to be unquestioningly obedient to his decrees. Bishops throughout the world were to look for guidance to the pope rather than to any national authority. Papal legates were to carry abroad his pronouncements and to take precedence over all other churchmen. Disputes were to be submitted to the final jurisdiction of the pope. He had the right to depose bishops and to annul the decrees of any lesser authority, while no one might judge him. No church council could accomplish general legislation without his consent. In short, Rome was to be the undisputed mistress of the Christian world, the pope, unique and universal, was to be the sole fount of church doctrine and law.

In the temporal realm, Gregory's first concern was to maintain inviolate the territories of the papacy. His guiding principle was that all lands held by the Church should be put to the uses of the Church. This meant that all church estates should be freed from the secular demands customarily made on landlords in the 11th century—for instance, the levying of a contingent of men for warfare. To ensure this freedom, the administrators of church estates—be they bishops or abbots—must not be obligated to lay overlords. They must owe their appointments and their allegiance directly to the Church. This held true even of the pope himself, and Gregory upheld the unconditional right of the cardinals to elect whom they would as pope, secure from any secular influence.

In his heart Gregory was worried by the evil conditions of the world and the weakness of the Church. At the outset of his papacy he wrote to the patriarch of Aquileia:

> The rulers and princes of this world oppress the Church as if she were a vile slave. They do not blush to cover her with confusion if only they can satisfy their cupidity. The priests . . . completely neglect the law of God, are neglectful of their obligations towards Him and towards their flocks. In aiming at ecclesiastical dignities they seek only worldly glory. . . . The people, like sheep without a shepherd, are unguided and fall into error and sin, and Christianity is a mere name to them.

Undespairing, Gregory planned a council, "that we may not see irreparable ruin and destruction fall upon the Church." By taking a strong position, the pope dominated the synods and met each spring at Rome, and he soon achieved success in giving effect to his aims. His councils denounced simony and clerical marriage in the strongest terms and made them punishable by excommunication—the dread measure by which a sinful person was cast out from the society and banned from the services of the Church. In 1075 excommunication was pronounced on five German bishops who had paid for their appointments, and France was threatened with interdict (a sort of national excommunication) if her king continued in the "detestable guilt of oppressing the churches."

Thus the pope exercised his rule over the Church. Meanwhile, he secured his temporal position. His strongest potential opponent, Henry IV, enmeshed in a revolution of the Saxons, wrote a letter acknowledging him as rightful pope, and humbly confessing, "I have sinned against heaven and before you with fraudulent disloyalty and am no more worthy to be called your son." Within Italy, the principalities of Beneventum and Capua swore allegiance to the papacy—Richard of Capua expressly giving preference to the pope over the Emperor. With these to form a papal guard, Gregory laid claim to the lands which had in years gone by been alienated from the Church by the avaricious Normans.

These successes in both the religious and political spheres encouraged Gregory to indulge in his fondest hope—to reunite the eastern and western churches, which had formally separated in 1054, by reclaiming the Holy Land from the Turks. "I would rather expose my life in delivering the holy places than reign over the universe," Gregory announced. There was a strain of military ambition in his character, and he pictured himself as commander-in-chief of a Christian host, delivering Jerusalem, which would be "a worthy domain for the papal monarchy." He thought of leaving Henry IV in charge of European Christendom. But Gregory's position was not secure enough to permit his departure on a distant expedition. "It was a splendid dream," Milman has written, "fruitful, like all Gregory did, for later times; but with a sigh he renounced his dream for the harsh realities of his actual position."

The reforms Gregory fostered were bound to seem troublesome and unfair to many churchmen. They presented a severe problem to many laymen who had been in the habit of benefiting from their control over church affairs. The pope's claim of unrestricted authority over the international Church conflicted with the policies and rights of secular governments. Gregory's program could not fail to arouse serious opposition. Powerful bishops in different countries were not anxious to submit to papal dictation or supervision. "This dangerous man thinks fit to order bishops as though they were stewards on his estates," complained the archbishop of Bremen. Rulers were unwilling to dispense with the counsel of able churchmen just because they had practiced simony. Married churchmen refused to abandon their families.

But it was obvious that the fiercest contention would arise concerning the most vital matter—the control of church lands. To survive in the lawless 11th century you must be strong. Strength depended on your wealth and the manpower you could command. Wealth was measured in land, and the land supported the fighting men you could raise. Over the centuries a great deal of land had been given or bequeathed to the Church until in parts of Europe it held almost half the land. It was Gregory's intention to free this land from all claims of secular rulers upon it.

Naturally enough, however, the secular rulers, intent on increasing their own wealth and power, wanted to retain their rights over as much land as possible. They could not give up their control over land without fatally weakening themselves. It was the aim of the strongest of them to consolidate their holdings and centralize their government. These things they could not do if their domains were cut up and blocks of their richest lands were under church rule. They held on to their land with a tenacity born of the deepest need.

The Church's position was equally logical. "For a priest to place his hands, sanctified by the body and blood of the Lord, in the blood-stained hands of a layman is to dishonor his order and holy consecration." If a churchman held possession of an estate under the overlordship of a layman—that is, if to be permitted to administer his bishopric a bishop must promise allegiance to a baron—then there always existed the probability that the produce and manpower of that bishopric might be diverted from the service of the Church to less worthy purposes, at the will of the overlord. The lay patron might demand special favors for himself. He might even force the churchman to assist him in seizing other lands belonging to the Church! This was a situation intolerable to a Church declaring its independence.

Here, renewed with bitterness in the 11th century, was the age-old conflict between Church and State. People were torn between two obligations: loyalty to the Church and its moral commandments; duty to obey and serve the duly appointed rulers. Even today, when Church and State are clearly separated, we face the same problem when we must choose between the belief of our conscience and the law written on the statute book. It was worse in the Middle Ages when the Church was closely involved in the same daily politics as the State. Then, to obey the Church often meant to attack the State, or vice versa. Both Church and State laid claim to supremacy, demanding the ultimate loyalty of men and women. It was inevitable that the plan of a strong pope like Gregory to rule the entire Church from Rome should collide with the plan of a strong king to rule absolutely his undivided realm.

At this point, we had better review briefly the history of this conflict. We remember Bishop Ambrose's successful defiance of Emperor Theodosius. Ambrose was clearly of the opinion that the Church's responsibility for souls made it superior to the State. "Bishops are wont to judge of Christian emperors," he suggested, "not emperors of bishops." His further statement—"To compare kings to bishops would be far more unworthy than to compare base lead to gleaming gold"—became the standard assertion of the supporters of the Church.

About a century after Ambrose, Pope Gelasius wrote to Emperor Anastasius at Constantinople:

There are two powers by which the world is ruled, the sacred authority of the priests and the royal power. Of these, that of the priests is the more weighty, since they have to render an account for even the kings of men in the divine judgment.... The priests obey your laws, recognizing the supremacy granted you from heaven in matters affecting the public order.... While you are permitted honorably to rule the human race, yet in divine matters you bow your head humbly before the clergy and await from their hands the means of your salvation.... You obey them in the sacred mysteries of religion, especially the bishop of that see which the Most High ordained to be above all others, and which is consequently dutifully honored by the devotion of the whole Church.

Apparently Gelasius was confident that Rome was at a safe distance from Constantinople, for the emperor could hardly be expected to rejoice at the receipt of this arrogant letter. We would say, further, that as regards the internal government of the Church the pope's wish was father to his thought. For here is a definite and extreme statement of two principles about which controversy had long raged. Rome, announced Gelasius, rules all Christendom, and the Church is superior to the State. Nicholas I later acted on these two principles, asserting the papal authority over all churchmen and over princes as well. Actually, however, the case was not as simple, or as simply solved, as these popes desired. As a matter of fact, Church and State had undergone what we might call parallel development. They were sometimes closely allied, as under Charlemagne, but for the most part they had grown up as separate powers, more or less equal. Now it was Gregory who was confronted with the problem of defining and defending his rights, for in 1075 the papacy and the Empire met in head-on collision.

4. The Investiture Struggle

We have now come to the beginning of the most famous single episode in Gregory's papacy—the bitter Investiture Struggle. This struggle was based on the seemingly easy question of who should have the right to nominate a man to a church office, the Church (ultimately, the pope) or the State (ultimately, the Emperor). Normally, we would answer, the Church. But, in point of fact, throughout Europe, the right of appointment had come to be exercised, to a greater or less degree, by the State. The reasoning behind this was that the bishop administered property and ruled people that were, basically, parts of the State. Therefore, the bishop must cooperate with, and be satisfactory to, the rulers of the State. From a practical standpoint, furthermore, Rome was far away and the papacy often distracted.

Before passing judgment, let us look at two typical nominees. If the Church appoints to a rich bishopric a pious and ascetic scholar, he may well send his revenues to Rome and refuse to provide men and supplies for the use of the ruling prince, who may then be unable to protect his territory from warlike neighbors. Efficient government will be impossible. The bishop's flock will have their spiritual needs carefully ministered to but may find they have lost their physical freedom. If the prince has the power of nomination, on the other hand, he will incline to choose a trusted adherent who may be counted on to enhance the glory of the princely court in peace and to lead forth the men of the bishopric in war. The state will be rich and strong, and the cathedral gloriously decorated, but the subjects will have no adviser to bring them closer to God. The question, then, was by no means a simple one. It had profound religious, political, economic, and social significance. And in 1075 there seemed no chance of compromise; neither papacy nor Empire was willing to sacrifice its "rightful" prerogatives.

The danger signal to the effect that "all was not well" between them came when Henry disregarded Gregory's excommunication of the five bishops guilty of simony. Instead of treating them as sinful outcasts, Henry continued to rely on their advice and to reward their service. They retained all their ecclesiastical honors, in direct insult to the papal court. The reason for Henry's intransigence is not far to seek. A crushing victory over the rebellious Saxons at Hohenburg freed him from internal peril and permitted him to show his true colors, which were to accept no domination from Rome. But there had already been published, with a special copy sent to Henry, the decree of Gregory's council prohibiting lay investiture. This word "investiture" means clothing, or putting on, and refers to the act of conferring on an ecclesiastical appointee the ring and the staff which are the insignia of his office. In 1075 it included nomination to ecclesiastical position, and lay investiture meant nomination by a person outside the church hierarchy. This widespread custom was now to be discontinued, the Church was "to return to the decrees of the holy fathers." This was necessary, thought Gregory, because "I scarcely find any bishops lawfully appointed and of regular life. . . . And among all the secular princes there is hardly one who prefers the honor of God and righteousness to his own advantage."

Gregory may well have suspected that he would have trouble enforcing this decree in Henry's realm. After all, it had been impossible to criticize nominations to bishoprics made by his father, Henry III, the savior of the papacy, and it could hardly be expected that the proud and wilful son would easily surrender the power of nomination which was of such great help in establishing his rule over the Empire. Gregory anticipated that Henry IV would "repay our love with hate and show contempt for Almighty God for the high office conferred upon him." And so, to begin with, Gregory seems to have been willing to reach some compromise agreement. "Lest things should seem unduly burdensome or unjust to him," Gregory might have considered "moderating the decree as passed by the holy fathers." But Henry had sought no conference and had not given any "respectful attention to the master of the Church, to Peter, prince of the Apostles," in whose "place of power" stood Gregory.

The pope knew he had one key weapon in his armory. Henry wished to be crowned Emperor, and the coronation could be performed only by the pope. By December, 1075, brandishing this weapon, Gregory had decided to make no concessions. Why? The pope may have thought that Henry was implicated in the deed of one Cencius, who wounded and kidnaped Gregory during midnight mass on a stormy Christmas Eve, only releasing him the next day at the angry insistence of the Roman mob. At any rate, Gregory's attitude hardened to severity. He informed Henry that he could not hope to be crowned until he ceased interfering in church appointments. Gregory went further to suggest that Henry's disregard of the papal decree rendered him unworthy to be ruler of Germany. Was it a threat of deposition? Henry so interpreted it and was stung to immediate reprisals.

Early in 1076, Henry summoned the German bishops to a meeting in his loyal city of Worms. If Gregory hinted at Henry's unworthiness to be king, Henry would question Gregory's right to be pope! The German bishops, of course, had all been invested by the State; many were guilty of simony; some were married. The meeting could scarcely be called impartial and its action could safely have been predicted. Because Gregory's despotism had caused discord in the Church, because he was unduly friendly with Beatrice and Matilda of Tuscany, because Henry's consent had not been secured to his elevation to the papacy, the German bishops declared that Gregory was not rightfully pope and despatched to him a message of accusation:

> Since your pontificate was begun in perjury and crime, since your innovations have placed the Church of God in the gravest peril, since your life and conduct are stained with infamy; we now renounce our obedience. . . . You have declared publicly that you do not consider us to be bishops; we reply that no one of us shall ever hold you to be the pope.

The complaints of his bishops emboldened the young king to immoderate action. In a separate letter to Gregory, he declared:

> Henry, not by usurpation but by God's ordinance King, to Hildebrand, no longer Pope, but a false monk: You have dared to make an attack upon the royal authority which we received from

God. You have even threatened to take it away, as if we had received it from you. Our Lord Jesus Christ has called us to the government of the Empire, but he never called you to the rule of the Church. By craft thou hast obtained money, by money influence, by influence the power of the sword; by the sword thou hast mounted the throne of peace, and from the throne of peace destroyed peace, arming subjects against their rulers, bringing bishops appointed by God into contempt, and exposing them to the judgment of the laity. Us, too, consecrated of God, amenable to no judge but God, who can be deposed for no crime but absolute apostasy, thou hast ventured to assail, despising the words of that true Pope, St. Peter, "Fear God, honor the King!" Thou that honorest not the king, fearest not God! St. Paul held accursed even an angel from heaven who would preach another gospel. . . . Thus accursed, then, thus condemned by the sentence of all our bishops and by our own, for your evil rule, come down! Leave the apostolic throne which thou hast usurped. Let another take the chair of St. Peter, one who preaches not violence of war, but the sacred doctrine of the Holy Apostle. I, Henry, by the Grace of God, King, with all the bishops of my realm, say unto thee, Down! Down!

This letter specified the points at issue between Empire and papacy. First, as to papal rule over the Church, Henry denied Gregory's principle that the bishops were subordinate to him alone and condemned the violence of Gregory's measures against the bishops who disobeyed him — threatening French bishops for the misdeeds of their king, releasing the laity from obedience to certain German bishops. Second, as to relations between pope and king, Henry ridiculed Gregory's "right" to depose him. No! The king was king "by God's grace," accountable to none but God, wholly independent of the pope. Further, Gregory must defer to the ruler of the Empire, without whose approval he was "false pope." Gregory had claimed the pope could depose a king. The imperial monarch, said Henry, could make or unmake a pope.

At the opening of the synod at Rome in February appeared one Roland of Parma, bearing the German accusations. To Gregory he spoke: "The king and our bishops bid thee come down from the chair of St. Peter, which thou hast gained by robbery." Turning to the cardinals he went on: "Ye are bidden to receive another pope from the king . . . for this man is no pope but a ravening wolf." Outraged, the churchmen shouted: "Seize him!" Roland would not have escaped with his life had not Gregory himself restrained the fury of the assembly.

Gregory was insulted in his person, but more important for history was Henry's assertion of his right to name the pope, which—if allowed—would transfer control of the Church from Rome to Germany.

Confidently, Gregory took the one measure available to him that was commensurate with the glory of the cause. Small and frail in body he might be, and homely in countenance, but he was no coward. His fiery spirit aroused, and convinced of the righteousness of his cause, he announced to the assembled clergy: "It behoves us to draw the sword of vengeance . . . [and] smite the foe of God and of His Church." In answer to Henry's challenge, he declared:

> In the name of Almighty God, I prohibit Henry the King, son of Henry the Emperor, who has risen with unheard of arrogance against the Church, from ruling in Germany and Italy. I release all Christians from the obligation of the oaths which they have taken to him. I forbid all men to serve him as king. . . . And since he has scorned to obey as a Christian. . . . has had intercourse with the excommunicated. . . . spurned the counsels which I sent him for his own salvation, separated himself from the Church and endeavored to rend it asunder, I bind him with the bonds of anathema.

So, Gregory excommunicated Henry. Private persons dreaded excommunication. For a ruler to be placed under the ban was disastrous. Obviously, an outcast from the Church had no right to govern Christian subjects. His counselors and officials, under threat of excommunication for themselves, were instructed to ignore his orders and despise his person. To excommunicate a ruling prince was, in effect, to remove him from his throne. Gregory had asserted two of the rights he claimed for the pope: to cast out of Catholic society a man who did not agree with the *Roman* Church, and to absolve the subjects of an unjust ruler from their allegiance.

Henry's only hope was that his subjects would disregard the papal ban. His faithful bishop, William of Utrecht, attacked Gregory as "the perjured monk, who had dared to lift up his hand against the Lord's anointed," and declared the excommunication invalid because Gregory was not truly pope. But the political situation in Germany joined with the general strength of religious convictions to crush Henry's hope. The temper of the times in the 11th century was unfavorable to political unity. The feudal nobility were delighted with an opportunity to throw off the supremacy of Henry and assert their independence, under the legal cover of the papal excommunication. Gregory had given the signal for a renewed uprising of the fractious nobles of the Empire.

This disaffection from Henry did not lead directly to full-scale revolution, but the nobles determined to meet and consider their action. The meeting convened at Tribur, on the Rhine, in October. It is possible that the nobles might have chosen another occupant for the imperial throne had they been able to settle on an intrepid candidate. Gregory himself had proposed such a course if Henry did not "with whole heart turn to God" and correct his wicked ways. Henry has been pictured as pacing the other bank of the Rhine to await the decision of the conference. As it was, the threat implicit in the meeting of the nobility forced Henry to back down from the high-handed position he had assumed at Worms, and wrung concessions from him. In a declaration, Henry deemed it wise to recognize Gregory as the rightful pope, to promise obedience to him in ecclesiastical matters, and to do penance if he could not prove his innocence of the sins for which he had been excommunicated. In an edict to the people, Henry averred that mistaken counselors had caused his break with the pope, and he advised his excommunicated supporters to seek absolution of their guilt.

Despite these submissive statements, under the terms of the papal ban Henry remained unable to exercise his rights as king. And the nobles made plans to discuss the future of the nation at another meeting, the following year in Augsburg, which Gregory should be invited to attend. Such a prospect must have been eminently pleasing to the pope, who saw in it the two-fold opportunity to establish his absolute control over the German bishops and to keep the peace by his personal arbitration of the quarrel between Henry and his princes.

5. Canossa—1077

After Tribur, Henry's cause was not lost, but he stood on the edge of disaster. He could not afford to remain under the ban, which permitted everyone to disregard at will his kingly authority. He could not afford to let the meeting at Augsburg take place, for the combined strength of the pope and the rebellious princes would limit his authority if it did not hurl him from his throne. Bitter though it was to his pride, Henry had to confess his peril and take drastic action to escape it. As Gregory moved slowly northward in Italy, demanding an escort from the princes before he would venture into Germany, Henry took the sudden resolve to cross the Alps himself. At all costs, he must prevent the pope from dictating a settlement. If Henry could not risk Gregory's coming to him, he must go to Gregory.

So, in the dead of winter, Henry climbed the snowy Alps. The crossing of Mt. Cenis was arduous. Most of the horses were lost, and Henry's wife and son had to be lowered down the mountain on skins of oxen. But the difficulties seemed as nothing when the royal party was warmly greeted in Lombardy. Many of the important people there, jealous of the house of Tuscany and smarting under harsh rebukes from the pope, were well-disposed toward the king. These friends suggested that Henry raise an army to chastize Gregory, but Henry refused. He was sensible enough to realize that he could accomplish nothing until he regained his authority at home. He would go to the pope, not as a conqueror but as a penitent. Gregory, doubtful of the effect of Henry's sudden appearance in Italy, had retired to the impregnable stronghold of Matilda of Tuscany. There, high in the Apennines, Henry sought him out, and there unfolded the memorable drama of Canossa.

Henry's excommunicated counselors had preceded him to Canossa and received absolution from Gregory. For the most important sinner, the process of forgiveness was longer drawn out. Barefoot and in a rough garment—as was customary for penitents—the ruler of the Empire stood in the snow, begging admittance to the castle in which sat the ruler of the Church. The gate stood closed. For three successive days Henry came "beseeching us with tears to grant him absolution and forgiveness." Gregory was unmoved, until even his friends murmured at his inhumanity. As a priest, while he had the authority to punish a sinner, Gregory was also bound to grant absolution to a sincere penitent. And so "at length his persistent declaration of repentance, and the supplications of all who were there, overcame our reluctance, and we removed the ban of excommunication from him and received him into the bosom of the Holy Mother Church." It is clear from Gregory's words that his pardon was grudgingly given. He had not expected Henry at Canossa. He realized that Henry, freed from the ban, would be an opponent more implacable and dangerous than before.

Canossa has been since 1077 a name to conjure with. The striking scene of the Emperor in the snow outside, and the obdurate pope inside, has made such an impact on the world's imagination that it is difficult to evaluate its true historical significance. Canossa is the symbol of the conflict of Church and State, and some see in Henry's humiliation the crowning victory of Church over State. But Canossa was far from providing a final settlement, and it is important first of all to remark those aspects of the quarrel which the meeting of Gregory and Henry did not settle. By his action Henry confessed that Gregory was pope, but he made no promise about lay investiture and he had no intention of abandoning his claim to nominate to church office. He did not swear allegiance to the pope, and he in no way admitted that Gregory had any right to depose him from his kingship. On the other hand, Gregory did not commit himself to crowning Henry as Emperor, nor did Henry gain Gregory's aid in suppressing the internal dissensions in Germany.

Simply stated, Henry went to Canossa an excommunicated king and departed from Canossa a king freed from excommunication. Politics were not discussed. The action at Canossa was purely religious. Henry humbled himself as a penitent before Gregory to secure absolution from the guilt of his moral sins. This absolution, once granted by the pope, was unconditional. Gregory had no further hold over Henry. On the temporal plane, the opposition between the two men went on as before.

Who won at Canossa? Was Henry's humiliation worth more to Gregory than the removal of the papal ban was worth to Henry?

For the time being, most of the profits fell to Henry. He returned to his realm as lawful king. He regained the initiative in his disputes with the princes, and the dangerous meeting of them and the pope was deferred. Their opposition again took on the doubtful colors of rebellion. Henry had promised that he would put no obstacles in the way of Gregory's entering Germany for a conference, but would Gregory now dare to go? He could expect no escort from the princes. They had hoped to persuade Gregory to depose Henry, but now Gregory could do them no good. Gregory's Italian enemies might regret that Henry had not chosen to attack the pope and humble the power of Tuscany, but now they freely criticized Gregory for his undue pride. Many Germans resented the lack of mercy he showed their king. Canossa so exalted the prestige of the pope that it consolidated the lay and clerical opposition to his supremacy. Gregory, thus, had climbed to a height that was dangerous because so many were anxious to push him off, while Henry had gained his immediate end—the recovery of his kingdom.

In the long run, however, Canossa was a triumph for the Church, because of its effect on public opinion. The greatest earthly monarch had been forced to submit to the pope, to bow at least to his superior spiritual authority, because the Church exerted an influence over the minds and deeds of humans which no temporal power could resist. At Canossa Henry may simply have done an act of free-will penance, but he did it because of the universal force of the papal ban. Until his excommunication was removed, Henry was politically helpless. After Canossa, no king could disregard the pope, every king must shape his policies with an eye to the reaction of the pope. The papacy stood forth to the world as a potential force for justice, as a bulwark against the iniquity and oppression of temporal rulers.

Bryce, the greatest historian of the Empire, thinks that the climactic event of Canossa worked the undoing of both sides. The Empire was dishonored, and in the future would be undermined with the support of the pope. But the papacy had raised itself to a position which the logic of reason and of history made it impossible to maintain. The cooperation of papacy and Empire which Charlemagne had created was broken forever at Canossa. From then on, papacy and Empire were enemies, and their opposition caused their ultimate ruin. If the absolute Church and the absolute State could not unite to govern, men and women would one day rise up to overthrow them both. But that is to look too far ahead of our story.

6. Aftermath of Canossa: troubles and death of Gregory

Canossa did not pacify Germany. Strife continued between Henry and the princes, in which, of course, the Church as a temporal power was involved. The princes were to meet in March in Forchheim. Gregory thought it his right to be there to serve as a sort of umpire in the German disputes. The princes invited him but urged him not to come without the safe-conduct of the king. (So much had Henry already profited from Canossa.) Gregory did not go, and he was much chagrined when the princes took action without recognizing the need for his advice and approval. They declared Henry deposed and elected as their new sovereign Rudolf of Swabia. Civil war followed.

Gregory was convinced that it was his duty to act as peacemaker and demanded from both sides a safe-conduct to Germany. But delays and obstacles were put in his path. Henry and Rudolf each felt that Gregory should declare in his favor, but the pope was in an embarrassing predicament. Rudolf was surely a usurper and Gregory had reason to distrust the princes, but Henry would never be a reliable friend to the papacy. Gregory hesitated to commit himself, and his hesitation was increased by the insecurity of his own position. Most of Lombardy hated him as a reformer, and the unreliable Norman, Robert Guiscard, was ravaging the papal domain of Beneventum. Gregory was deeply discouraged by his failure to solve the German problem. He said, "This life is a weariness to us, and death desirable." So far had he lost his usual vigor and aggressiveness of spirit.

Germany remained in turmoil for three years, with the pope's reputation suffering from his forced vacillation and with Henry gradually rallying the stronger forces to his more lawful side. Gregory made no compromise in the matter of principle; his council issued a full prohibition of lay investiture. Both the investing layman and the invested cleric were to be punished by excommunication from the Church. But in temporal affairs it was Henry who initiated a new series of decisive events. As the rightful ruler of Germany, Henry insisted in 1080 that Gregory should excommunicate the usurping Rudolf. In his ultimatum Henry expressly threatened to find another pope. This revival of the threat to the independence of the Church stung Gregory into action. He would again demonstrate that no king may stand up against the pope, who holds "the keys of the kingdom of heaven." He addressed a plea to his synod in Rome: "So act, I pray you, holy fathers, that all the world may know that if ye can bind or loose in heaven, ye can also give or take away kingdoms and all other possessions according to the merits of each man. Ye have often taken away bishoprics from the wicked to bestow them on the good. And if ye judge in spiritual things, ought ye not to be deemed able to judge in worldly things?"

Rudolf was still in the field against Henry; he might still win a final victory. Henry's insolence convinced Gregory of the righteousness of Rudolf's cause. The papal decree came forth:

> I excommunicate and anathematize Henry, so-called king, together with all his supporters; in the name of the omnipotent God, I depose him from the kingdom of Germany and the government of Italy, and strip him of all regal power and dignity. I forbid any Christian to obey him as his king and I absolve from their oaths those who have sworn or who should hereafter swear loyalty to him. May he, with all his supporters, be impotent in battle, and may he gain no victory so long as his life shall last. . . . If Henry, by his disobedience, his pride and his insincerity, has been justly deprived of the kingly dignity, so in reward for his humility, his submission, and his candor, Rudolf now receives the title of king and the regal power. . . . Let your judgment then be accomplished upon this Henry so promptly that all the world may see and acknowledge that he falls, not by chance, but by your power. May his confusion lead him to repentance. . . .

Obviously another Canossa would not have satisfied Gregory. This second decree of excommunication is much more sweeping than the first. In it Gregory asserts far more than spiritual control over Henry. He is also Henry's temporal overlord. Gregory takes his kingdom away from him and gives it to Rudolf. Gregory attempts to guide the future course of history by calling down earthly disaster on Henry's head. His unhappy future is to come, as "fire from heaven," because of the power of the Church over the king. Clearly, Gregory's own logic had pressed him into a highly exaggerated position. His demand for papal independence—the Church is co-equal with the State—had led to the assumption of papal supremacy—the Church is superior to the State and may direct it. Since the human spirit is of a higher order than the body and since the papacy controlled men's and women's spiritual state, Gregory made the further assumption that the Church surely could control men's and women's temporal state.

First, unfortunately for Gregory, these assumptions were impractical. The pope had no mighty army at his disposal. He could determine the fitness of Henry to go to heaven; he could not ensure the defeat of Henry's army. Moral power alone seldom accomplishes material ends. Second, Gregory had misjudged the temper of the times, and people were not ready to act on his assumptions. Even though in principle they might acknowledge his doctrines as desirable, they were not ready to follow them consistently in practice. They were not ready to accept the will of God, as interpreted by the pope, as the only law governing the world. 11th-century men and women were selfish and often barbarous, and these traits counterbalanced their religious idealism.

Here was the conflict between theory and practice of which Bryce writes. Men and women were glad and proud to be Christians; they were not willing to recognize the omnipotence of the ruler of Christendom in all matters. If Gregory were given the power to "bind and loose" in earth as well as in heaven, the Church would be able to interfere in all the contracts by which society achieved some security and stability in its daily living. Men and women had not yet so purged their hearts of worldly ambitions and suspicions as to be willing to take such a risk.

This is not to imply that Gregory was seeking tyrannical control over people's daily lives in order to increase his own, or the Church's, temporal power. Extreme though it might seem to others, there can be no doubt that Gregory was convinced of the logic, the righteousness, and the desirability of papal supervision over the affairs of people. How else could God's purposes be accomplished? As the head of God's Church, the pope was God's chosen representative on earth, superior to all mere humans. To him, as the successor of St. Peter, God granted authority over all Christian people. To this rule, even the Emperor could be no exception. After all, who made the Emperor? Was it not the coronation of Charlemagne and of Otto by the pope that showed God's favor toward these rulers at the same time that it legalized their position in the eyes of their subjects? Was it not the decision of the pope in 800 which had transferred the imperial crown from the head of a murderous usurper in Constantinople to the head of Charlemagne in Rome?

It was clear then, to Gregory, that the imperial power was granted by the papacy to a particular prince, and what a pope had granted, a pope could later revoke. It was Gregory's assertion that, as the earthly Peter, he was the universal overlord. All kings and princes were subject to the supervision of the Church. Gregory did not want to be himself king or Emperor. The royal power was as nothing compared to the pope's. But it was his right, as it was his duty, to ensure that kings exercise their power to forward the establishment on earth of the City of God, in which the divine will alone would reign.

As the overlord of kings, the pope was the supreme judge. Gregory assumed that earthly rulers would bow to his guidance. The Church was greater than the State, the laws of the Church were eternal, those of the State merely temporary. The State must obey, and must also protect and defend, the Church. If kings failed to be governed by the papal will, it might become necessary to punish them. This the pope was competent to do, not only spiritually—in their persons—as had been done

before by excommunication, but also materially—in their possessions—
as Gregory now tried to do by stripping Henry of his kingdom.

Gregory did not assert lightly or for his personal profit that all
rulers were responsible to the pope. The pope's function was to bring
all to God, by the shortest possible road. He was responsible for the
souls of the subjects of the king. Therefore, he must demand that the
king exert his temporal rule according to the laws of God, for the
welfare of the subjects. The king must be moral and good, to retain his
kingdom. Gregory explained this in a letter to William I of England:

> Lest the creature whom His goodness hath formed after His own
> image in this world should be drawn astray into fatal dangers, He
> hath provided in the apostolic and royal dignities the means of rul-
> ing it through divers offices. . . . If I, therefore, am to answer for
> thee on the dreadful day of judgment before the just Judge who
> cannot lie, the Creator of every creature, bethink thee whether I
> must not very diligently provide for thy salvation, and whether,
> for thine own safety, thou oughtest not without delay to obey me,
> that so thou mayest possess the land of the living.

This demand of Gregory for the right of supervision over national
politics was new. Earlier theory described Church and State both as
representative of God's authority, the one in spiritual, the other in temporal, affairs—each possessing equal dignity. While Gregory admitted
the need for an imperial power, he considered it as inferior, as delegated
by the pope. There could be no comparison between papacy and empire. They were the "two lights in the firmament of the militant church";
but the power of the Empire, like the rays of the moon, was borrowed,
weak, and intermittent; whereas the power of the papacy, like the rays
of the sun, was everlasting, unquenchable, and brilliant, by its own
nature.

The temporal overlordship which Gregory demanded could be enforced in the 11th century only by the weight of arms. Kings—especially
Henry—could not be expected to relegate themselves to a secondary
position without a struggle. The ruin which Gregory had decreed for
Henry could be brought down on his head only by war, and so the conflict in Germany was renewed.

Henry again took the initiative. A synod of the German Church met
at his command in Brixen in June 1080. If Gregory thought he could
dispose of the German monarchy, Henry would prove that he could
dispose of a pope. The German bishops formally deposed Gregory—
for heresy (Gregory had been entirely too lenient with the heretical
Berengarius)—and elevated in his stead as Clement III one Guibert
(whom Gregory had once insisted that Alexander II consecrate as bishop
of Ravenna).

Gregory rashly resorted to prophecy. Within a year, he predicted, the erring Henry would fall in battle. In October the forces of Henry and Rudolf met in battle near the Elster River. Although Henry's army was worsted, it was Rudolf who was killed. Here, said many, was the judgment of God! Gregory had been overbold. God was punishing him for his rash and unjustifiable presumption.

Lacking a really strong champion in war, Gregory was truly in a desperate position. Henry was preparing another descent into Italy, this time at the head of an army. Already, seeking allies, Gregory had stooped to a reconciliation with Guiscard the Norman. This unscrupulous and rapacious duke had been, alternately, friend and enemy of the papacy, as expediency dictated. His one real aim was self-aggrandizement. For his seizure of papal lands several years before, the pope had placed him under the ban. Now, to secure his alliance, Gregory freed him from the ban, even though Guiscard made no promise of restoring stolen Salerno and Amalfi. Thus Gregory patiently suffered a minor wrong — a rape of church property — to prevent a major wrong — the extinction of church independence.

By condoning a wrong, the pope weakened his moral position. He felt he was defending the right, but it was unfortunate that he should try to obtain a good end by the use of evil means. Guiscard was "a bandit without religion," and he did not prove trustworthy as an ally. His ambition took him off to the east, where his daughter was the wife of a deposed emperor of Constantinople and where the Normans hoped to build a mighty power. He thus was not available to help Gregory in his campaign to recover Ravenna, captured by Henry. And, in 1081, it was not Guiscard but the people of Rome who supported Gregory in defiance of Henry when the king had reached the very gates of the city.

Gregory stood firm in the face of disaster. He renewed his excommunication of Henry because, as he had said, "We are not at liberty to prefer the favor of any man to the law of God, or to swerve from the straight path for the sake of advantage." But, militarily speaking, Henry was too strong for Gregory, with Guiscard absent. In 1083 Henry captured a large part of Rome. The following year he had Clement III crown him as Emperor, while Gregory was cooped up, a virtual prisoner, in the castle of Saint Angelo. At last, Guiscard joined the contest. With "a strange army of the faithful," consisting very largely of Saracens, he marched on Rome in overwhelming force. Henry fled at his approach, and Gregory looked forward to his freedom.

But the Norman army was unruly, and its unopposed entry into Rome was followed by the most tragic event in Gregory's papacy. With Gregory helpless, and Guiscard unwilling, to check their ferocity, the army ravaged the population and sacked the city. Hundreds were killed or sold into slavery; ten years later the city was still ruinous. "The cruelty of the Normans," says an ancient chronicler, "gained more hearts for the Empire than 100,000 gold pieces." The once-popular Gregory was now so reviled that he could not show himself in the streets of his capital without his foreign guard. Here we see a tragic paradox, a great pope vindicated by a robber baron—the right upheld by wrong, so as to make men hate and fear the right.

When the Normans retired southward, Gregory had to accompany them. His resources were exhausted, and he dared not remain among the angry Romans. He was taken to Salerno, which Guiscard still held from the papacy. There he was stranded when Guiscard departed on another eastern expedition. There, on 25 May 1085, Gregory VII died. As he lay dying, bitter disappointment filled his heart. Twisting the biblical verse, he said, "I have loved righteousness and hated iniquity; therefore I die in exile." Instead of the glorious victory which he had confidently expected, he had met with mortification and defeat. While Henry reigned unchecked, Gregory had had to flee from Rome and now died in a land he could no longer call his own. He had failed in his task of redeeming the wicked world.

7. Gregory's influence

If the history of the papacy ended in 1085, we might agree that Gregory had been a failure. At his death, he left incomplete the major reforms he had projected. The pope had not secured unquestioning acceptance of his absolute power over the universal Church. His appointments were often opposed, his jurisdiction denied, his decrees flouted. Nor had he established his supremacy over all temporal kingdoms. Henry IV stood out against him, and other rulers would follow the imperial example whenever they felt strong enough.

Although the rough civilization of the 11th century did not provide fruitful soil for reforms, Gregory cannot escape some blame for failing to accomplish more than he did. He can rightly be criticized for mistakes in policy and for weaknesses of character. There was a basic, and perhaps unavoidable, confusion in his mind between the spiritual and temporal. He wanted a purified Church, and he apparently did not realize that a Church with enormous temporal possessions could not but be affected by material ambitions and worldly politics. He denied to kings any voice in church appointments but claimed for the pope the unconditional right to intervene in the appointment of the highest officials of the national churches. To attain his spiritual ends, he did not balk at the use of temporal means—forcibly to compel a reform, violently to oust a bishop. And the tools he used—the barbarous Guiscard, the self-seeking Rudolf—were seldom worthy of his lofty principles.

Even were we to admit the necessity of Gregory's mixing so much in politics, we should have to criticize him as being, while pope, a poor politician. Lacking in shrewdness, he was apt to misjudge human nature and miscalculate existing conditions. He underrated his opponents and "backed the wrong horse at the wrong time," like Rudolf in 1080. Those whom he considered the champions of the papal cause were all-too-often using Gregory as a front for their own personal schemes for advancement. Even when people acknowledged the justice of Gregory's purposes, they were alienated by his autocratic methods and his unscrupulous adherents.

There was a bluntness and imperiousness in Gregory; despite his eloquence and energy as a spiritual leader, his inflexibility repelled supporters. He was impatient for success, even if he had to bludgeon the world into agreement with him. He was callously indifferent to the material needs and the moral hesitations of lesser humans. His ardent temperament and his excess of zeal pushed him into untenable positions, where those who wanted to be his friends found themselves his enemies. A wise statesman or stateswoman never coerces when he or she can persuade. It seems only reasonable that Gregory could have gained far more from Henry if he had endeavored to understand the imperial viewpoint and had met it in a spirit of moderation instead of resorting at once to his strongest weapons. But Gregory was one who wished "to have the whole cake, and have it all at once." His courage and his faith made him dangerously single-minded. Once his course was decided upon, he followed it with headlong fervor and energy, and with never a thought of delay or compromise. Those of less-strong convictions, or of more worldly wisdom, fell away from him as though he were indeed a "Holy Satan."

But the papacy outlived Gregory's exile and death, and his tremendous influence on future events refutes his opinion that he had failed. At Clermont only ten years later, Pope Urban II, a follower of Gregory, preached a crusade. It was too bad that the Emperor, alienated from the papacy, did not take his proper place at the head of the armies of Christendom. But the expedition went forth and triumphantly liberated the Holy Land from the Saracens, as Gregory had dreamed it would.

In 1122 the Concordat of Worms put an end to the Investiture Struggle. Although the triumph of Gregory's ideas was not complete, Henry V signed away most of the control which Henry III had exercised. The Emperor could no longer nominate bishops. They were to be elected at a meeting of churchmen, at which, however, the Emperor's representative might be present and might exert a powerful influence. The actual investiture of the nominee with the ring and the staff was the exclusive prerogative of ecclesiastical officials. The authority of the

Church was thus rendered independent of the State.

Less than one hundred years after that, Innocent III raised the papacy to the peak of its power. His word determined the selection of the German Emperor; his legates effectively ruled England, the rest of Europe acknowledged his ultimate sovereignty. Only France resisted the papal authority, and even its powerful king, Philip Augustus, felt the restraining influence of the papal command. Innocent was the fully-realized Gregory. His beliefs were identical with Gregory's. In a more favorable time, he was able to put them into more effective practice.

After his death, then, Gregory's influence was productive of the greatest days in the history of the Church. The reason is that, despite unworthy means and unfortunate faults of character, Gregory worked for enduring principles, not for temporary advantage. He lived for God, not for himself. He was bravely willing to disregard past customs and precedents and to appeal to "the truth and the life." While he was determining that he must excommunicate Henry, it is recorded that he prayed to St. Peter: "And so I *bind* him, in trust in thee, that the peoples may know and be convinced that thou art Peter and on thy rock the Son of the living God has built his Church and the gates of Hell shall not prevail against it."

Like Augustine, Gregory realized that no earthly empire could compare with the City of God. His aim was to bring the kingdom of God more nearly into actuality for the people of this world, to infuse into people the spirit of Christ, to replace the prevalent rapacity, cruelty, and chaos with peace, order, and morality. This ideal may well be ultimately unattainable, but it is nonetheless noble; to it with steadfast purpose Gregory devoted his life. Because his intense faith made him obstinate and unyielding in the face of fierce opposition, the Church was able to make real advances toward the attainment of its ideal.

At the time of Gregory's death, the papacy was much greater than it had been at the time of his birth. It was a stronger force in the world, motivated by a nobler ideal, more influential for the right. In Gregory's spacious mind there had existed a vision of what the Church might become—universal, unified under papal rule, guiding society in the Christian spirit. Gregory's career determined the direction in which the Church would develop and advanced it on the road to becoming the most important and most glorious institution of the civilization of the Middle Ages. Over this Church the papacy maintained an absolute domination. The pope was infallible—he could not err; all bishops were subordinate to his authority and dependent on his favor; no church decree was valid without his consent; from his judgment there was no appeal; and his legates enforced his will on the various national churches.

At the same time, the papacy established its dominance over secular princes. "Instituted by divine grace" and "aspiring ever toward the heavenly life," the Church was of a higher order than the State, which with "human lust of power constantly strives after empty glory." So Gregory had written in 1076 to Herman, Bishop of Metz. Almost a hundred years later, Thomas Becket, Archbishop of Canterbury, made a definite statement of the papal position:

> The Church of Christ is constituted of two orders—the Clergy and the People, the one having the care of the Church that all may be ruled for the salvation of souls; the other consisting of kings, princes, and nobles who carry on the secular government that all things may lead to the peace and unity of the Church. It is certain that kings receive their power from the Church, and the Church not from them but from Christ.

According to this doctrine, the State is only semi-divine; it is really nothing more than a department of the Church; it exists solely to serve the purposes of the Church. Medieval people could therefore rightly presume that they might appeal to the papacy for justice against the depredations of lawless rulers. All kings trembled at the thought of papal rebuke, from which there was no escape. As Bryce has put it: "With his authority, in whose hands are the keys of heaven and hell, whose word can bestow eternal bliss or plunge in everlasting misery, no earthly potentate can compete or interfere."

In the possession of such sweeping powers by one human being there were seeds of corruption—of pride, of tyranny, of injustice. These were to bear bitter fruit in the 15th century. But throughout the Middle Ages the Church as an institution did far more good than harm. It preserved ancient learning; it elevated moral principles above brute force; it encouraged the practice of Christian virtues such as the service of others; it provided a refuge for the poor and the homeless, the sick and the aged, whom secular society did not bother to look after.

The Church of the Middle Ages benefited all humankind, because Gregory imagined it as embracing all peoples, not as a local, partisan institution. The people of the Middle Ages saw in the divinely-created Church the realization on earth of the City of God. This Church, with its beautiful buildings and gorgeous ceremonial, with its carefully ordered government, with its code of pure morality, was the ideal community, which all secular communities should try to imitate. This Church was God's commonwealth, directed by the divine spirit. The head of this Church, the pope, was God's earthly agent, who would interpret and execute God's will. To disobey the pope was, by implication, to disobey God.

As we have suggested, it was the papacy of Innocent III at the beginning of the 13th century which represented the peak of the

Church's power and prestige. "The Lord left to Peter the governance, not of the Church only, but of the whole world," wrote Innocent to the patriarch of Constantinople. Again, said Innocent, the pope "stands in the midst between God and man—less than God, more than man. He judges all, is judged by none." The pope, humble before God whose servant he was, stood unchallenged as the ruler of the world. This was the papacy as Gregory VII dreamed of it. Innocent could describe it in these terms in the 13th century because of what Gregory had accomplished in the 11th. Perhaps, despite his humble origins and his unimpressive appearance, Gregory was indeed, as he has been called, "the greatest pope of the Middle Ages."

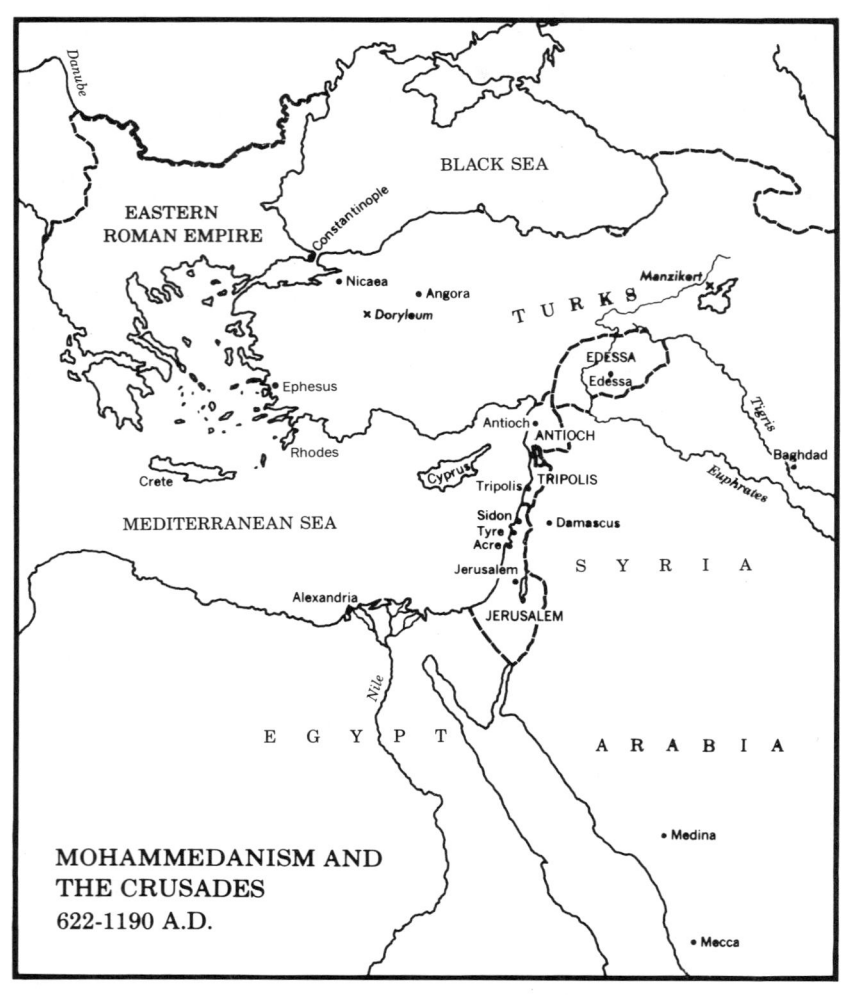

BLACK SEA

EASTERN
ROMAN EMPIRE

Danube

Constantinople

• Nicaea   • Angora

x Doryleum

T U R K S

Manzikert
x

EDESSA
• Edessa

Ephesus

Tigris

Antioch •
ANTIOCH

Baghdad

Rhodes

Cyprus
Tripolis
TRIPOLIS

Euphrates

Crete

MEDITERRANEAN SEA

Sidon
Tyre
Acre

• Damascus

S   Y   R   I   A

Jerusalem

Alexandria

JERUSALEM

Nile

E   G   Y   P   T

A   R   A   B   I   A

• Medina

**MOHAMMEDANISM AND
THE CRUSADES**
622-1190 A.D.

• Mecca

Chapter Six

BERNARD
OF CLAIRVAUX
AND
THE MONASTIC IDEAL
(1090-1153)

The story of Bernard of Clairvaux reveals the chief characteristics of medieval life as it approached its fullest development, far removed from the chaos of the Dark Ages. Civilizing forces are overcoming barbarism. The standard of living is rising. Kings are battling against the independent power of their feudal lords. The pope has asserted authority over both spiritual and temporal rulers. Nearly everybody is enlisted in the Catholic Church, and many people are devoting their lives to the service of God. Although some people, having emerged from the insecurity and fears of earlier times, are beginning to think and hope for themselves, the Church is able to unite European Christendom in the crusades to recover the Holy Land from the Turks. With all these movements Bernard was closely connected.

Probably the group of people which did most to shape the life of the Middle Ages was the monks. Before everything else, Bernard considered himself a monk. So let us start our story of his varied career with a study of monasticism.

1. Benedict and his Rule

At various times in history, when adverse conditions make life seem stale and unprofitable and human endeavor seem wicked or futile, certain people have chosen to retire from the world. Turning their backs on the greed and inhumanity of their usual society, they have sought to lead more satisfying, righteous, and useful lives. The early centuries of Christianity, coinciding with the decay of the Roman Empire, were such a period. Harsh laws, high taxes, and increasing barbarization of life made the job of leading a decent existence apparently hopeless. So, many sincere but discouraged Christians withdrew from normal activities, seeking fulfillment of their inner desires to discover the will of God and to live in accordance with it. Their retirement might be solitary. Going off into the wild spots of the desert or the mountains, like St. Anthony in Egypt, they might live as hermits. Enduring fearful hardships, such hermits impressed their contemporaries by their holiness, but their material accomplishment was negligible. To others, solitude did not seem essential to a good life. St. Pachomius in Egypt and St. Basil in Greece organized those who desired to stay apart from the world in small communities in which they might live and work together according to a fixed regimen. The man who adapted this idea of monasteries to the practical genius of the Europeans, the real founder of western monasticism, was Benedict of Nursia.

Benedict was first a hermit. Born of good family in Umbria about 480 A.D., he was sent to school in Rome. There the barbarians had just displaced the last emperor, and Benedict was struck by the aimlessness of the people around him. He fled to an isolated cave in the hills, where he passed three years in prayer and contemplation. He became an extreme ascetic: he denied himself all comforts and scourged his body unmercifully whenever he felt the slightest desire for self-indulgence.

Gradually people began to hear of this recluse, whose holiness enabled him to perform miracles like those reported in the Bible. Other men dispirited by the chaos in Rome and anxious to lead good lives, came to Benedict as disciples. He formed them into groups, and before long in the neighborhood of Rome there were under his direction twelve monasteries, each with twelve monks. Later he traveled south, converted to Christianity the country people whom he found celebrating a feast of Apollo, and erected his most famous monastery, Monte Cassino. Before he died in 543, this simple Italian monk had dared to rebuke a Gothic king for his cruelty.

The great strength which Benedict imparted to the monastic movement was the establishing of a uniform way of life, which was followed in all his monasteries and could be copied in any other monastery. To begin with, a three-fold vow was required of each man who, after a trial period of a year, desired to enter the monastery. First, he must be chaste, so that his mind might be free from the temptations of the flesh and the obligations of family life. Second, he must be ready to obey without delay or argument. "Let no one in the monastery follow the inclination of his own heart: and let no one boldly presume to dispute with his abbot, [for] 'I am not come to do my will but the will of Him that sent me.' " Third, he must accept utter poverty. "He should have absolutely not anything: neither a book, nor tablets, nor a pen—nothing at all. For indeed it is not allowed to the monks to have their own bodies or wills in their own power." By thus placing his life wholly in God's hands, the monk hopes to save his soul from wickedness and make himself worthy of the heaven which was the great promise of Christianity.

But the Benedictine Rule does not end with the three-fold vow, for Benedict hoped his monks would inspire others by their example of virtuous living. Idleness is bad for the idle individual, and provides no benefits for the world; Benedict called it "the enemy of the soul." He did not prohibit his monks from sin, but he kept them "busy with righteousness" by setting up a routine that would make their lives productive. In each day, after subtracting enough time for meals and sleep, five hours were devoted to religious services, and ten hours were divided between useful manual labor and reading in the Bible and in the works of the Fathers of the Church. "They are truly monks," said Benedict, "if they live by the labors of their hands." But neither study nor labor in the fields should ever be permitted to interfere with prayer. Monasteries were founded for the service of the Lord, and the monks' religious duties were "the work of God to which nothing is to be preferred."

Beyond supporting themselves—and each monastery was to have the mill, the bakery, and the gardens to make it self-sufficing—Benedict enjoined his monks to extend hospitality to any who might come to their door. "Chiefly in the reception of the poor, and of pilgrims, shall care be most anxiously exhibited," when the monks could expect no reward.

The Rule also contained provisions for the permanence and the internal order of the monastery. The monks took the vow of stability: they could never leave the house of which they had become professed members. Thus, no Benedictine monastery would be suddenly deserted. By way of compensation, the monks were protected as well as possible from the degeneration of their house on account of the folly or vanity of the abbot. The monks were to choose their own abbot. Then they owed him unquestioning obedience. But the abbot was not exempt from observance of the Rule. He must take counsel with his fellow-monks before making any important decision. "As often as anything especial is to be done, the abbot shall call together the whole congregation" and hear their opinions, beginning with the youngest. "On lesser matters" the abbot should "employ the counsel of the elder members alone."

As a further restraining influence on the abbot's dictatorial powers, the Rule stressed his responsibility for the welfare of his house and the salvation of its inmates. His duty was "to rule the souls and aid the morals of many, [knowing] that from him to whom more is committed, more is demanded." As a chosen leader, his aim should be "to carry out with his deeds the name of Superior. . . . Even as it behoves the disciples to obey the master, so it is fitting that he should providently and justly arrange all matters. . . . The abbot shall do all things fearing the Lord and observing the Rule; knowing that he, without a doubt, shall have to render account to God for all his decisions." If the job of the Benedictines is to serve God, the job of the abbot is to serve and guide his brothers. Like Benedict himself, the abbot must be loving as well as wise and firm.

The Benedictine Rule makes no impossible demands of the monks. It does not cut them off from all human companionship; rather it stresses the idea of fellowship and communal living. It does not require excessive mortification of the flesh; rather it sets up a healthy routine of existence. The monk's life was no doubt hard and self-denying, but it was not immoderately austere, especially if we compare it to the miserable and uncertain conditions of life outside the monastery. The monk was to have sufficient clothes and food and time to rest. And the Rule was to be made flexible by common-sense application of its provisions. "Let all things be done with moderation, on account of the fainthearted. . . . The weakness of the feeble or delicate is to be taken into consideration by the abbot." He was cautioned not to overtax the moral or physical strength of his monks by too rigorous regulations or too burdensome requirements.

Because Benedict's Rule was so sound, it began to be put into successful operation over a wider and wider area. Pope Gregory I called it "conspicuous for its discretion." It is to Gregory, who wrote Benedict's biography, that we owe most of our knowledge of the monk's career. Gregory himself, rich and patrician, held high civil office in Rome and then devoted his life and wealth to founding monasteries. When Gregory became a monk himself, he was a Benedictine. At about this time Rome was crowded with refugees from Monte Cassino, which the Lombards had just sacked. Later, in 590, the people compelled an unwilling Gregory to become the bishop of Rome. Gregory saved Italy by his diplomatic dealings with the Lombards. He acted as civil governor of Rome, establishing its defenses, and he broadened and administered the papal territories. He found the Church in imminent danger of dissolution, with many dioceses overrun and severed from connection with Rome. Over these he reasserted his control, as metropolitan or archbishop. He thus began the process of restoring the ties which bound the various churches in Europe to Rome, gaining some recognition for the rights and privileges of St. Peter and for the bishop of Rome as the patriarch of the whole Church. He was the last of the great Latin Fathers of the Church, whose writings determined its doctrine and practice.

Gregory wrote a manual of *Pastoral Care*, prescribing for the conscientious bishop the method for the good ordering of a diocese. This book has been compared to Benedict's for the good ordering of a monastery. To his manifold tasks Gregory brought the single-minded devotion of the monk. He yearned to return to the monastery, where his soul might "soar above things corruptible, and though enclosed in mortal body, would yet pass beyond its fleshly bars." But his own desires must be disregarded, even though he was "overwhelmed with the trouble of worldly business." As pope, he called himself "the servant of the servants of the Lord," and he was motivated by his sense of responsibility for all Christians.

Gregory gave the papal stamp of approval to Benedictine monasticism, and he found in the monks the most loyal, fervent, and hard-working adherents of his policies. High among these was his aim to convert to Christianity the barbarians who then occupied Britain. He had wanted to go among them himself as a missionary, and in 597 he dispatched Augustine to them with a band of forty monks. So was the Benedictine Rule transplanted to England; in the 7th century it took firm root in France; and in the 8th, English missionaries established it in Germany. By the time of Charlemagne, the Benedictine Rule was acknowledged as superior to any other, such as the Columban Rule first followed in Ireland. As monasticism was then the most highly regarded way of life, it follows that the Benedictine monks—everywhere in Europe—were regarded as the best examples of men who lived according to the precepts of Christ himself. The influence of the Benedictines was enormous; in converting the heathen, caring for the sick and poverty-stricken, educating the young, preserving learning, setting a Christian example, it was a beneficent influence.

Strictly speaking, the Benedictines never comprised a monastic order, as there were no legal ties among the monasteries. No monastery was considered superior to the others; no abbot had authority over the other abbots; no monk might be ordered to transfer to another house. Rather, the goal of the Benedictine monasteries was to achieve autonomy—the right of complete self-government—free not only of each other but of interference from any outside power. It was precisely this autonomy, we realize, which was hard to attain in the lawless days of the Dark Ages. The well-tilled fields of the monks were rich prizes to attract ambitious feudal lords. So, gradually, many of the monasteries underwent a process of feudalization, by which they fell under the influence, if not into the actual hands, of a feudal lord. Treated as a fief, the monastery would be drawn back into worldly affairs and would be expected to forward the private schemes of its overlord. As they were feudalized, the monasteries lost their purity and vigor. Their abbots began to ignore the Benedictine Rule. More and more, men joined the monastery, not from desire to give unselfish service to the cause of Christ, but hoping to find a refuge from the ills of the everyday world. Such monks were not happy to submit to strict discipline. The monastic ideal seemed in the process of decay.

The first of many efforts to revive the pure ideal was the establishment of a monastery at Cluny, in France, in 910. The specific purpose of the founder was to establish a house totally free of lay interference, both in elections and in administration of its property. The rule at Cluny was the Benedictine Rule, but with one important difference. All monasteries founded on the Cluniac idea were to remain subordinate to the mother house. The abbot of Cluny would be the "general" of an entire Cluniac order, which would have the strength to resist feudalization. This idea met with enthusiastic response. For two hundred years the abbots of Cluny were great men; Cluny was the effective center of Christian influence in Europe; and Cluny gave its support to the reform of the Church as undertaken by Gregory VII.

It is difficult, even among monks, to maintain reforming zeal. As time went on, Cluny grew into a splendid institution, mixing in politics and forgetting its primary mission to serve God. Some people felt that life in a Cluniac monastery was too luxurious and that the troubles which beset the world in the late 11th century were caused by the sinfulness of men and women. The desire to atone for sin provided a new impetus to asceticism: the good life was the life of hardship. The Cluniac monks had neglected many of the duties, both religious and physical, of the Benedictine Rule. A new monastic reform was needed.

In 1098 a group of Benedictine monks headed by Robert, Abbot of Molesme, moved into a new monastery built for them by Count Odo of Burgundy at Cîteaux. Their purpose was to go back to the strict observance of the Rule, to simplicity in religious services, and to hard labor in the fields. Such a purpose held a strong moral appeal and called forth respect for the character of those professing it, but it could hardly hold much attraction for ordinary weak and sinful people. "Everybody revered the life of these monks for its sanctity but held aloof from it because of its excessive austerity and the poverty which prevailed" at Cîteaux. The new ideal was too uncompromising to be popular and the new Cistercian monastery welcomed few converts. It was still a small and feeble institution when the able Englishman, St. Stephen Harding, became abbot in 1109. But the Cistercian order was not destined to premature collapse.

2. Bernard at Clairvaux; the Cistercian Order

Near Dijon, in 1090, there had been born one Bernard, son of a knight who later died on a crusade. The young boy was delicate and sensitive in body and spirit, and it was not strange that plans should be made for his entering the Church. His family had visions of his attaining the high ecclesiastical position which was appropriate for a member of the aristocracy and sent him to Châlons to be educated.

But Bernard was an unusual young aristocrat. Material advancement and pride of place meant nothing to him. The more he thought about his future the more he was convinced that despite the opposition of his relatives he should become a monk. If he was to be a churchman, he wanted to give his whole heart to his calling. Religion should not be a mere matter of form or convention, of holding important office and wearing handsome robes. Bernard felt called to abandon the fickle, jealous, petty world and to devote himself to the service of God. The most proper home for a sincere Christian was the austere monastery at Cîteaux, which might scare away the lackadaisical monk, but, "had no terrors for the soul truly seeking God. Without hesitation or misgivings, he turned his steps to that place, thinking that there he would be able to find seclusion and escape the importunities of men, wishing particularly there to gain a refuge from the vain glory of the noble's life and to win purity of soul."

This last purpose—to win the salvation of his own soul by denying the selfish demands of his own body, to save his life by losing it—has always been the highest ideal of the monk. In 1113 Bernard presented himself at the doors of Cîteaux and "entered the monastery, poor in spirit, still obscure and of no fame, with the intention of there perishing in the heart and memory of men." But no one is wholly the master of his or her own fate. Medieval people, especially, thought God was very close to them; he was imminent in their lives, and they did as they did largely through his intervention. Thus it was God's purpose, even more than Bernard's, that was fulfilled when he entered Cîteaux.

At his arrival, the monastery was "made glad by the Lord, for that day God prospered the house." In the first place, Bernard did not present himself to St. Stephen Harding unaccompanied. His own eagerness had communicated itself to others. He had persuaded some thirty young friends to join in his resolution of sharing in the labor and worship of the monks. So eloquent were his words that women are reported to have hidden their husbands and sons from him lest they renounce the world forever. In the second place, it was soon apparent that Bernard was to be no ordinary monk. He may have sought solitude and peace, "but God ordered it otherwise and prepared him as a chosen vessel, not only to strengthen and extend the monastic order, but also to bear His name before kings and peoples to the ends of the earth." Bernard would have said that it was God's will that he became a monk. It was also by God's will that he became the most important monk of his century.

In the decade of Bernard's arrival the Cistercian order sent forth its four great daughter-houses. The most famous was to be Clairvaux, of which Bernard was chosen to be abbot. In June 1115, "Stephen placed a cross in Bernard's hands, who solemnly walked forth from Cîteaux" with a little band of twelve followers. Northward they walked for nearly a hundred miles until they found a shady valley with a gushing stream—a location promising them solitude. There "with their own hands" the monks raised the "rude fabric" of the single building which was to serve them as chapel, dormitory, and refectory. The earth was the floor, and in the loft were box-like beds strewn with dried leaves.

The first winter was hard. Their clothes and shoes wore out; their salt-supply dwindled; their diet was limited to beechnut and roots. The courage of some failed, but not their abbot's. "Presently Bernard heard murmurs. He argued and exhorted, he spoke to them of the fear and love of God, and strove to rouse their drooping spirits by dwelling on the hopes of eternal life and divine recompense. Their sufferings made them deaf and indifferent. . . . Bernard, seeing they had lost their trust in God, reproved them no more; but himself sought in earnest prayer for release from their difficulties. . . . And presently came a stranger who gave the abbot ten livres." Bernard had not argued that life at Clairvaux would ever be comfortable, nor had he been shocked by the frailty of his companions. Instead, he had turned to God for assistance, and once again God had intervened decisively in the affairs of the Cistercian Order. Now the crisis was past; Clairvaux would survive.

Bernard brought to his task a saintly devotion and the humble sense that he was merely an agent to carry out God's purposes. In his eyes there was no higher mission, no greater opportunity, than to be guardian of the souls and welfare of his monks. His decisions would affect the lives of many; his example must show the true way to God. Bernard was harder on himself than on his fellow monks. His cell was the poorest in Clairvaux, set in an angle between the stairs and the roof, so that he could scarcely stand erect in it; his bed was simply a board.

He won his monks to him by his genuine desire to work for their good, coupled with his deep pity for their weaknesses. As abbot, Bernard was not like Benedict, whose discipline had caused his first monks to try to poison him, nor like Gregory the Great, whose uprightness made him relentless in the punishment of erring brethren. To their nobility of nature Bernard added the essential Christian virtue of charity. He knew when to temper justice with mercy.

"His zeal for conversion crowded his order with recruits." Bernard wanted to enlist monks in order to save them from the suffering that would be the fruit of their own sinfulness. Men can aspire to nothing more perfect, he thought, than the bliss of being a monk. A man who enters a monastery "from rich, becomes richer; from being noble, becomes still more illustrious; from a sinner becomes a saint. . . . Clean from the filth of living in the world, earth's dust shaken off, he may become fit for the heavenly mansion." So Bernard cannot excuse a family which tries to prevent a son from becoming a monk. But for the young monk himself, whose resolution weakens in the face of the strict requirements of the monastery, Bernard has sympathy. So he writes to plead with one Robert who had fled from rigorous Clairvaux to luxurious Cluny. But charity does not suggest for such a fainthearted monk any lowering of standards, any relaxation of the demands on his spiritual and physical exertion, for these are the road by which he marches to salvation. A life of ease gains one nothing; on the other hand, hardships—even death—can joyfully be endured, for they open the doors to the more wonderful life hereafter.

Bernard explains why it is good for the departed monk to return to the rigors of the life at Clairvaux: "Is it safer to be caught alone and sleeping than armed with others in the field? Before the enemy's darts, the shield is no burden, nor the helmet heavy. . . . Only flight loses the victory which death does not lose. Blessed art thou, and quickly to be crowned, dying in battle. Woe for thee if, recoiling, thou losest at once the victory and the crown." This is the letter which Bernard was dictating to a scribe in the open air when rain began to fall. "It is God's work," said Bernard, "write and fear not." And no rain spotted the letter.

Bernard insisted on the close observance of the Benedictine Rule. The Cistercians earned their name of Grey Monks by wearing habits of undyed wool. Their diet was meager: at Clairvaux, there was no white bread, no spices to make the food more palatable, very little wine. Each monk took his turn as cook, and many of them were far from skillful. The Cistercian monasteries could not buy land but could own only what was given them; the monks, of course, could have no personal property. Their religious services were of the utmost simplicity and their chapels, with no stained glass windows and no pictures or images of saints, were stark. Bernard disapproved of any display. "The Church is resplendent in her walls, beggarly in her poor," he lamented. "She clothes her stones in gold, and leaves her sons naked." The only ornaments at Clairvaux were statues of Christ on the Cross.

Bernard was not even interested in forming a library in his monastery. "You will find more in the woods than in books," he said. If the Cistercians were to collect libraries, as they did despite Bernard's feelings, at least they should exclude the works of pagan authors. Bernard was as narrow in condemning the classics of Greece and Rome as had been Gregory the Great, who said, "The same mouth should not sing of both Jupiter and Christ." In his zeal for self-denial, Bernard outdid his own monks; he "reduced his body to a shadow by austerities and so detached himself from the world of sense that he could drink oil for water without noticing the difference."

Bernard was ardent in the movement against the laxness of monastic discipline, the pride of bishops, the worldliness of the whole Church. "Whom can you show me among the prelates," he asked, "who does not seek rather to empty the pockets of his flock than to subdue their vices?" He was horrified at the thought that "foul rottenness crawls through the whole body of the Church." He did not hesitate to criticize his friends or those in high places. He spoke of the important Abbey of St. Denis as "a school of Satan, a den of thieves." From Clairvaux, under the impetus of Bernard's driving spirit, spread the reforming mission. Before Bernard died, he had sent out sixty-five bands to establish new monasteries, uniform with Clairvaux in discipline. There was then a total of two hundred and eighty Cistercian houses, and the order had replaced Cluny as the dominant religious force in Europe.

Among the Cistercian houses Bernard had made Clairvaux preeminent. Its location was famous throughout Christendom, its disciplined life universally admired. "The still silent valley bespoke the unfeigned humility of Christ's poor. . . . In this valley full of men, where no one was permitted to be idle, a silence deep as night prevailed. The sounds of labor, or the chants of the brethren in the choral service, were the only exception. . . . The solitude in a certain sense recalled the cave of our father St. Benedict, so that while they strove to imitate his life, they also had some similarity to him in their habitation and loneliness." Many noblemen, even, entered famous Clairvaux and altered their lives and characters: "I knew them proud and puffed up; I see them walking humbly under the merciful hand of God," said Bernard.

The Clairvaux monks were considered "perfect followers of Christ. . . . Singing, without fatigue from before midnight to the dawn of day, with only a brief interval, they appear a little less than the angels, but much more than men." To enter Clairvaux was to take part in a life purer and better than that outside. About 1150, William of Malmesbury wrote: "The Cistercian Order is now both believed and asserted to be the surest road to heaven . . . a model for all monks, a mirror for the diligent, a spur to the indolent." As Gibbon puts it, "By a vow of poverty and penance, by closing his eyes against the visible world, by the refusal of all ecclesiastical dignities, the Abbot of Clairvaux became the oracle of Europe."

As a monastic order, the Cistercians had an organization that was a compromise between the Benedictine congregation of independent monasteries and the highly centralized Cluniac system. The Cistercian order resembled a family tree. The mother-house at Citeaux established four daughter-houses, as we have seen, and these in turn established daughters of their own. As a mother watches over her children, so Clairvaux—for example—retained some rights of inspection and supervision over her own daughters because "for love's sake we desire to retain the care of their souls." But the control from above was not absolute. The Cistercian Charter, as sanctioned by the pope in 1119, was aristocratic rather than autocratic in principle. The abbot of Citeaux was not a "general" like the abbot of Cluny. The Cistercian Order was governed, rather, by an annual conference of abbots.

The Cistercians did not have as widespread an influence as the earlier Benedictines or Cluniacs, nor were they as successful in raising the general moral and intellectual tone of European life. They have been criticized for being more interested in the salvation of their own souls than in improving the world around them. But they made at least two significant contributions to medieval civilization. Returning to the Benedictine tradition of farming, they concentrated on the breeding of domestic animals and raised the healthiest cattle in Europe. But their chief claim to worldly fame was as wool-growers; for quantity and quality, their wool was unsurpassed. Also, in arranging for the sale of their product across international boundaries, the Cistercians contributed to the expansion of trade that was an outstanding characteristic of the late Middle Ages. Seeking solitude, the Cistercians usually founded their houses in inaccessible places. Then they worked indefatigably to cultivate the fields that had hitherto lain waste. In so doing they "turned thickets into cornfields and osier-beds into vineyards," increasing again the production of wealth.

3. Mysticism or rationalism?

With such material matters Bernard was not much concerned. It was not to them that he owed his success in recruiting the Cistercian order, in governing Clairvaux, in spreading his influence throughout

Europe. His influence derived from the nobility of his soul. Bernard exemplified the highest monastic ideal. He was a true monk, who abandons this world for the love of God. Walking in the cloister, in prayerful meditation, he feels himself closer to God, more aware of God's purposes, readier to execute God's will, than he could possibly be in the fields, the market place, or the feudal castle. His religion is stimulated by the communal services of the monastery; but at bottom it is very personal, based on contact between God and the individual, an affair of feeling and sentiment.

Bernard's was the faith of medieval people at its best and purest. His heart reached out for intimate friendship with God. He did not adore him because of his particular characteristics—his omniscience or omnipotence. He did not want to dissect God or to argue about him, because it was via the emotions, not via the brain, that one could know the nearness and the kindness of God. Bernard turned away in distaste from theological argument. A religion that had to be rationally explained was not really a religion at all. Religion is faith. The essence of faith is belief—belief beyond, independent of, and impervious to, reason. "The faith of the righteous believes," said Bernard, "it does not dispute."

So Bernard cared nothing for "scientific proofs" of God's existence or nature. He needed no evidence beyond what his heart told him, which included everything important: God existed and God loved the world so deeply that he gave his only Son to redeem the world from sin. And Christ the Son loved humans so deeply that he willingly suffered death as a man that we might thereby be given the chance to be redeemed. It is clear that the essential element in the relation of God to his world, and in the relation of Christ to mortals, is love. It is correct to speak of God as living by a law only if we remember that that law, holding the universe together, is love.

A man's goal as he enters a monastery is to feel, closely, this love of God for him and to respond to it by his own love for God. This experience of the love of God does not come to an individual because he or she is learned in scripture or because he or she does good works in the world. It can come only by the grace of God. Nothing will accomplish our salvation save the grace of God, which was exhibited once and forever in the sacrifice of Christ for all. The story of that sacrifice, in fact the basis of all the Church's doctrine, is to be found in the Bible, which was to Bernard the supreme source of truth and bulwark of faith. In the Bible are to be discovered both the deeds and the purposes of God.

Bernard gladly echoed the words of the great Christian Father on whose works the whole fabric of medieval Christianity was founded.

St. Augustine, Bishop of Hippo had said: "Nothing is to be accepted except on the authority of Scripture, since greater is that authority than all the powers of the human mind." Faith comes before reason; faith is superior to reason. Like Augustine, Bernard was indifferent to the knowledge of "natural laws." To try to penetrate the mysteries of the universe, to search beyond the truth as miraculously revealed to humans in the Bible, would be to fall into a maze of uncertainty. "The fuller my faith," on the other hand, "the more will I understand."

All the thoughts of Augustine and Bernard, far apart in time but close together in doctrine, revolved around God. As they meditated, there grew in both a profound love of God. Augustine said, "Thou hast made us for thyself, and we cannot rest until we rest in thee." He thought of God as the inspiration, the creator, and the center of that City of God of which we may all one day be joyful inhabitants. Augustine's feeling has been described as his "grandly reasoned love of God." Bernard's feeling was even more fervent. "No 12th century soul loved God more zealously" than Bernard, but his was a God humanized in Christ, who could experience the emotions of fear and pity. If it were possible to divide the indivisible, we might say that Bernard loved Christ more than he loved God. His faith was based first on his estimate of Christ, the loving God-man, immeasurably superior in moral splendor to all others. This Christ loves Bernard, and all people, with a love that truly passes understanding.

"Jesus, the very thought of thee with sweetness fills the breast," Bernard wrote. "How kind thou art to those who fall, how gentle to suppliants, how good to those seeking thee! What must thou be to those who find thee!" And Bernard felt a deep personal yearning for communion with this Christ:

> Beneath Thy cross abiding
> For ever would I rest,
> In Thy dear love confiding,
> And with Thy presence blest.

Bernard's life was thus a continuing search for Christ. Self-discipline and asceticism might be hard, but the monk's life was not forbidding. Rather it was what he most wanted and what he considered most worthwhile. His religion was not a list of prohibitions, but a series of fulfillments. And his zeal was joyous because, while he searched, Christ was also seeking him.

Bernard, as we have been describing him, was a mystic. "The essence of mysticism," writes a modern scholar, "lies in the surrender of a human personality to a spiritual power beyond itself.... The mystic hopes to arrive at a feeling of deliverance from the world and...

to enter into the knowledge of God and into God's very existence." The surrender is personal and emotional; his or her knowledge of God cannot be demonstrated; rather it is intuitively felt. Through private prayer and contemplation, the mystic *experiences* God, and finds peace and salvation.

Bernard, the mystic, lost his soul to God, but he had no intention of retiring as a hermit. He tried to share his experience of God in his sermons. He felt that Christianity depended on "the experience of the vision of God," but he knew at the same time that the mystic's vision of God is not alone enough to regenerate the world. The vision must inspire the real Christian to devote himself or herself to the service of humankind. The love of God demands also the love of one's neighbors.

In the Middle Ages the universal goal was to get to heaven. The sincere lover of one's neighbors felt impelled to strive to save their souls from sin. The way to salvation was fixed. The individual was made deserving of the grace of God by receiving the various sacraments of the Church at the hands of her ordained ministers. The surest way to lose your soul to the Devil, on the other hand, was to fall into heresy. The heretic who denied the teachings of the Church, who doubted the efficacy of the sacraments, who refused the ministrations of the priest, was surely destined for eternal punishment. Love of neighbor, therefore, compelled a fierce hatred of heresy. The average citizen feared heretics and approved harsh treatment of them. A Spanish bishop was praised who "sent them to the fiery stake as they merited, in order that these workers of iniquity should perish with their wickedness as a wholesome lesson to others."

It as far worse to be a heretic than a non-Christian. People rated the shame and ignominy of heresy as an "unspeakable evil, in comparison with which all other crimes are as trifles." A popular story related how God had sent loathesome toads to eat out the tongue of a heretic who suffered death, showing thereby "how foul and infamous are the teachings of heretics."

It was natural for Bernard to share the sentiments of his era about heresy. There was much human sympathy in his character. We have noted that he was gentle to sinners like weak-willed monks. He grieved unabashedly at the death of his brother, Gerald, even though monks were supposed to ignore all family connections. But, against heretics, his very concern for his fellow's good demanded that he should be firm.

Heretics, wrote Aquinas, the greatest of all the medieval scholastics, "deserve not only to be separated from the Church by excommunication, but also to be severed from the world by death, [for it is] a much graver matter to corrupt the faith which quickens the soul than to forge money, which supports temporal life." Bernard would have concurred in rating spiritual welfare far above mere physical, eternal far above mere temporal. To be sure, Christ had preached mercy, and therefore the Church seeks to redeem heretics. Bernard said, "It is not by force of arms that we must crush them, but by argument . . . by education and persuasion." But his patience with heretics went only so far. A heretic who repents may be saved, but if he or she refuses repentance his or her own soul must be sacrificed in order to save the souls of others. A relapsed heretic, one who repents and then reverts to an unauthorized opinion, is particularly dangerous. If that heretic repents a second time, he or she "may be admitted again to penance, but not spared the pain of death."

4. Bernard, Abelard, and papal politics

Peter Abelard was a well-known teacher in the schools of Paris. As a youth he had attended the lectures of the great scholars of his time but had soon become dissatisfied with their teaching. Abelard challenged them as being neither willing nor able to support their statements with any proof. His brilliance in debate forced them into confusion, and the charm of his personality attracted followers who heaped ridicule on his antagonists. Abelard argued that scripture—on the literal truth of every word of which the schoolmen were insisting—was in places inconsistent, or even obviously foolish. If he could expose such blemishes in any part of scripture, said Abelard, then it followed that people should not unhesitatingly accept the authority of scripture. Rather, they should subject scripture to rational criticism to find out what parts of it they may accept as logical and true. Here was a horrifying suggestion! The teachings of the Church were being doubted! The church authorities planned to investigate this dangerous teacher, to discover evidences of heresy for which he might be condemned. Abelard was constantly harassed, until finally he demanded a showdown.

The place and time chosen for the trial of Abelard was the Church Council at Sens in 1141. Here there was to be a great exhibition of holy relics, so that a vast congregation of the most important religious and civil dignitaries was assured. It was essential to find a defender of orthodoxy outstanding in both ability and prestige. Obviously—the abbot of Clairvaux, "the giant of the Church." Modest of his learning, Bernard was not anxious to contend in argument with a trained logician. But his participation was represented to him as a public duty: "All men had prepared for the spectacle . . . his absence would cause scandal." Putting his trust in God, Bernard prepared to attend the Council. In truth, fearing for his beloved Church, he could not resist applying "all his vehement energy to stay the progress of this great plague." In Bernard's eyes, Abelard was clearly a heretic, with whom the Church could make no compromise.

The world awaited expectantly the combat of these two famous men. Both were noted for their skill in oratory, their interest in human nature, their ability to win the hearts of their hearers. It was truly to be a meeting of giants. The case of Abelard appeared strong. He had been anxious to confront Bernard "in fierce logical combat." Convinced that truth was on his side, he arrived at Sens attended by a worshipful and notable "troop of disciples." As a matter of fact, however, Abelard's case was hopeless. His judges, among whom were some personal enemies, stood only to lose if he should be acquitted. Although Bernard came to Sens "with only two or three monks, as it behoved a Cistercian abbot to travel," he had behind him all the weight of position, of tradition, of recognized authority. The world was not impartial; Abelard "addressed the reason of a few; Bernard inflamed the hearts and passions of all classes." Bernard was the child of light and man of God, facing Abelard the fiend.

Bernard opened the case by reading passages from Abelard's work for which he was charged with heresy. Abelard, despairing of justice from the unsympathetic audience, suddenly appealed his case to Rome and left the assembly. The council was thrown into confusion. Were its hands now tied? The pope, as we saw in the case of Gregory VII, claimed for his court jurisdiction superior to that of any provincial council, but there was still some doubt as to the legitimacy of his claim. If Abelard's appeal were heard, how would the papal curia decide? Under Bernard's leadership, the council determined upon a curious half-way measure. Abelard was permitted to depart from Sens without hindrance, but his works were condemned as heretical. It was assumed that Pope Innocent II owed so much to Bernard, as we shall shortly see, that he must validate a decision that was agreeable to the great abbot. As a matter of fact, Abelard never reached Rome to make his appeal. His health broke down and he took refuge at the monastery of Cluny, where in 1142 he died.

Berengarius of Poitiers addressed to Bernard a justification of Abelard in which he sneeringly described the bishops of the council as "these moles, judging a philosopher." Bernard himself was emphatically not a philosopher; he was a churchman who did not pretend to distinguished learning. In the combat between the churchman and the philosopher, the specific heresies of Abelard which were condemned are no longer of much interest, even though Bernard accused Abelard of imitating the doctrines of Arius, Pelagius, and Nestorius — three of the most notorious heretics in all church history. What gives the combat its significance is that it was one of the earliest battles between religious faith and secular reason. Bernard was shocked by Abelard's "laughing contempt for authority." Abelard maintained that no authority, however sacred, can be permitted to stand in the way of the search for truth—truth that commends itself to human reason and that, upon examination, can be proved. The venerable Fathers of the Church, the authors of the Bible itself, being human, were prone to err. Their works, therefore, should be freely subjected to scientific criticism. Faith is dependent on reason.

By contrast, thought Bernard, faith can only exist if it is separated from reason. Faith is better, stronger, surer than reason. The authority of the church Fathers cannot be questioned, much less refuted. Outside the framework of church doctrine, there is no such thing as knowledge. To try to explain the "sacred mysteries" of the Christian faith is to desecrate and destroy them, and ultimately to detach people from the love of God. The battle between the unhesitating faith of a Bernard and the rational inquiry of an Abelard continues to this day. In 1141, Bernard's cause was victorious. To read his opinion of Abelard is to learn much about his faith and about the temper of his times.

Bernard thought Abelard presumptuous for "rushing in upon the hidden things of faith," which should be kept hidden. "Abelard is trying to make void the merit of the Christian faith when he deems himself able by human reason to comprehend God altogether. The man is great in his own eyes." In Bernard's view God, being God, has purposes which are not, and should not be, comprehensible to the human intellect. God can only be perceived in the vision of the mystic, and then not clearly. The Christian faith is greater than the mind of any individual Christian can compass. Bernard objected to Abelard because "this man has no mind to believe what his reason has not previously argued." His self-assurance was as outrageous as his teachings were intolerable.

After condemning Abelard's views, Bernard attempted a final refutation of them. He wrote:

> He defines faith as being opinion. As if anyone might think or say what pleased him concerning it; or as if the sacraments of our faith, instead of reposing on certain truth, depended on wandering or various opinions. . . . If the faith is unstable and rests not upon most undoubted truth, is not our hope in vain? . . . God forbid that we should think as he does, that there is anything in our faith and hope which hangs on a doubtful opinion. . . . Differently indeed writes St. Augustine: "Faith dwelleth in a man's heart, not by guessing and thinking but by certain knowledge, conscience bearing witness." His definition of faith, I confess, pleases me: "Faith is the substance of things hoped for, the evidence of things not seen". . . . You may not think or dispute on the faith as you

please.... By the name *substance* something certain and fixed is placed before you; you are enclosed within unchanging limits. For faith is not an opinion, but a certitude.

Bernard could have Abelard's opinions condemned as heretical and he could support himself with quotations from St. Augustine. For the person who did not hold his faith, however, Bernard could not make it "a certitude." On the whole, though, the 12th century did not mind. Earthly life was hard then for almost everyone, but heaven promised much. The 12th century world agreed with Bernard that, without faith, there would be nothing to live for.

Bernard did not enjoy his conflict with Abelard. Away from Clairvaux he was always homesick. Regardless of personal health or inclination, however, "the eager watchdog of the faith" could never fail to respond to a summons to serve his beloved Church.

Like Gregory, Bernard thought that the pope should be the shepherd of Christendom rather than its prince. So he was acutely unhappy whenever the papacy became mired in political disputes. But we have already seen that medieval Rome was, as Bernard called it, a center of war and discord. When its quarrelsome nobility and unruly populace rose in opposition to Pope Innocent II and set up an anti-pope, Innocent appealed to Bernard for help. Bernard won for Innocent the support of England, France, the Empire, and the cities of northern Italy. It is said that the Milanese were so impressed by Bernard's personality and oratory that they wanted him to be their bishop. Finally, with reluctance, Bernard went to Rome and persuaded the anti-pope to abandon his pretensions.

In 1145 a former monk of Clairvaux was elected pope as Eugenius III. Here was testimony to the influence of Bernard, who had swayed the policies of kingdoms and ended the disturbing papal schism. It might well have been of this particular point in Bernard's career that Gibbon wrote, "Princes and pontiffs trembled at the freedom of his apostolic censures." The prestige of Clairvaux now surpassed that of Rome itself. Bernard complained that all those who sought favors of the pope came first to him rather than to Eugenius, as though Bernard were the veritable ruler of Christendom.

Bernard warned Eugenius of the trouble he would face in Rome. "Who is ignorant," he wrote, "of the vanity and arrogance of the Romans? A nation nursed in sedition, cruel, untractable, and scorning to obey, unless they are too feeble to resist...." But the worst was yet to come, for Eugenius was driven out of the city by the mob under the leadership of Arnold of Brescia.

This Arnold is an interesting revolutionary. He and Bernard shared one basic opinion—that the Church must cleanse itself of worldliness and corruption. Both wished for a return to the time when, as Bernard described it, "the Apostles cast their nets to catch, not gold and silver, but souls." But Arnold went much farther than urging moral reform. A pupil of Abelard, he preached the complete overthrow of the hierarchy of the medieval clergy. He said the churchmen should live in apostolic poverty, abandoning all their landed property and their secular authority. He denied to the pope that "fullness of power"—both temporal and spiritual—which was the basis of Bernard's thinking about the Church.

Arnold's denial of the pope's supremacy was too much for Bernard, who enlisted against him the power of the French king. The vehemence of Bernard's condemnation of Arnold attests the heat of his passions, burning usually in love but now turned to hate. Bernard harried this dangerous radical throughout Europe. Here we see exhibited a rather unappealing aspect of Bernard. So fierce were his feelings that, if he could not convert his opponents, he sought to destroy them. His denunciations were picturesque. Arnold, he wrote, "whom Brescia vomited forth, Rome abhorred, France repelled, Germany abominates, Italy will not receive." But Bernard was wrong. Arnold was acclaimed by the mob of Rome, where he created a "republic" over which he ruled as virtual dictator. The pope was unable to return to Rome until after the capture and execution of Arnold, which did not occur during Bernard's lifetime.

5. Mohammed: the spread of a new religion

It was not only in combatting heresies and making popes that Bernard traveled and preached. It was inevitable that he should take part in that most romantic enterprise of the Middle Ages, which evoked the full energies of both Church and State, the Crusades. These were a series of expeditions, covering a period of two hundred years, devoted to the recovery of the holy places of the Christian faith from the Mohammedans. Before talking of the Crusades, it is necessary to learn something of the history of the Mohammedans.

Mohammed was one of those very few people whose lives have had a profound effect not only on their own time and country but on the history of the world. He was born in 570 A.D. in Mecca, the holy city of the Arabs, where was located the great black sacred stone, the Kaaba. Mecca was a trading center, and the young Mohammed soon started traveling with caravans to Syria, Egypt, and Mesopotamia. He received little formal education but spent much of his time in the desert, observing the majesty of nature and mingling with the independent Bedouin tribesmen. The keen-witted Mohammed made an early success in the caravan business and was able to marry a rich widow named Khadija, who gave him the security and the loyalty which were vital to his future career.

At about the age of forty, Mohammed grew conscious of a new mission. He was prone to fall into trances, during which he felt that God was speaking to him. He became convinced that he was chosen to be the mouthpiece of God, revealing God's intentions to the people of Arabia. Out of natural timidity, Mohammed spoke of his vision at first only to a small band of friends. They became his secret followers and wrote down the words which he uttered in his states of trance. When these sayings were later collected, they comprised the Koran, God's disclosures of himself to his prophet Mohammed. The Koran emphasized the futility of idol-worship and the command to worship the one god, strong and all-knowing, yet compassionate and merciful. "God alone is; God alone has power. . . . His will is the best and wisest for you."

Fear of ridicule and suppression delayed for several years the publicizing of Mohammed's teaching. But, as a matter of fact, the ground in Arabia was already prepared to receive his message. Christianity, Judaism, and Zoroastrianism had penetrated into the Arabian peninsula, and the Arabs were ready for a monotheistic religion, based on sacred writings, which provided them with a firm moral code. Furthermore, a single faith would help to bind the various tribes together and give them strength to face their enemies.

Obviously, however, Mohammed's new ideas would not gain immediate popularity among the people or, more especially, among the traditional authorities. To cease worshiping the Kaaba would be to take from Mecca its distinction as a holy city. To listen to Mohammed as the oracle of God would be to cease obeying the dictates of the established government. Naturally, therefore, Mohammed aroused opposition, which his persistence changed to persecution. Many of his followers sought safety in exile, and Mohammed planned his own flight to Medina. At just this time the authorities had perfected a plot to kill Mohammed, but he and his faithful follower Abu Bekr made good their escape by night and reached Medina after weeks spent as desperate fugitives.

This flight from Mecca to Medina, known as the Hegira, 622 A.D., is the beginning of the Mohammedan calendar. It marks the turning point in Mohammed's career, when he was transformed from a hunted fanatic into a triumphant prophet. The people of Medina welcomed Mohammed as their leader. He demanded nothing extraordinary of them—only that they should believe in one God, Allah, and in Mohammed, his prophet, and should pay an income tax. He allied the new converts in Medina, the Helpers, to his original followers from Mecca, the Emigrants, by banding them together in brotherhoods. Mohammed's cause was based on a simple, universal faith, bolstered by a vigorous *esprit de corps*.

The situation could not remain static. The supremacy of Mecca depended on the suppression of Mohammedanism. Conversely, the survival of Mohammedanism depended on its expansion. Mohammed began the conflict by attacking the caravans from Mecca, and this soon developed into war. An initial victory gained prestige for Mohammed, and a later truce gave his followers the right to enter Mecca peacefully on the annual pilgrimage to the Kaaba, which Mohammed had accepted as one of the duties of the faithful. On these occasions Mohammed made many converts, even among prominent Meccans, and the idea spread that he could not be defeated. By 630, when he led an expedition against Mecca, the city was ready to open its gates to him. When Mohammed commanded that all Arabs accept his faith, it was clear that his victory over Mecca symbolized both the victory of Mohammedanism over idol-worship and the unification of the Arabian tribes under a single leader.

Despite the death of Mohammed only ten years after the Hegira, the main principles of his new religion were firmly established. Arabia was converted to Mohammedanism. Mecca remained the holy city and the Kaaba remained the central shrine, but the new faith—Islam—meant the surrender of the Arabs to Allah, the one, all-powerful God. Islam bore certain resemblances to the faith of the Hebrews and the Christians, from which it was descended, but was based on God's final revelations, made to the latest and greatest of the prophets, Mohammed. To Mohammed, who superceded the prophets of the Old Testament and Jesus Christ, Allah revealed his commandments for the government of the faithful. Arabia, under Mohammed, became a theocracy with Church and State combined. Only the followers of Islam could be citizens of the Arab state; only the faithful could serve in the army of Islam to which Allah called them.

The army of the faithful was to be the weapon by which Islam would spread its new word. Already it had reached to the borders of the Byzantine and the Persian empires, and Mohammed had written bold letters to their emperors, promising that they would not be harmed if they embraced his faith. Mohammed had seen the folly of ruthless destruction succeeding conquest. Even the implacable enemies captured in Mecca he welcomed as converts to Islam. Non-Arabs need not even be converted; they would be tolerated as a laboring caste. Their produce would maintain the state and sustain the army of believers. By 632, Mohammed had given to Islam its creed and its code of laws, its goal and the policies by which the goal was to be attained.

How are we to account for the extraordinary success of Mohammed, hunted as an outlaw in 622, revered as the sole prophet of an inspiring and expanding new religion in 632? First, there was his character. Mohammed was a visionary, but there was nothing impractical in his mastery of the art of handling people. Tactfully adapting his manner to his audience, he attracted the interest of all classes and roused their loyalty to him and his ideas. No hypocrisy or selfish ambition degraded his approach to others. His demand for their support was sincere and produced a sincere response. "No emperor with his tiaras was obeyed as this man in a cloak of his own making."

Furthermore, the rules to which Mohammed commanded obedience were definite and simple, appropriate to the Arab nature and to the spirit of the times. The righteous citizen will believe in Allah, and to demonstrate this faith will abide by Allah's universal moral law, will pray regularly, will fast and refrain from self-indulgence, will make a pilgrimage to the Holy City, will give alms to the poor. He or she will be rewarded for this constancy at the last judgment by being assigned to a cool and shady Paradise, where comfort and pleasure will be enjoyed eternally. And even in this life, obedience to Mohammed's commands "raised the standard of living." The popular historian Will Durant echoes Gibbon as he sums up the improvements which Mohammedanism brought to the Arab world: it "raised the moral and cultural level, promoted social order and unity, inculcated hygiene, lessened superstition and cruelty, bettered the condition of slaves, lifted the lowly to dignity and pride, and produced sobriety and temperance."

Above all, Mohammed's teaching served as a timely stimulant to a vigorous people whose energies had long lain sleeping. Mohammed blew the trumpet-call which reawakened the civilization of the Near East that had submitted for a thousand years to the successive domination of Persia, Greece, Carthage, Rome, and Byzantium. He called the waiting Arabs to action. The Mohammedan must disregard danger, outdo all others in endurance, accept hardship without complaining. Most important, the True Believer must be ready to fight and die for the faith. This was not a harsh duty but a glorious opportunity. Here lay the fulfillment of the Mohammedan's highest destiny. "Marching about morning and evening to fight for religion is better than the world and everything in it," Mohammed taught. The fighter for the faith, pursuing the most noble career open to men, is sure of salvation. "The sword is the key of heaven and hell: a drop of blood shed in the cause of God, a night spent in arms, is of more avail than two months of fasting and prayer. Whosoever falls in battle, his sins are forgiven." "Paradise is before you," a Moslem commander promised his troops on the eve of a battle, "the devil and hell fire behind."

What Arab could resist the appeal of this fighting faith? The imperatives of Mohammed's teaching opened limitless vistas to a people who had been poor and oppressed. At one stroke they might ensure both their spiritual and their material well-being. "The roving Arabs," says Gibbon, "were allured to the standard of religion and plunder." To fight under Mohammed's banner, to spread abroad the new faith, was their duty. To win a victory over the decaying power of Persia or the Eastern Empire, to capture a famous city, was to lay hands on the fabulous spoils of the oriental world. To die while fighting was inevitably to exchange the difficulties of this life for the perfect bliss of heaven, where one might recline in the shade and enjoy forever the highest pleasures imaginable. So the Moslems "advanced into battle with a fearless confidence; there is no danger where there is no chance." Their fate was in Allah's hands; win or lose, their future would be better than their present.

Mohammed's teaching and the state of the world in the 7th century combined to make it certain that the followers of the new faith would be energetic, warlike, fanatical in their devotion. Good Moslems knew that they must surrender to the will of God; it turned out that this will was for them to conquer the world for Allah.

At the time of his death Mohammed had set afoot schemes for the expansion of Islam beyond the natural boundaries of Arabia. The confident fighting spirit of the Arabs found expression in the wills of Abu Bekr and Omar—the leaders who successively assumed the task of executing the Prophet's commands. This spirit resulted in a spurt of expansion that for speed and extent and permanence is without parallel in history.

The first forward rush of the Moslem armies met with almost incredible success. Attacking Syria from behind, they found their opponent's finances disordered, fortifications dilapidated, morale weak, as a result of political and religious disagreements. The great cities of Damascus and Antioch fell to sieges, the aging Emperor Heraclius not having a strong enough army to succor them, and in 637 Jerusalem surrendered. Attacking Egypt, the Mohammedans again met little popular resistance and overran that rich province by 641. Then they turned eastward to conquer Persia, already exhausted from her warfare with the Empire, in a quick campaign. Operating from the ancient seaport of Alexandria, the Mohammedans constructed a fleet that was able to challenge the imperial navy, to assist in the capture of Mediterranean islands like Cyprus, and to send out raids in the direction of the great capital of Constantinople. By the end of the century, the fall of Carthage had left the Moslems supreme in all of North Africa; by 714 they had crossed the Straits of Gibraltar, occupied Spain, and reached the Pyrenees.

A combination of factors serves to explain the progress of the Mohammedan power. Their armies moved with unexpected speed. Careful breeding of horses provided them with good mounts for their armored cavalry, equipped with javelins. Instead of bulky wagon trains, they employed camels for their transport. Often they lived off the lands they conquered. Divided enemies seldom put up whole-hearted opposition to their advance. By contrast, the Mohammedans were carried forward by their newly-developed purposefulness and by their strong-willed leaders, and each overhelming victory added to their sense of the exaltation of their mission. Their caliph, the title taken by the successors of Mohammed, was the commander of the faithful—king, high priest, commanding general all at once. There was no problem of Church and State; in Islam political law and religious doctrine did not need to complement each other because they were one. Above all, of course, it was the inspiration of the Prophet himself that drove them on. Belief in Mohammed's message brought Arabia to life, says Carlyle. "Belief is great, life-giving. The history of a Nation becomes fruitful, soul-elevating, great, so soon as it believes."

The effects of the Mohammedan conquest were by no means all bad. In many cases their living faith replaced an uncertain Christianity. The Mohammedans were seldom cruel. Those they overcame were offered three choices: become Mohammedans; pay tribute to the Mohammedan treasury; or be killed. Very few people found it impossible to accept one of the first two opportunities. The conversions were, on the whole, genuine, and the tax revenues increased enormously.

Nor were the Mohammedans as a rule intolerant, at least of people. Omar permitted the Christians to live on in Jerusalem and to retain possession of most of their holy places, although he ordered a mosque built on the site of the Temple. This does not mean, to be sure, that there could possibly be any true religion other than Islam. When he captured the world-famous library at Alexandria, the same Omar said scornfully, "If these writings of the Greeks agree with the book of God, they are useless and need not be preserved; if they disagree, they are pernicious and ought to be destroyed."

For almost a hundred years the Moslem armies swept everything before them, until "Arabia is at Granada on this hand, at Delhi on that." "Allah Akbar!"—God is great—was their war-cry. One brilliant success followed another, until Moslem and enemy alike became convinced of the invincibility of Allah's host. Early in the 8th century, writes Gibbon, "The Caliphs were the most potent and absolute monarchs on the globe . . . their prerogative in no way circumscribed . . . the supreme judges and interpreters of the Koran . . . reigning by right of conquest over the nations of the East, to which the name of liberty was unknown." In habit and in thought, the greater part of our ancient world had been Mohammedanized in less than a century.

Then, within a single generation, at the frontiers of their empire, the Moslems met two decisive defeats. These set the limit to their conquests and drew lines on the map beyond which the Arabs were never able to advance. The first defeat came in 718 under the very walls of Constantinople. The Arabs had mounted a combined military and naval offensive against the Byzantine capital. The emperor, Leo the Isaurian, earned undying fame by his indomitable defense. The superiority of the imperial fleet and the secret weapon of the day, known as Greek fire, were too much for the 80,000 Arabs. Faced with starvation, they raised their siege and retreated. The other defeat, at Tours in 732, we have already noted. The embattled Frankish infantry halted the 75,000 Arabs under Abd ar-Rahman, slew their leader, and rolled them back to the Pyrenees.

The Arabs had never before met such solid resistance as Leo and Charles the Hammer had put up, and it was this solid resistance that had stemmed the tide of their advance. But it is also true that a change was taking place in the spirit of the Arabs. Their first youthful vigor was exhausted; the offensive impetus that had carried them to the eastern and western gates of Europe was spent. The great days of Mohammedan civilization were far from over. Indeed, the development of their most extensive commerce, their contributions to learning and the arts, the full flowering of the gorgeous life of *The Arabian Nights*, were still in the future. But the expansion of the Arabian Empire was finished. Increasingly, the energies of the Arabs were to turn to indulgence of their appetites and mistreatment of their subjects.

The defeats at Constantinople and Tours, the high water marks of the Arabian Empire, left serious wounds and started a process of internal bleeding from which the Arab power was never able to regain its fullest strength. The Ommayad family which had held the caliphate was overthrown by the Abbasid. The new caliphs moved the capital from Damascus to Baghdad, more remote from the dangerous frontiers, but the Empire was no longer united. Spain, still in the hands of the Ommayads, became an independent power; and later Egypt also, under the Fatimite dynasty, broke away from Baghdad.

There were occasional upsurges of offensive spirit and active achievement. One such occurred in the reign of Charlemagne's contemporary. Haroun-Al-Raschid, whose court far surpassed the western emperor's in splendor. It was Haroun who sent a water-clock and an elephant as gifts to Charlemagne. Partly for his own political purposes, the sophisticated Haroun recognized Charlemagne as the patron of the Roman Church in Jerusalem, and Charlemagne established a hospital and library there. As a military leader, Haroun marched his army into western Asia Minor and captured Angora, but his expeditions have been described as raids in force rather than as serious invasions. Their object was plunder, not permanent annexation. After Haroun such raids continued: Sicily fell to the Arabs; the Spanish Moslems took Crete; and African Moslems raided Italy and burned Monte Cassino. Even these successful raids testify to increasing disunity. The 9th century on the whole was a period when weak caliphs permitted civil disturbances to waste the resources of the state and to increase the spirit of separatism which could only culminate in the dismemberment of their unwieldy Empire.

In their magnificent capital at Baghdad, the Abbasid caliphs resorted to two dangerous expedients. They placed their personal safety in the hands of a mercenary bodyguard. They assigned their ruling power to a chosen assistant—a vizier, or emir, or sultan. Abdicating their responsibility, they could abandon themselves to a life of pleasure. Gibbon describes the effect: "The luxury of the caliphs relaxed the nerves and terminated the progress of the Arabian Empire. Temporal and spiritual conquest had been the sole occupation of the first successors of Mohammed; and . . . the whole revenue was scrupulously devoted to that salutary work. The Abbasids were impoverished by the multitude of their wants and their contempt of economy." Halted in their victorious course, excluded from Europe, Allah's warriors found nothing further to accomplish. Lacking the discipline of a serious purpose, they ceased to be militant and so ceased to be creative. Mohammed had failed to tell them what to do after they had conquered the world.

The dying of the Arab creative urge did not extend to the "arts of living." As so often happens in history, a period of political decline is a period of flowering in the arts and crafts. Life was far more comfortable and agreeable in Baghdad than in Aachen. There were more *things* to be enjoyed; more *ideas* to consider. Commerce thrived, with few trade barriers and a stabilized currency. Canals and windmills irrigated the soil to produce citrus fruits, sugar cane, cotton. Spiced foods graced the tables, and rare jewels graced the persons of the rich. Household ornaments were of delicately carved wood and ivory. Silk-weaving and metal-work were raised to the status of arts. The development of paper permitted a diffusion and conservation of learning unimaginable in the west. The Arabs preserved the works of Greek philosophers, especially Aristotle. Their calculating devices and scientific instruments permitted them to experiment in mathematics and the physical sciences. They improved upon the medical and astronomical knowledge they had acquired from India. The Arabs of the 9th and 10th centuries lived in a highly cultured world.

But riches and learning do not weld a state together or invigorate its leaders. Political disintegration continued. The old Byzantine empire was able to seize the initiative and put the Moslems, for the first time, on the defensive. The Greek rulers recovered the islands of Crete and Cyprus, reconquered most of Asia Minor and parts of Syria and Mesopotamia, and annexed the exposed territory of Armenia on the eastern frontier. Meanwhile, the caliphs at Baghdad had grown more impotent under the domination of their emirs and bodyguards.

Then a new force appeared in the east, to threaten both Greeks and Arabs. This was the rugged warrior race of the Seljuk Turks. Starting as nomads in Central Asia, they had migrated from the steppes around the Caspian Sea, across the Volga River, to the Black Sea area, and finally to Persia, where they displaced the Mohammedan rulers. In the meantime, as they were moving westward they were learning to make use of the superior knowledge of the Arabs and they were converted to Mohammedanism. Finally they were invited to Baghdad by the Caliph. They rescued him from the hands of his old courtiers, only to place him under their own control. The newcomers from the east did not destroy the Arab empire; they simply became its new masters.

New converts to Islam, the Seljuk Turks brought to Baghdad a fervid zeal for Allah, a raging hatred for the infidel. A new racial strain, they brought a new vigor and ambition. With a new military discipline, they reestablished the unity of the empire and revived its aggressiveness. Having with comparative ease dominated the Moslem world, they prepared confidently to overwhelm the Christian. Under their great leader Alp Arslan, they defeated the Greek emperor at the battle of Manzikert in 1071 and occupied Jerusalem. Alp's successor as Sultan, Malik-Shah, took Antioch in 1084, and the Greek empire was once again reduced to little more than Constantinople. The Turks had mastered Persians, Arabs, and Greeks. The eastern world was in their hands, reunited and strong. Then, in 1091, Malik-Shah died, and quarrels broke out among the subordinate leaders as to who should succeed him.

6. The First and Second Crusades

An interesting conjunction of circumstances existed in the world at the end of the 11th century, pregnant with possibilities. A renewed concern for their spiritual welfare (responsible, we have seen, for the Cistercian monastic reform) caused an unusually large number of Europeans to desire to make a pilgrimage to do penance on the holy ground of Jerusalem, at the same time that the fanaticism of the Seljuk Turks had made it newly difficult and dangerous to visit the holy places. The clever diplomat and schemer Alexius Comnenus had acceded to the throne of the Greek empire at the same time that the death of Malik-Shah had left the Moslem empire leaderless. And in Rome Pope Urban

II, in the tradition of Gregory VII, was anxious to assert the influence and prestige of the papacy.

It was Alexius who took the first significant step in initiating events. Regardless of the split that had separated the Greek from the Roman Christians in 1054, he appealed to the pope for assistance in recovering the Holy Land from the Turks. But it was the action of Urban II that was critical. He cared little for reinforcing the Eastern emperor, but he seized the opportunity to call forth the feudal forces of Europe to serve under the papal banner in a great religious war that would augment his own power as it spread the Christian faith.

Late in 1095 Urban went to Clermont in northern France. One day he addressed a vast crowd in the fields outside the town. A Frenchman by birth, the pope spoke to the people, not in learned Latin, but in popular French. He told of the shame of having Christian churches in the hands of pagans. He emphasized the special irritation to the pilgrims of the Turks' presence in Jerusalem. He condemned the bigotry of these ferocious Moslems who robbed, imprisoned, or tortured the helpless and innocent Christians. He mentioned the peril in which western christianity stood, now that its eastern defences had been so disastrously breached. Then he appealed to the spirit of chivalry which he knew was in the heart of every one of his hearers. Having exposed to them the obvious wrongs which the Moslems had done to their Church, he urged the crowd to act forcibly and promptly to right these wrongs. "Come forward to the defense of Christ." You, who are so well accustomed to fighting, "fight now a just war," a war which God himself approves. In offering these medieval men a chance to indulge their fighting instincts, Urban promised them a new and certain path to heaven. "Labor for everlasting reward," he cried. "If any should lose their lives . . . their sins will be forgiven them. I grant this to all who go."

The effect of Urban's magnificent speech was immediate and electric. No one heard it unmoved. A contemporary ballad puts it:

> From son to sire, like holy fire,
> God's spirit spread his word;
> Was not one eye of thousands dry,
> Was not one heart unstirred.

When Urban held aloft the Cross, a great shout arose from the multitude: *"Dieu le veut* — God wills it," and each man signed himself with the sign of the cross. Urban appointed Bishop Adhemar as his papal legate to command the First Crusade.

A wave of crusading fervor swept Europe. Everyone wanted to go — rich and poor, noble and serf, devout churchman and sinful layman. Some dreamed primarily of their personal salvation, some of the possibility of plunder; some, especially men from the Italian cities, saw new markets for trade; others, especially younger sons of knights, hoped to win lands of their own. Some glimpsed an opportunity for glamorous adventure—an escape from tedium or unhappiness. The Crusade was such a vast enterprise that there was room for them all. On the whole, the impulse behind the Crusade was generous and commendable. "With one passionate outburst the people sought to free themselves from the pressure of earthly wretchedness." Here was a chance to serve God, to rise above the sordidness of everyday living to a higher level of devotion and achievement. They were led on by "the flaming zeal of feudal Christianity. . . . Overmastering and unifying all was the passion to wrest the sepulchre of Christ from pagan defilement and thus win salvation for the crusader. Greed went with the host, but it did not inspire the enterprise." Urban had kindled a true flame in the heart of Europe.

Crusading was a brand new adventure for western christendom, and it is not to be wondered at that the initial effort gave rise to confusion and delay, waste and heartbreak, especially among the ignorant. Where is Jerusalem? How can we get there? Who is to lead us? Will we really have to fight? Why not set out at once, and get it over with? Some did set out, too soon, and many got lost and never reached their destination. There was unnecessary bloodshed and persecution along the way, as the crusaders clashed with local inhabitants, and crime and starvation—as well as simple wavering of purpose—reduced their numbers. One motley group, under the leadership of Walter the Penniless and Peter the Hermit, is known to history as the Peasants' Crusade. The peasants reached Constantinople, but they were pushed from pillar to post by the Byzantines, and their efforts ended in frustration.

The real First Crusade began later. It was a typical feudal host, led by a group of powerful barons under the nominal command of Adhemar. Here again the tale is one of confusion; progress eastward was slow, and when Constantinople was reached the political wrangling began in earnest. The various forces constituting the Crusade had differing aims. Urban and Adhemar thought of it is a great movement of religious enthusiasm that would establish the preeminence of the papacy. Alexius cared little for the Church but wanted to regain his empire. Many of the barons had ambitions of their own.

At last the Christian army moved into Asia Minor, and the first real battle—at Doryleum in July 1097—resulted in a narrow victory for the crusaders over the local Moslem force. Promptly the conflicting purposes of the barons resulted in the division of the crusading army, but the main body laid siege to Antioch. Not until June 1098 did Bohemond the Norman manage to occupy the city and besiege the citadel. The Moslems, meanwhile, had surrounded the besieging army, and despair spread in the Christian ranks. Many of the crusaders slipped down the walls by night to desert, earning themselves the picturesque title of "rope-dancers." When the Christians were on the verge of surrender, a youthful zealot dug under St. Peter's Church and discovered a rusty lancehead. This relic, proclaimed to be the lancehead which had pierced Christ's side, inspired the crusaders to redoubled efforts. A desperate assault broke the Moslem siege.

Now the death of Adhemar, quarrels between Bohemond and Raymond of Toulouse, and grumbling by the rank-and-file caused further delay. It was not for still another year that the crusading army came in sight of its main objective—Jerusalem. Of the 250,000 who had originally taken the cross, perhaps 30,000 were now in the army of Godfrey of Bouillon. In July 1099 the attackers successfully stormed the walls and swept through the city. Mercilessly they cut down everyone they could find, giving vent to the emotions that had been building up since the occasion of Urban's call to arms at Clermont. They waded through blood to the Church of the Sepulchre, which they reached "sobbing for excess of joy."

The Crusade was accomplished; the Holy City was liberated. But among the victors there was no voice of authority acceptable to everyone. Therefore, in deciding what to do with their newly-acquired territories, they naturally followed the customs in which they had been educated. The eastern world—Outremer, as the Europeans came to call it—was cut up according to the feudal pattern. On Christmas Day 1100, Godfrey's brother Baldwin was crowned king of Jerusalem. But his realm was not unified, and the feudal rulers of the other principalities, Antioch, Edessa, and Tripoli, thought of themselves as the equals of the king. Meanwhile, successive contingents of reinforcements setting out to march from Constantinople to Jerusalem were cut off by the Moslems and destroyed. Although the Christians enjoyed individual successes at Acre and Ascalon, at Tyre and Sidon, the land route to Jerusalem was never secure.

In 1118 the death of Baldwin—virtually the last of the original leaders—marked the end of the spirit of dedication to a cause which had brought the First Crusade to its goal. Outremer was still no more than a loose collection of fiefs, whose lords might quarrel with each other as well as with the Moslems. How long could the Christians of Outremer, so far distant from their sources of spiritual and material strength, maintain themselves in a hostile, unfamiliar world?

Western Christendom was struck with astonishment and horror by the report that at Christmas, 1144, the Moslems had reconquered

Edessa. The Christian states which had been so confidently established in the East were not safe. Unaided by Europe, they could not hope to survive. A plea for assistance came to Pope Eugenius III at Rome. There was need for a renewed effort by the Church, a regeneration of the crusading spirit. Eugenius resolved to enlist the whole weight of the Church in the cause. And so we come back to Bernard of Clairvaux.

Bernard trusted little in the value of pilgrimages; a better way to find God was through prayer and self-denial. But he was, of course, acquainted with the idea and the events of the Crusade. He had played a chief part in the founding of one of the institutions designed to give permanent effect to the accomplishment of the First Crusade—the religious-chivalric order known as the Knights Templar. He had secured official recognition of this order in 1128. An intimate friend of its Master, Hugo of Champagne, he had probably had a hand in compiling the stern rules the Templars were to live by. There was a close similarity of spirit, purpose, and manner of living between a knightly order like the Templars and a monastic order like the Cistercians—above all, a sense of selection and consecration. "All who despise your own wills and with purity of mind desire to serve under the supreme and veritable King and with minds intent choose the noble warfare of obedience, whom God in His mercy has chosen out of the mass of sinners for the defense of the Holy Church, hasten to associate yourselves perpetually." So reads the prologue to the Templars' rules. In one of the rules there is a harshness we would deplore today. "The Christian who slays the unbeliever in the Holy War is sure of his reward, more sure if he himself is slain. The Christian glories in the death of the pagan, because Christ is thereby glorified." If the loving Bernard wrote that, we might well say that he had been influenced by the fighting creed of Mohammed.

Bernard was never really content working "in the world." In 1146, he was worn and frail, tired by many journeys and controversies, ready to return to the beloved peace of his monastery. But he had become, as we know, the most prominent and influential churchman of his day. It was inevitable that the pope should summon him, once again, to work for the Church. Bernard, ready to sacrifice everything for "a matter which concerns the service of Christ, in whom is our salvation," saw his duty clear.

So, forgetting his weariness, he became the "prophet and missionary of God" and went forth to preach the Second Crusade. The first great gathering was in Vézelay at Easter. Pale and emaciated though Bernard was, his appearance stirred the people as he and King Louis VII stood on the platform together and he sought to arouse the enthusiasm of the multitude. "When the light from that thin, calm face fell upon them, when the voice flew from those firm lips, and words of love, aspiration, and sublime self-sacrifice reached their ears, they were no longer masters of themselves or their feelings.... Presently rose a shout of 'crosses, crosses,' and Bernard began to scatter among the people the large sheaf of them which had been brought for the purpose. They were soon exhausted. He was obliged to tear up his monk's cowl to satisfy the demand."

Bernard traveled about northern Europe, preaching with consummate skill. He pictured the infidels prepared momentarily to burst "into the very city of the living God," which would be "an irremediable grief to all time, an irrecoverable loss, a vast disgrace, and an everlasting shame." What were his brave hearers going to do? Here was their real chance, especially for those among them who were sinners. "The Lord, your God, is trying you. O ye sinners, He wills not your death, but that you may turn and live.... Now He seeks occasion for your benefit.... God is kind.... I may call it a highly favored generation which has happened upon a time so full of indulgence." Bernard urged them not to give up fighting but to fight in the service of God. For this, they could not fail to be rewarded. "Let not your former warlike skill cease, but only that spirit of hatred in which you are accustomed to kill one another.... Now, brave knight, now, warlike hero, here is a battle you may fight without danger, where it is glory to conquer and gain to die.... Take the sign of the cross and you shall be pardoned for every sin that you confess with a contrite heart."

And Bernard preached with phenomenal success. His charm, his sincerity, his humility acted as a magnet. "Wherever he appeared, the usual bonds of society seemed loosed, and all moved around a new center of life." In Spires, at Christmas, he persuaded Emperor Conrad III to take the cross, a feat that ranked as a miracle. "His progress from Constance to Cologne," reports Gibbon, "was the triumph of eloquence and zeal." At Frankfort so great was the press around him that he was in danger of being suffocated. "At last, laying aside his cloak, Conrad gripped Bernard in his brawny arms and hoisting him over his shoulders, carried him away to safety." The experience of 1095 could not be repeated. The time was past for a spontaneous uprising of the people, fresh with hope and ignorant of risks. But the zeal that was aroused, the armies that were recruited, the leaders that were enlisted—all were Bernard's doing.

The story of the Second Crusade is short and full of woe. It does not directly involve Bernard, for he did not himself go to the East. There was, to be sure, some talk of making him commander-in-chief, but Bernard, "in wonder where the popular excitement would stop," wisely declined to serve in that capacity. Every sensible person then must have applauded his refusal, and we are happy now to be spared what could only have been the tragic sequel. So Louis and Conrad were to share the command.

Disputes between French and Germans broke out before they had even left Europe. The Greek emperor antagonized the westerners with his demand that any lands they might seize should be fiefs of his empire. In a related controversy, he promoted the land route toward Jerusalem over the open sea route favored by Roger of Sicily. Conrad elected to move overland from Constantinople, and Louis shortly followed his dangerous lead. Advancing into the barren hills of Asia Minor, each met with near-disaster. Then the two monarchs decided to join the expedition that King Baldwin III was preparing against Damascus. Here was another blunder, for this city had been friendly toward the Christians and might have allied with them against the marauding Moslems of the interior. In front of Damascus there were bitter clashes of temperament and purpose between the eastern christians and the newly-arrived crusaders. In July 1148 Baldwin abandoned the half-hearted siege. The Second Crusade had petered out.

Bernard, of course, had had nothing to do with the military errors that had dissipated the strength of the Crusade: poor strategy, bad timing, and a fatal lack of concerted effort at crucial points. But someone had to be blamed for the debacle and Bernard, as the prime mover of the whole enterprise, was held responsible. Because he had foretold the glorious destiny awaiting the crusaders, he was now accused as a "false prophet." All those who had ever trembled before the severity of the high-minded monk now hastened to revile him. Even Bernard felt the sting of their criticism.

7. Bernard and "lost causes"; Bernard the Saint

The collapse of his Crusade proved to be a blow too dreadful for Bernard to withstand. His plans and hopes, prayers and trust, had fallen into "an abyss so deep that I call him blessed who is not scandalized" by the disaster. He could not recover the full vitality of his spirit. In truth, Bernard's work was finished. He had never given thought to his own comfort or safety, and his body was now broken by his austere living and endless labors. His loyal Cistercians claimed him, and he returned with relief to his monastery. He had found that in this disappointing world even a person of the greatest reputation is really but a "pilgrim and stranger." He would place his reliance, not on humanity, but on God's grace. In 1153, Bernard of Clairvaux died, a simple and faithful monk who had spent his life in the service of his God and his neighbor.

In this chapter we have mentioned famous men—princes, crusaders, thinkers, Benedict of Nursia, Gregory I, Mohammed. Unlike the kings and popes, Bernard never held a position with broad ruling authority. Nor was his life creative in the sense of originating something new, as Benedict with a monastic order or Mohammed with a new religion. Does Bernard belong on this list of famous men, indeed near the top of it?

Let us begin with a simple recital of his deeds. He ended a schism in the Church and made a pope. He led a monastic revival and promoted the reform of the clergy. He put down the most notable heretic of his time and won a place among the great mystics of the Christian faith. He launched a crusade. This bare list of accomplishments is evidence of his ability, versatility, and effectiveness. Here was a man whose concerns ranged over the whole European world and whose opinions made a difference to people of various careers and classes. Kings and popes listened to his admonitions. There can be no doubt of Bernard's importance to his time. He exercised power, not by force, but by the firmness of his convictions – eloquently expressed, compelling obedience. He "swayed Christendom as never holy man before or after him."

An estimate of Bernard's impact on his era nevertheless awakens the modern reader to the sense of tragic irony. Famous though his deeds were, it is interesting to observe how his career is representative of a civilization then approaching its highest peak of development and before long to begin its decline.

Bernard's name is associated with beliefs and institutions soon to decay, with what we might call a succession of "lost causes." For example, he gave his energy to the crusading movement which already had outlived its original inspiration and was doomed to ultimate futility. He defended the cause of faith against inquisitive reason, condemning the pursuit of scientific knowledge for its own sake. But Abelard was preparing the way for an intellectual revolution that cast aside authority and was to give to the 18th century the name of the Age of Reason. Bernard upheld the pope in his demand for universal obedience against the rising surge of nationalistic ambitions. He asserted the power of the Church over the State; today the State may consult the veterans, the farmers, or the unions, but it prefers not to bother with the Church. By word and deed, he maintained the unity of the Church, which the Church itself was to destroy by its blindness, its pride, and its rapacity in the days before the Reformation. He derided the carved animals of Cluny as "ridiculous monsters," but such carvings were to grow in popularity and lend fascination to the Gothic style. He himself had prophesied as much when he wrote of the gargoyles presenting "so rich and amazing a variety of forms that it is more delightful to spend the whole day in admiring these things piece by piece than in meditating on the Divine Law." Bernard believed—probably above all else—in self-renunciation, in submerging one's own will in the will of God, but the gratification and the glorification of the individual were to become, with the Renaissance, the chief motives of modern society.

Such a view of Bernard not only suggests the irony of our most intense strivings, but also calls to our minds outstanding differences between the civilization of the Middle Ages and our own. Bernard gave himself to causes which we have very largely abandoned as either hopeless or misguided. Our lack of sympathy with his aims—the inevitable idea that he was foolish or intolerant—makes it harder to evaluate his achievements accurately.

One measure of a person's greatness is that different eras, each from its own point of view and for its own reasons, should agree in their evaluations. Bernard's contemporaries were convinced of his greatness: the high and the mighty admired him for his forthrightness; the poor and the humble were awed by his holiness. An early medieval chronicler, Otto of Freisingen, true to his religious tradition, wrote of him as "venerable in life and manners . . . renowned for signs and wonders." Bernard was a miracle-worker; he had interrupted his crusade-preaching to restore the sight of a blind man and thus had convinced the people that he spoke with the voice of God.

At the dawn of the Renaissance, Dante wrote his *Divine Comedy.* In his imagined visit to the other world in the company of Virgil, Dante climbed up through the various stages of Purgatory, meeting many famous people along the way. In the very highest position of Paradise, Dante found Bernard, who presented the poet to the Blessed Virgin.

Modern authorities, more sophisticated than the 12th century, less credulous than Otto, and less prone to flights of fancy than Dante, still assert the value of Bernard's contribution to our world. For example, this summary: "He upheld Christian civilization against barbaric violence and worldly legalism without fear. . . . [He was] a beneficient influence in a world of passionate misdoing."

The occasions have been rare, then, when individuals have denied that Bernard fairly won his name of Saint. Noble of mind, he staunchly defended the right as God gave him to see it, and yet he was humble of heart. Vehement against worldly pride or wrongdoing, he was fierce in his denunciation of the wicked heretic, the cruel pagan, the arrogant ruler, the self-indulgent monk, and relentless in the campaigns he waged against them. But he was charitable to weakness and he took pity on the sinner. The steady motivation of his life was his gentle love of humankind, growing out of his understanding of the love of God for him.

Architecture and the Decorative Arts

THE CRUCIFIXION - *Enamel plaque, approximately 11 x 7 inches, early 13th century. In her town of Limoges Eleanor of Aquitaine patronized the production of such striking enamels, intricately designed and decorated and sometimes studded with jewels.*

175

The Bettmann Archive

CELTIC CROSS - *Missionaries carried Christianity into distant Ireland c. 600 A.D. The people would be reminded daily of the central role of their faith by monumental crosses like this one, 17½ feet tall, erected in the 12th century at Moone Abbey in County Kildare.*

PROCESSIONAL CROSS - *A silver cross that was mounted on a staff and carried in all church processions is shown. It is decorated with local plant forms, symbols of the apostles, and the Lamb of God. From the cathedral treasure at Essen.*

The Bettmann Archive

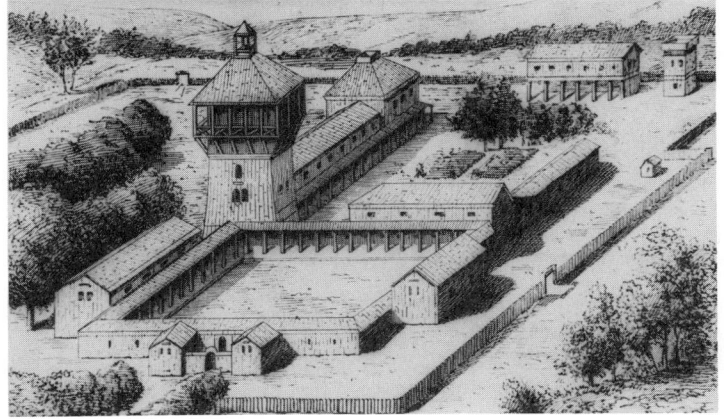

The Bettmann Archive

MEROVINGIAN VILLAGE - *A simulation of a settlement of Clovis' time, including fortification, storehouses, and buildings for communal living. Fields for cultivation and pasturage lay outside the village perimeter.*

The Bettmann Archive

CHINON - *This view across the River Vienne shows the full development of the medieval fortress on a commanding hill. Townspeople clustered in dwellings well below the walls, along the river bank. The Angevin Treasury was kept under heavy security at Chinon, the favorite castle of Henry II.*

The Bettmann Archive

S. SOPHIA - *An east-west cross section of the cathedral. Byzantine architecture emphasized columns and round arches, with delicate and colorful decoration of ivory, marble, gold, and mosaic. The central dome covered a vast open space. The statue of Justinian outside was destroyed in a later war.*

The Bettmann Archive

CANTERBURY CATHEDRAL - *By contrast to Byzantine, 13th-century Gothic cathedrals emphasized the Latin cross shape, towers, buttresses, pointed arches, large stained-glass windows, and a west front crowded with statuary and stone-carving.*

SAN VITALE - *Interior of the cathedral in Ravenna, 6th century. Small arches, decorated columns, and a profusion of ornament are typical of the Byzantine. On the north wall leading to the apse (to the right in the photo) a mosaic depicts Justinian meeting with church officials. On the opposite wall is a mosaic of Theodora and her retinue.*

VEZELAY - *Interior of the church. Typical of the Romanesque style of the 11th to early 12th centuries are rounded arches, transverse arches in the outer aisles, and the use of stone of contrasting colors. Compared to the later Gothic, the vaulting is not as high and wide, the pillars are heavier, and the ratio of glass to stone in the outer walls is much lower. Outside Vézelay, Bernard preached the Second Crusade.*

Part Three

Politics in Western Europe

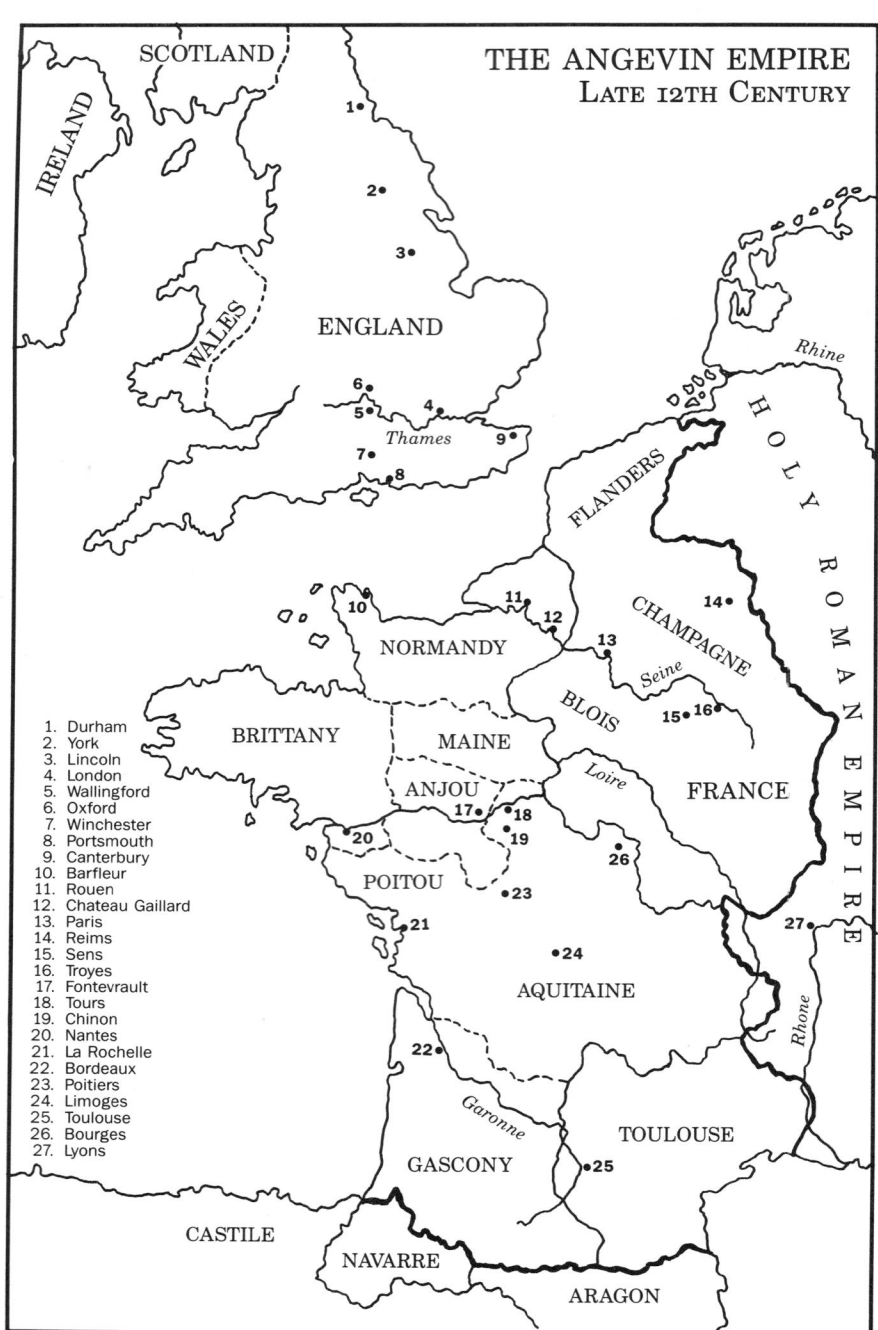

THE ANGEVIN EMPIRE
LATE 12TH CENTURY

SCOTLAND

IRELAND

WALES

ENGLAND

1• Durham
2• York
3• Lincoln

6•
5• •4 London
Thames 9•
7•
•8

Rhine

FLANDERS

HOLY ROMAN EMPIRE

10•
11• •12
NORMANDY 13•
Seine
CHAMPAGNE 14•

BLOIS 15• •16

BRITTANY MAINE *Loire* FRANCE

ANJOU
17• •18
•19
20•
•26
POITOU •23

•21

•24
AQUITAINE

27•

Rhone

22•

Garonne

TOULOUSE

GASCONY •25

CASTILE

NAVARRE

ARAGON

1. Durham
2. York
3. Lincoln
4. London
5. Wallingford
6. Oxford
7. Winchester
8. Portsmouth
9. Canterbury
10. Barfleur
11. Rouen
12. Chateau Gaillard
13. Paris
14. Reims
15. Sens
16. Troyes
17. Fontevrault
18. Tours
19. Chinon
20. Nantes
21. La Rochelle
22. Bordeaux
23. Poitiers
24. Limoges
25. Toulouse
26. Bourges
27. Lyons

Chapter Seven

ELEANOR
OF AQUITAINE
AND FAMILY POLITICS
(1122-1204)

First Phase: PERSONAL RELATIONSHIPS IN FRANCE

1. Women in a world of warriors

Although Bernard of Clairvaux preferred to remain aloof from worldly affairs, we know that his compelling personality and spiritual preeminence inevitably embroiled him in the main problems of his time, political as well as religious. Indeed, his irresistible preaching of the Second Crusade was an extraordinary political achievement. "You ordered and I obeyed," he reported to the pope. "I opened my mouth and the crusaders multiplied. . . .Villages are deserted and you will scarcely find one man for every seven women." Among those whom he influenced was Queen Eleanor of France, who took the cross in 1146 with her husband Louis VII.

Nor was their meeting at Vézelay the first encounter of Bernard and Eleanor. Leaders of Church and State were frequently in direct contact with each other. Sometimes their responsibilities seemed to overlap and it was difficult to tell one from another. Political leaders wielded power and gave protection, using the intellectual abilities of churchmen and offering them material rewards. Clerical leaders wielded the influence of the Church and controlled the road to salvation, as well as offering personal counsel.

Eleanor and Bernard had seen each other at the trial of Abelard. They had both attended the rededication of St. Denis, reformed by Abbot Suger at Bernard's suggestion. Bernard's example had prompted Suger to lay aside his own sumptuous attire and comfortable furnishings in favor of simpler living. Eleanor and Louis had probably worried how Bernard would react to the magnificent architecture and colorful ceremonial of the new abbey, but he had kept his personal feelings in public restraint.

Meanwhile, Eleanor and Bernard had held a private conference on several troublesome matters — Eleanor's reputed baneful influence on Louis, her failure to bear a child, the blood relationship between husband and wife. Many churchmen of that era held women to blame for introducing evil into the world. Bernard himself, afraid of women, said, "To live with a woman without danger is more difficult than raising the dead to life." At the same time he must have been fascinated by women and he criticized most sharply what he found most fascinating. Of the court ladies he wrote in a letter:

> Their garments are fashioned from the finest tissues of wool or silk. A costly fur...forms the lining and border of their cloaks. Their arms are loaded with bracelets; from their ears hang pendants enshrining precious stones. For headdresses they have a kerchief of fine linen which they drape about their neck and shoulders, allowing one corner to fall over the left arm. This is the wimple, ordinarily fastened to their brows by...a circle of wrought gold. Gotten up in this way, they walk with mincing steps, their necks thrust forward...adorned as only temples should be, they drag after them a tail of precious stuff that raises a cloud of dust....Some you see are not so much adorned as loaded down with gold, silver, and precious stones, and indeed with everything that pertains to queenly splendor.

Eleanor adored the display and luxury which were the very aspects of life that Bernard had forbidden himself. And he was sure that she should keep out of politics. But he was impressed by her forthright manner and practical mind. She was not overwhelmed by his gaunt appearance and reputation for spirituality. She must be treated as a person of importance. So Bernard told Eleanor: "Work for peace in the kingdom, and I tell you that God of His great mercy will grant your request." Within a year a child was born. But the excited expectations of the populace dissolved in bitter disappointment when the long-hoped-for heir turned out to be a girl instead of a boy.

We must remember the small and local scale of life in the Middle Ages. A circle around Paris with a radius of 250 miles easily encompasses most of the places to be mentioned in this chapter. Paris and London were very large cities, Paris with less than 100,000 people, London with about 50,000. The population of England was something over 2 million; of France about 6 million. The political and social organization of this small world was very largely dependent on personal relationships. The lord of the manor, we know from the pattern of Norman feudalism, held the virtually absolute authority in his local domain that counts and princes wished for in their larger territories. Local rivalries were intense and often directed major policies.

In such a society a dominant factor was the prowess of the individual. Success depended on courage and strength, determination and stamina, and on the good fortune to avoid the sudden accidents of daily life brought on by contaminated food or water, blood poisoning, a chance arrow, or a fall from a startled horse. A second dominant factor was the personal magnetism that would attract the loyalty of friends and hold the support of dependents. Status was determined by birth; it could be raised by a favorable marriage; it was enhanced by feats of arms or openhandedness. Every important person was the center of a network of family and friends, each of whom commanded a larger or smaller number of their own adherents. The immediate interests of holders of nearby castles might be confounded by the broader ambitions of their overlords. Would the small vassal remain loyal to his count? Would the count aid the duke or the king? Might popularity or force dictate a shift in alliances?

Issues were settled by war or the threat of war. When weather permitted, local skirmishing was a daily occurrence. Men devoted their lives to preparation for personal combat, knightly tournaments, training of war horses, repairing of equipment, confrontations between nobles, agreements that postponed conflict, and — sometimes — war itself. One must readily have grown accustomed to death in combat, wounds that turned gangrenous, the treacherous surrender of a castle, the massacre of a garrison, or the seizure of women and children as the spoils of war.

In a world so dominated by military campaigning and the "manly virtues", it is not as strange as it would be today that women were normally excluded from affairs of state and played little part in government. If no male heirs were in existence, however, women in most places were entitled to inherit property. So they were important as heiresses. In such cases they became marriage targets for ambitious men, although usually they and their lands were at the disposal of their overlord. Beauty and charm and a loving nature might be desirable attributes, but they were insignificant compared to the property or vassals that a noblewoman might bring as her dowry.

After being given in marriage to a lord whom she might never have seen before, it was only rarely that a wife's understanding and good sense gained her the trust of her husband and participation in planning his policies. But a woman's primary obligation was to produce one or, better, several male heirs. This, of course, involved the discomforts of pregnancy, sometimes intensified by her accompanying her lord on his journeys, followed by the acute dangers of childbirth. After performing the essential task of child-bearing, mothers in the highest ranks of society were often shunted aside, as their children were removed early from their care. Young boys must start their training for knighthood. Young girls might become hostages of international diplomacy. Betrothed as infants, they were taken to be brought up in the court in which they might one day reign. So for many noblewomen the duty of child-bearing was not even compensated by the joys of nurturing the children they had borne.

If a noblewoman failed in her duty to provide heirs, she might be summarily dismissed from the family. Ecclesiastical officials could be persuaded to decree that her barrenness was the result of consanguinity, too close a blood relationship between husband and wife. Her marriage, then, had been contrary to canon law and should be annulled. The wife could be consigned to an abbey. She might serve, perhaps as abbess, with devotion and dignity, but her chance to make an impact on the world of war and diplomacy would be gone.

As heiresses, as mothers of kings in their minorities, as famous abbesses or mystics, women of rank occasionally enter the pages of medieval history. It was generally recognized, however, that by law or custom or the particular demands of a military society, women could safely be counted out of a man's world.

Good and bad fortune were mixed at Eleanor's birth in Aquitaine in 1122. She suffered the initial critical disadvantage of being female. The early death of her only brother made her heiress of the duchy but did not put her in control of her own destiny.

Her forebears were extremely talented but erratic in action, courageous as fighters, skilled in poetry and music, domineering in personality, ardent in their passions. Her grandfather was Duke William IX, crusader and troubadour; her father, William X, immensely strong and independent-minded. Despite the extravagant caprices and scandals of their private lives, despite quarrels with the Church and their vassals, they maintained dominance over their restless nobility and their extensive territories, including the provinces of Poitou and Gascony.

According to the chronicler Ralph of Diceto, "Aquitaine overflows with riches of many kinds, excelling other parts of the western world to such an extent that historians consider it to be one of the most fortunate and flourishing provinces of France. Its fields are fertile, its vineyards productive, and its forests teem with wild life." Moderate climate and abundant streams made Aquitaine a pleasant land. Its long, protected seacoast produced the vital salt. Its gentle hills grew the grapes which, as wine, would be exported in ever-increasing quantity from the new port of La Rochelle. Poitiers, Bordeaux, Limoges were growing as centers of crafts and trade. Control of trade through fees and taxes, added to feudal dues and the produce of his own lands, made the Duke of Aquitaine a man of great wealth.

So the court of William X was a political, financial, and cultural center. The death of her mother made young Eleanor the first lady of the court, companion to her father, hostess to prominent visitors, patroness to artists and scholars. Daily experience in this focus of culture and power, witty and learned conversations, flirtations with young noblemen, reading in classical and modern poetry, all combined to give Eleanor an informal but effective education.

As heiress, Eleanor went with Aquitaine, or Aquitaine went with Eleanor. A young lady of beauty and knowledge and poise, as well as of most unusual worldly prospects, she was the most desirable "catch" of her generation. To whom would her father and his overlord, Louis VI, marry her? Who would share with her the wealth of Aquitaine, the delights of its rolling hills, thriving towns, and splendid court? Obviously a suitor must be of the highest rank and potential.

The hazards of medieval living made Eleanor's marriage a matter of immediate significance. In the prime of strength and prosperity, William X undertook a pilgrimage to Saint James of Compostela. En route, he fell ill. He sent an embassy to Paris, offering Eleanor as bride for the son of the king, and then he died.

In the tradition of the family of Capet, Louis VI had tirelessly worked to expand the royal domain and influence. Here was a not-to-be-missed opportunity to double the land over which a future king would one day have direct powers. Realizing that his own health was failing, the king ordered preparations begun for young Louis, hitherto a scholar in the hands of the monks, to go to Bordeaux to take a dazzling bride.

The departure of Louis in the early summer of 1137 was the commencement of an "event of the century." Under the guidance of Abbot Suger, his escort of hundreds of young knights and experienced churchmen formed the nucleus of a colorful cavalcade on the winding journey of perhaps 400 miles from Paris to Bordeaux. Local lords provided food and wine at the frequent stopping points, and alms were distributed to the crowds gathered at bridges to see the royal heir and his gorgeous entourage.

On 25 July 1137 Eleanor and Louis sat on velvet thrones during the brilliant marriage ceremony at the Cathedral of Bordeaux and then held a banquet for a thousand guests in the Ombrière Palace overlooking the Garonne River. At the gates meat and wine were distributed to the crowds of peasants who had come for the greatest holiday of their lives.

A week later the marriage party headed back to Poitiers, where Louis received the ducal crown of Aquitaine and the homage of its nobility. And there a message from Paris brought news of the death of the king. By September, when she herself finally reached the capital, Eleanor Duchess of Aquitaine was—even more impressively—Eleanor Queen of France.

2. Eleanor as queen of France

Only fifteen years old, Eleanor had been thrust by an almost dizzying succession of events into the very highest position. She was attractive, vivacious, perhaps already falling in love with her studious and decorous husband, and bursting with the opportunities which life had suddenly opened to her. She was also mature, with her endowment of family talents and considerable knowledge of the world. Certain intentions must have been taking shape in her mind and heart. She wanted to create in Paris a court in which she would be the central figure, leading activities and establishing tastes. She wanted to share with her husband in making their royal power preeminent. This would entail maintaining her own supremacy in Aquitaine so that her vassals would contribute their strength to that of the king. She expected, we can be sure, to relish life and to favor those who gave her joy and entertainment. And, of course, she planned to have children who would one day carry on the dynasty in which France and Aquitaine were newly joined.

Delighted by Eleanor's wit and radiance, Louis was happy to share in her intentions and in planning how to achieve them. He had not expected to inherit the throne until his brother Philip had died in a hunting accident. So he was acutely aware of his new responsibility for the maintenance of royal authority in his own domain and now for the assertion of royal influence in Aquitaine. So he gladly found occasions for travel throughout his realm, holding courts to show off the young queen and remind the vassals of the power and interest of the royal couple, recently crowned at Bourges.

As a child Louis had been sober and earnest. Religion had been the core of his education, under the direction of Abbot Suger. Louis was impressed by the regular habits and simple life of the monks. Given to solitary study and meditation, he appeared naive and humble, particularly by contrast with the lively Eleanor. But he was handsome, reputedly with blond hair and blue eyes, full of energy, and fond of hunting. He was straightforward and courteous, kind and generous — thoroughly likable, despite a tendency to moodiness and sudden anger.

As soon as her mother-in-law, disapproving of Eleanor's forward southern style, departed from Paris, Eleanor set about redecorating the old palace on the Ile de la Cité in the midst of the river Seine, commissioning tapestries from Bourges and summoning troubadours from Provence. The Ile was the heart of the capital, where were centered the powers of both Church and State. Despite Roman ruins, crumbling walls, and unpaved streets, Paris was a thriving city, astir with activity and stimulation for its crowded inhabitants. On the Right Bank were the growing businesses of merchants, craftspeople, and money-changers. The Abbey of St. Denis was being rebuilt to unimagined height with the ribbed vaults of the new Gothic architecture. On the Left Bank were international communities of scholars. Louis and Eleanor enjoyed talking with monks of the various orders, hearing lectures on Greek philosophy and Roman literature, attending learned theological disputations. At court Eleanor had plays performed in Latin, but she listened also to the music of Provençal verse and brought a new elegance to manners and bright color to fashion. The 12th century was a time of awakening and discovery.

Probably it was inevitable that differences of taste and attitude and policy should develop between the scholarly, sometimes sombre Louis and the sociable, high-spirited Eleanor. The queen was headstrong and imperious. The burghers of Poitiers attempted to establish a self-governing commune. Angered by their sedition, Eleanor was pleased when Louis planned to punish them by sending their heirs into exile. Suger, who had received weeping delegations from the city's populace, persuaded Louis not to impose so harsh a penalty.

No doubt Eleanor was displeased that her own sovereignty had been flouted and that the burghers had not been severely punished. But her true resentment was personal: Was a frail and aging monk, who had risen by resourcefulness and good fortune from serfdom, to have a greater influence on her husband than she?

A far more serious crisis grew out of a marriage controversy. Eleanor gave ardent support to the proposed marriage of her younger sister and Raoul of Vermandois, son of the powerful count of Flanders. Flanders was a significant potential ally of France in any dispute with Normandy. The unfortunate obstacle to the marriage was that Raoul was already married to the niece of the count of Champagne. Geography, family relationships, and his status as Louis' most powerful vassal made Champagne even more essential than Flanders to the welfare of France.

Conflict between Champagne and Flanders was unavoidable, for honor and prestige were involved as well as property. Approval of the marriage by the overlord Louis and strong opposition to the marriage by his vassal-in-chief Champagne turned this marital dispute into a civil war that threatened the structure of the kingdom.

Despite his reputation for mildness and kindness, the king was readily aroused into action in support of Eleanor's wishes and aroused into anger when those wishes were resisted. Louis led his forces into Champagne and assaulted Vitry. As the town was quickly taken and given to the torch, the inhabitants sought sanctuary in the church. Suddenly—in an event for which responsibility can never be firmly fixed—the church was ablaze. Over a thousand men, women, and children perished.

The impact of this appalling event on public opinion was devastating. So it was, too, on Louis. The vision of the awful conflagration was ever before his eyes. The feeling of guilt for the senseless massacre of innocent people overwhelmed him. He sank into a state of inaction and despair. There should be no more singing and dancing in his palaces. His attendance at prayers increased. His days were spent in fasting. He appeared only in the drab habit of a monk.

Meanwhile, Louis was involved in another fierce argument with the pope and Bernard concerning the appointment of a new bishop of Bourges. This was a recurrence of the lay investiture quarrel. In support of his own favorite, Louis ordered the cathedral locked against the nominee of the clergy. The pope excommunicated Louis, but the bishopric remained vacant.

It must not seem that Bernard disapproved of kings. On the contrary, he had high respect for the royal power, which was ordained by God, from whom all power comes. A subject should not oppose his ruler, for "who resists the ruling power, resists the ordinance of God." But like Gregory VII, he believed that the king's power must be held within proper limits. The temporal sword was inferior to the spiritual. "This sword the prince receives from the hand of the Church. . . .The prince is then, as it were, a minister of the priestly power."

So Bernard always worked on behalf of the Church and the pope. He denied that there was no higher legal authority than the royal court, asserting the independence of church courts and the supremacy of papal jurisdiction. In the matter of ecclesiastical appointments, he maintained that election should be wholly in the hands of the Church.

It is no wonder then that Bernard was moved to write a strong reprimand to Louis:

> You are evidently kicking with too much haste and inconstancy against the wholesome advice you have received, and you are hurrying, under I know not what counsel of the devil, to your former evil courses. . . .For from whom except the devil can I say

that this counsel proceeds that adds fire to fire and slaughter to slaughter; which lifts the cry of the poor, the groanings of captives, the blood of the slain, to the ears of the Father of the fatherless and the Judge of widows?...Do not, my king, with rash audacity lift your hand against the terrible Lord who takes away the breath of kings. I speak sharply because I fear sharp things for you.

In fact, the celebration at St. Denis had begun to revive the king's spirits and offered Abbot Suger the chance to work out a compromise to settle the outstanding controversies between king and Church. Louis accepted the Church's nominee as bishop of Bourges. He would do his best to restore the ravages in Champagne. But there was tacit acceptance of the marriage of Eleanor's sister and Raoul of Vermandois.

After St. Denis, however, there was a distressing change in Eleanor's way of life. The palace was gloomy, without music and festivals, and life was austere rather than exhilarating. Bernard had threatened Louis with God's vengeance. He had found Eleanor to blame for Louis' mistakes and demanded that she give up her role as partner in royal policy-making. Louis had named Suger "the Father of the Nation" and had presented to his abbey the jeweled crystal vase which had been her wedding gift to him. Eleanor deeply resented the influence of these monks on her husband, who continued to seek ways of doing penance for his sins. It may have been at this time that Eleanor is reputed to have said, "Sometimes I feel I have married a monk." Louis did not disguise his disappointment when her baby was a girl.

3. The Second Crusade: problems and disappointments

In 1145 news spread rapidly through Europe that Moslem warriors had captured the northern stronghold of Edessa, exposing the kingdom of Jerusalem to mortal danger. The first threat would be to Antioch whose prince was Raymond of Toulouse, youthful uncle of Eleanor. Would the houses of Capet and Aquitaine take the lead in offering relief to the threatened Christians in the Holy Land?

Both Louis and Eleanor welcomed the timely opportunity to embark on crusade. For Louis it was the best of all chances to do everlasting penance for the fiery massacre of Vitry. For Eleanor it offered relief from boredom in Paris and the dissatisfactions of her marriage. She would help in the planning. She would inspire her own loyal adherents from Aquitaine. She would go on crusade herself with a train of ladies and would have her first view of the rich and glamorous East. As the earliest western monarchs to take the cross, she and Louis would share in the glory of defeating the Moslems and saving Jerusalem. The

Crusade would open a new world to her senses; it would test her heart and mind; it promised to be the finest achievement of the century. All in all, it was a thrilling prospect.

Eleanor participated vigorously in the preparations for the vast expedition. Vassals who had taken the cross must pledge the services of their fighting men. Treasure must be donated by bishops and abbots and great lords, special taxes collected, baggage trains constructed, arrangements made for food supplies and river transport along the way. Many noblewomen had vowed to go with her. It was rumored that they might form a troop of Amazons. In any case special furniture and equipment must be provided so that they would not lack for creature comforts. Many other women planned to follow the fighting men. It was June 1147 before the host commenced its march. While Eleanor and her friends rode gaily ahead with the commanders of the day, Louis stationed himself with the rearguard, where he maintained rigorous discipline during the summer journey across southeastern Europe.

In September the army of Louis sailed down the Danube, crossed the plains of Thrace, and were struck with awe by their first sight of Constantinople, capital of the Byzantine empire. They were amazed by its splendid location and its unique size: more than half a million people dwelled behind its twelve miles of walls, punctuated by nearly 500 towers. A broad avenue stretched over three miles from the Golden Gate through a succession of forums to the great church of S. Sophia. At every turn there was a new wonder: the golden statue of Emperor Justinian, the lofty dome and gleaming mosaics of S. Sophia, the underground water system, the stupendous bulk and labyrinthine chambers of the imperial palace, the spectacular shows in the Hippodrome. Louis and Eleanor were lodged in the Blachernae Palace, whose shaded gardens stretched down to the Golden Horn, where ships from everywhere lay at anchor. The produce they had brought to the greatest trading center in the world was for sale in the myriad shops on the lower level of the colonnaded streets. Nowhere else could be found such riches of silks and spices from the East, medicinal drugs and dye-stuffs, textiles of incredible smoothness, gold, ivory, and pearls, along with the more mundane iron and timber and wool from the West.

Only a few of the crusaders had a close view of the emperor, Manuel Comnenus. This man of sublime majesty was treated almost as a god, served by hundreds of well-trained slaves, protected by the elaborate ceremonials presided over by dignitaries of various rank. He was gracious to Louis and Eleanor, offering incomparable luxuries and entertainment. Life moved dazzlingly as one shared in feasts and observed the dancers and acrobats. Eleanor would have reveled in a long stay at Constantinople, for it was like no place she could even have imagined. But the crusading army was wasting its time and sustenance. Surprisingly, the German Emperor Conrad had not waited to unite his force with the French. Manuel provided little clear information or material supplies. Neither the frivolity nor the formality of Byzantine society appealed to the devout Louis. Uneasy and impatient, he ordered the crossing of the Bosporus.

Not far along the hilly road Conrad had taken, the French were horrified to be met by the wretched survivors of the German defeat at Doryleum. Orders were changed. The French turned back to take the coast road toward Antioch, despite the steep defiles and rushing streams that would hinder their journey. Storms and flash floods carried away their tents and equipment. A second change of plan: they must move inland and cross the mountains to reach Antioch.

One afternoon soon after Christmas Louis and the rearguard of his army were toiling upwards to reach a plateau where they would rendez-vous with the van, commanded by his uncle and a Poitevin Geoffrey de Rancon, accompanied by the queen. Arriving at dusk, Louis no sooner discovered that there were no friendly troops on the plateau than his men were assaulted on all sides by the Turks. The attackers were re-pulsed only after a fierce struggle in which many French leaders were killed and Louis barely escaped. Geoffrey and Eleanor, disregarding in-structions, had pressed on into a farther valley which seemed to offer more comfortable shelter and better forage and had taken no part in the battle. Many put the blame for the disaster on the queen.

The disheartened crusaders retreated once more to the coast. The sea voyage to Antioch would not be long, but their Greek allies de-manded exorbitant passage money from them. Finally Louis decided that the nobles and ladies would embark. The bulk of the foot-soldiers, Bernard's long-suffering rabble, had to be left behind.

Antioch must have seemed like a second Constantinople to the wearied crusaders. Its charming prospect between the mountains and the sea and its warming breezes, added to ample supplies and rich gifts from Prince Raymond, restored them to health. Chaplain Odo of Dailio sent a favorable report back to Abbot Suger:

> The King has reached Antioch only at the end of immense danger. We now know that he can take care of himself and meet reverses with firmness. . . . He thinks only of the misfortunes of others and he has done his utmost to relieve them, for he knows that a king exists only to procure the common welfare. He is in good health. . . . He has never gone against the enemy without having received the Sacrament, and at his return he recites vespers. . . .

Sad to say, fresh discord arose. Raymond offered a good plan to recover Edessa and strengthen the Christians' northeastern frontier, but the French suspected him of selfish ambitions. Eleanor supported Raymond's proposal. Her sensible arguments, added to her sophistication and sociability of manner, made her overestimate her influence on the husband who so often had acceded to her wishes. She seemed determined to stay in Antioch, even if that meant that she and Louis would be separated for a time. She may have remarked that the life they had led in Paris lacked the novelty and excitement of the east. Perhaps, even, she mentioned that their joint descent from Robert the Pious put their marriage within the range prohibited by the Church.

But Louis remembered that he had vowed a pilgrimage to Jerusalem. He was troubled by the rumors circulated by his sober counselors of Eleanor's fondness for frivolity and flirtation. Despite her persuasion, Louis grew obdurate. The crusading army—or what was left of it—would proceed immediately to Jerusalem. Departure was under the cover of darkness, with an outraged Eleanor in "protective custody."

The arrival of Louis in Jerusalem raised the spirits of all the Christians. But they still lacked a single, clear objective. Louis agreed to the foolish campaign against Damascus, but the tedious siege made no headway. With strength and initiative exhausted, the Second Crusade wound down to its ignominious end.

4. Discontent leads to separation from Louis VII

Frustrated and unhappy, Louis delayed in Jerusalem for a year. Aware of Eleanor's discontent, he apparently complained to Suger. Urging his monarch to return forthwith to France, Suger wrote: "With reference to the Queen your wife, I think you should conceal any displeasure until you are back in your own kingdom, when you will be able to consider the matter more calmly." Finally Louis and Eleanor set sail for Rome and a meeting with the pope.

Eugenius III had invited their visit in the hope of healing the reported rift between them. Because the forces of Arnold of Brescia had driven the pope out of Rome, the royal pair met him in nearby Tusculum. Eugenius was kind and conciliatory. He greeted them with gracious hospitality, provided them with opportunities for intimate conversation, and told them not to worry that the Church would raise objections to the blood relationship between them. The still-devoted Louis was encouraged by the pope's confidence, but Eleanor did not conceal her personal dissatisfaction.

Eleanor and Louis traveled northward again, reaching Paris in early December 1149. They were safely returned from their pilgrimage to Jerusalem but with sadly little glory or achievement. Their crusade had consumed enormous quantities of people and material resources. It had not benefited France or strengthened the Christian monarchy in the east. And it seemed to intensify the discord between them. Although their second child was born within the year—another daughter, Alice— Eleanor continued in her discontent.

As we know, disorder and disloyalty were commonplace on the borders of medieval domains. One of Louis' greatest vassals, Geoffrey of Anjou, became unruly; like most medieval lords, he was bold and unscrupulous. He had married Matilda, granddaughter of William the Conqueror and daughter of Henry I of England, after her return from Germany as the widowed Empress. In 1133, they had a son, Henry.

Matilda's only brother William had been drowned years before in the loss of the White Ship in the Channel. Henry I then devoted his energies to assuring the loyalty of the English and Norman nobility to his heiress Matilda. But she was in Normandy when her father died unexpectedly in 1135 and her cousin Stephen, another grandchild of the Conqueror, seized the throne. The contest for the throne between Stephen and Matilda kept England in turmoil for almost twenty years, with marked erosion of royal authority. Stephen through carelessness, and Matilda through arrogance, each failed to establish a solid base of support. Meanwhile, unwilling to risk aiding his wife in her battles in England, Geoffrey concentrated on securing control of Normandy. When Henry their son grew mature enough, Geoffrey and Matilda gave him the responsibility of governing Normandy.

Louis was unable to enforce his will on Geoffrey. Although their quarrel was over a minor matter—Geoffrey's imprisonment of a royal seneschal—the contestants were of great prominence. So another call went out for Bernard of Clairvaux, and Louis and Eleanor met Geoffrey and Henry at Paris.

Meeting Henry for the first time, Eleanor saw a young man who was virile rather than handsome. Stocky and muscular in build, he was energetic and restless, an avid horseman, devoted to outdoor activity. He was also a man of wide reading and culture and an accomplished linguist. In Eleanor, Henry met a great lady, of seasoned intellect and courtly manners, who appeared to have grown apart from her husband but had retained her youthful beauty and dreams of happiness. Each seems to have been attracted to the other.

Whether or not Eleanor and Henry talked of the future and reached a secret understanding, Geoffrey proved uncharacteristically tractable and agreed to a settlement of his dispute with Louis. On his journey homeward, Geoffrey paused for a cooling swim after a particularly hot ride. Suddenly, he died. Henry, already duke of Normandy, became also count of Anjou and Maine.

Early in 1152 a synod of French churchmen annulled the marriage of Eleanor and Louis on the grounds of consanguinity. Probably Eleanor desired the annulment; she did not dispute it or the consequent separation from her two daughters. Louis, although disheartened, gave his consent. He needed a son and he may have thought he could direct the choice of a new husband for Eleanor and so maintain control over Aquitaine.

Freed from a marriage that had ended in disappointment, Eleanor realized that she must act with speed and determination. She set off immediately for Poitiers. An unmarried heiress, she would be a rich prize for any fortune-hunting nobleman. Indeed she had to escape from ambushes set in her way by Theobald of Blois and Henry's younger brother, Geoffrey. She would choose her own husband. On 18 May 1152, in Poitiers, Eleanor of Aquitaine and Henry of Anjou and Normandy were married.

Second Phase: THE RISE AND FALL OF THE ANGEVIN EMPIRE

5. Eleanor and Henry II of England

A modern scholar writes that Eleanor "was foolish to forsake a king who loved her to wed another, younger than she, who would prove to be unfaithful, choleric, and domineering." But a contemporary chronicler felt that her second husband was better suited to Eleanor's personality than her first. Both Eleanor and Henry were passionate, ambitious, and vigorous. Eleanor seized the opportunity to escape her frustrations with Louis and to risk with Henry her dreams of sharing in rule, exerting independence of judgment, and presiding as a woman over a court which nurtured the arts and courtly love. Would the coming years be a time of happiness and achievement?

Soon after her marriage Eleanor paid a visit of thanksgiving to the Abbey of Fontevrault, which she had visited before departing on crusade. This famous abbey, now under the rule of the Abbess Matilda (widow of William of the White Ship), housed numerous noble ladies. Although it accepted both men and women, it welcomed especially women of all classes who had been ill-treated or unfortunate and who needed defense of their rights as human beings. Eleanor renewed her favor to the abbey, confirming its charter and demonstrating her own enthusiasm at the prospect of a new life. She wrote:

> After separating, for reasons of kinship, from my lord Louis, the very illustrious King of France, and being united in wedlock to my very noble lord Henry, Count of Anjou, divine inspiration led me

to want to visit the sacred congregation of the virgins of France. . . .Thus I have come to Fontevrault guided by God . . .and here, with heartfelt emotion, I have approved and confirmed all that my father and forebears have given to God and to the church of Fontevrault, and in particular this gift of 500 sous, in the coinage of Poitou, made by myself and my lord Louis in the days when he was my husband.

Henry's intentions of going soon to England to advance the fortunes of his mother were thwarted by the aggressiveness of the king of France. Distressed by his former wife's prompt marriage to Henry and his consequent loss of Aquitaine, Louis invaded Eleanor's territory. Henry reacted promptly to repel the invasion. Louis, never pleased to engage in war, accepted a long truce.

Henry first arrived in England in January 1153. The civil war between Matilda and Stephen, waged intermittently, somewhat spiritlessly on both sides, and so far indecisively, had been costly to the country in destruction of property and decline of royal authority. In August, Henry learned that Eleanor had given birth to a son, named William. In September, Stephen's son and heir Eustace died. In November, the Treaty of Westminster ended the civil war: Stephen would remain king during his lifetime; at his death the crown would pass to Matilda's son Henry. Within a year Stephen died. Eleanor, again pregnant, went to England to be crowned with Henry at Westminster Abbey. By legal and undisputed succession Henry had added the realm of England to his extensive holdings, by inheritance and marriage, across the Channel. There could be no doubt that in land and wealth and power the new king of England far outdid the king of France.

It is significant that from 1154, even on the continent, Henry was known as "the King." He wasted no time in proving himself a forceful and effective ruler. He approached his task with zeal, turning back from no difficult problem or irksome responsibility; he reveled in his broad powers. The king with a handful of his chief officials and advisers was, in fact, the government, wherever he might be. Henry was incessantly on the move, on horseback or by boat (except when delayed by rough weather on the Channel), visiting the farthest corners of his domains. The proximity or, better, the presence of the ruler was the critical element in medieval government. Henry sought to make himself visible everywhere, receiving homage, asserting his privileges, dispensing justice—the most impressive of the royal duties. He led his soldiers and ordered castles built; he met with local officials and collected fees; he visited churches and talked with abbots. He enjoyed hunting and hawking, mixing affably with those of all degrees.

Henry's decisiveness and resourcefulness, which had seemed so attractive to Eleanor, came to be widely admired. His normal amiability was marked by occasional outbursts of scorn for hypocrisy and of fury at shoddy service. Impatient with excuses or blundering, he was open-handed in praise for duties well-performed. Physically he seemed tireless, requiring little rest, abstemious with food and drink, pushing luxuries aside. Surrounding him there was constant noise and activity. His staff complained bitterly about sudden changes in plan, rapid journeys, and nights spent in the open. But Peter of Blois wrote: "While other kings are in their palaces, resting their limbs, he is able to surprise and disconcert his foes and keep a sharp eye on everything."

Whenever she could Eleanor chose to accompany Henry, despite long hours of riding, the discomforts of 12th-century wagons, and her frequent pregnancies. None could complain that Eleanor failed to perform her first queenly duty with notable success. Although William died before his third birthday, Henry had already been born in 1155 and Matilda in 1156. They were followed by Richard and Geoffrey, Eleanor and Joanna, and John, the youngest, born in 1167. Even amidst feudal turbulence, the direct line of succession seemed assured.

As they traveled together, Eleanor and Henry found pleasure in their possessions and shared in their thoughts and hopes, their duties and diversions. In London, where all the nobles and educated people spoke French, they found strong defensive walls, bustling river commerce, numerous churches, and the vast—and newly rebuilt—palace of Westminster rising high above the Thames. The Londoners were proud of the "spacious and fair gardens" of the suburbs and the "pasture lands and pleasant open spaces of level meadows intersected by running waters which turn mill wheels with a cheerful sound."

Eleanor was happier when they were nearer home, at Rouen, Angers, Bordeaux, or—best of all—Poitiers. Here the climate was gentle, the music of the viol and lute soft, and the wine smoother than beer. Here there were tournaments for the boastful knights and bounteous feasts; acts by acrobats, jugglers, and conjurers; theatrical performances and learned readings; bright and lavish costumes. Here in her favorite language of the south troubadours sang their tales of noble deeds and fervent love, and life was a succession of joyous days. Here one could believe the Arthurian legend of knights of unequaled valor roaming the world in search of the Holy Grail and returning to receive the favors of their chosen ladies of incomparable grace and beauty. Here Eleanor was the patroness "whose kindness knows no bounds."

At their several courts, Eleanor controlled the staff and kept the domestic accounts, supervising the purchase of staples like food and oil and wine and of luxuries like spices and linens and jewels. For her private expenses she could draw on her "Queen's gold," a fund deriving from special payments made on receipt of a royal charter.

When military expeditions or other business of state decreed that they travel separately, Eleanor maintained the utmost dignity and composure, combining graciousness of manner with sympathy for popular feelings. With clear head and firm hand she represented the king. She dispensed justice in Henry's stead and fulfilled his other administrative responsibilities. She did not hesitate to issue royal commands. For instance, indicative of her particular concern for the rights and property of the Church, she writes to the viscount of London: "Should it be true [that the monks of Reading have been unjustly dispossessed of certain lands], I command you to ensure that their lands are returned without delay, so that in the future I shall hear no more complaints regarding deficiencies in law and justice; I will not tolerate their being unjustly deprived of anything that belongs to them." Again, in response to a plea from the abbot of Abington, she instructs his vassals: "I command that in all equity and without delay you provide the Abbot with those same services which your ancestors provided in the days of King Henry, grandfather of our sovereign lord; and if you do not do so, then the king's justice and my own will make you do so."

For ten or a dozen years, the match between Eleanor and Henry proved far more successful than might have been expected. Despite the substantial difference in their ages, they seemed to speak with one voice and to share dreams for the future for themselves and their children. They rejoiced together in their achievements and in the splendor of their courts. But Eleanor showed some signs of restlessness. Gervase of Canterbury, always an unfriendly critic, called her "a very clever woman and most noble of blood, but fickle." Would any husband meet her standards? Would life anywhere satisfy her expectations? Bishop Stubbs, more friendly, described her as "a very able woman of great tact and experience and still greater ambition." What were her worries? To be merely a wife and mother would never content her. She aspired to independent authority, at least in her own Aquitaine. At her urging Henry launched a campaign to bring to heel her most insubordinate vassal, Raymond of Toulouse. But Henry advanced listlessly; facing the added opposition of Louis of France, he withdrew, and Eleanor blamed him sorely for his failure.

Eleanor wanted to do more than represent her husband. Treated with deference at home and on her journeyings, she craved the prerogatives of a ruler. Writs might be sent out in her name, but how much personal power did she wield? How much influence in her husband's decision-making? She tended to be masterful, but Henry was accustomed to dominate. Because she was a woman, Henry undervalued her abilities and grew resentful of her desire to share in his statecraft. Dynamic and affable he might be, but he was also prone to moodiness and violent outbursts of temper.

As Louis of France had come to have more faith in Abbot Suger's judgment than in Eleanor's, so Henry of England came to place more and more reliance on the counsel and efficiency of his chancellor, Thomas Becket. This zealous statesman, talented in administration and in diplomacy, fond of magnificence, seemed to rule everything in the king's name. And he came to have a special place in the king's affections, anticipating his thoughts and desires, sharing in his daily living. Eleanor found Becket an unwelcome rival. He flaunted his position and the wealth and prestige it brought him. Perhaps she was jealous of his wit and accomplishment. Surely she was displeased when young Henry at age seven was entrusted to Becket's care, for nurture and education.

Were Eleanor and Henry troubled by the size of the royal family? Eight children born in fourteen years assured the future of the family, but they were a problem to bring up and to provide with suitable spouses. The intimacies and deep affection within families that we take for granted today—even common interests and mutual consideration— were rare in the 12th century. Rather, each family member was likely to act with brutal selfishness. The children, especially the boys Henry, Richard, and Geoffrey, close in age, became fierce rivals. They were distressed that their father, constantly on the move, seemed scarcely to know them as individuals. Later they grew resentful of his dictatorial manner. They seemed more fond of their mother, even though she tried to dominate their minds and monopolize their affections. Eleanor became increasingly possessive of the children as the years went by. She and her husband grew apart as the willful and headstrong Henry tired of her as his female companion. Eleanor's resentment reached a climax when Henry in 1166 established his mistress, the Fair Rosamund Clifford, in the royal castle of Woodstock.

6. The Angevin empire, in concept and in fact

The lands of England and Normandy, Brittany, Anjou, Poitou, and Maine, Aquitaine and Gascony came under the rule of Henry and Eleanor. Historians call their realm the Angevin empire, after Henry's native province. Obviously it was far different from the Roman Empire of the Senate and People, Augustus and Hadrian, Marcus Aurelius and Diocletian. Different, also, from the Eastern Empire struggling still to hold back both barbarians and Moslems, and from the Holy Roman Empire, striving to preserve the remnants of Charlemagne's glory. No master plan shaped the Angevin empire; rather, it emerged from a century of conquest and civil war, marriages and inheritances, primitive medical science, human folly, and chance.

The peoples of the Angevin empire were divided by languages and traditions, by economic patterns and social customs, as the lands were divided by the often turbulent waters of the English Channel. On the borders of England were unfriendly Scots and Welsh. The long stretch of land on the Atlantic coast was threatened by Flanders, Burgundy, Toulouse, even by the Spanish kingdoms of Navarre and Aragon, and above all, by the king of France. But the empire was rich in people; in wood and wool and wine and fish; in commerce and coastal shipping; in the arts and crafts of metals, textiles, and ceramics. Potentially, if it could maintain unity of government and policy, the Angevin empire was the greatest power in the western world.

The chief danger to the empire came from its internal structure. In the feudalized Europe of the 12th century, distance from border to border and diversity of people and local rulers constantly threatened dismemberment. Lacking centralized power—a standing army and a competent bureaucracy trained to enforce a single code of laws and taxes—the empire had only the feudal system by which to regulate itself. And the feudal pyramid, with the overlord rising only slightly above tiers of lesser and lesser vassals, was always likely to collapse as the result of the ambitions of its hierarchy, the greed of border enemies, or local animosities.

Insufficient power, inadequate experience among the governing classes, limited travel and communications facilities, all meant that there was not even a model of centralized monarchy to be tested in a large and diversified realm such as the Angevin empire. Even though a vigorous king like Henry moved with surprising speed and his presence at a scene was usually decisive, he could not be everywhere at all times of trouble. What he needed was a personal representative in each major district, with power enough to maintain discipline and order among the commanders of local strong points and with vision enough to subordinate the immediate desires of the local knighthood to the longer-term needs of the empire as a whole. These representatives of a sometimes distant monarch must be absolutely loyal not only to the ruler, whom they would obey during his lifetime, but also to the concept of unified power, so that they would transfer their loyalty at his death to his rightful successor. In an era when personality was the dominant element in government and when rights of inheritance were not clearly defined, there would always be temptation and opportunity to establish via feudal allegiances a base of personal strength and popularity that could be used either to create an independent political power or to challenge the authority of the legal heir.

Henry was the personification of strength and determination. He and Eleanor had every intention of preserving their empire. As their older sons matured, they seemed intelligent and brave, good exemplars of the chivalric ideals. Was each son committed to the idea of the empire and willing to serve with contentment in the position assigned by accident of birth or marriage contract? The security of the empire depended on Plantagenet family cohesion. Could Henry and Eleanor allot to each son a political role that would fulfill his desire for adventurous activity without tempting him to undermine the unity of the whole realm? Would family ties be close and strong enough so that the sons would work effectively under the leadersip of their father and in anticipation of enduring cooperation with each other? If so, the extended territories of the empire might be held together under the control of related leaders sustaining the single policy of upholding family pride and power.

Meanwhile, up and down the eastern boundary of the Angevin realm lurked the disgruntled Louis of France. He had no intention of allowing his kingdom to suffer further humiliating losses of territory. To strengthen his own family connections, he married Eleanor's daughters, Marie and Alice, to his close allies of Champagne and Blois. In 1154 Louis himself took a second wife, Constance of Castile, who gave him two more daughters before dying in childbirth. Louis was ever ready to dispute with Henry the possession of a castle, the overlordship of a county like Toulouse, or, especially, the control of the Vexin—the small area around the Seine River as it flowed from France into Normandy. At Paris Louis extended a welcome to any English or Angevin official—or to any son of Eleanor's—who was dissatisfied by his lot in life. A continuing source of irritation to Eleanor and Henry was that, for their territories in France, Louis was their suzerain.

Whenever open war broke out between the kings, Henry's speed and vigor usually gave him the edge. But Louis was a tenacious adversary. From time to time they met to make truces. Their meeting in Paris in 1158, for example, was important. Louis' daughter Marguerite was betrothed to young Henry. She would bring the Vexin as her dowry.

Henry and Marguerite were married as children in 1160 and lived, of course, in Angevin territory. Even into this new decade, when Louis and his third wife, Adela of Champagne, had still produced no son, the significance of such a marriage loomed very large. Eleanor and Henry could well have dreamed that when Louis died their Plantagenet family might extend its rule over his domain and its vassals—that France might be included in the far-spreading Angevin empire. But any such fancy of family aggrandizement was shattered in 1165 by the birth of a son, Philip, to Louis and Adela.

Although in the 1160's Henry was much in England while Eleanor remained on the continent, it appears that both were giving thought to the future of their children. They may have started from different motives: Henry from irritation with the demands of impatient youngsters, Eleanor from the desire to secure their fortunes. But they arrived at the same conclusion: it would be best to promise to each son his share of the patrimony, to give him a region with which he would feel a special relationship and for which he would one day have a special responsibility.

In January 1169 there was a meeting of the Plantagenets and Louis at Montmirail. The purpose was to have each of Henry's sons do homage to Louis for his inheritance in France, and to publicize the consent of the French king and the local barons to the proposed arrangement of the Angevin lands. At the magnificent Christmas court at Nantes Geoffrey had been betrothed to Constance, the heiress of Brittany. Now it was announced that Louis' daughter Alice would marry Richard, who was installed the following Easter as duke of Aquitaine. Henry, the oldest, was ultimately to have England, Normandy, Anjou, and Maine, the original inheritance of his father. In London in June 1170, he was crowned king of England, to reign jointly with his father. No particular territorial provisions were yet made for John, the youngest son, who already seemed to be Henry's favorite.

The grant of a title and the territorial base to support it was a matter of no small import for the princes. But it did not settle the question of how much actual authority they were to have. There is no doubt Henry intended to give them the show rather than the actuality of power. He expected them to be supervised by his own trusted officials. For instance, William Marshal, who had earlier vaulted into royal favor by protecting Eleanor from the rebellious Lusignan family, was now the head of young Henry's household. But the princes had opportunities for independent action and for exploitation of their new lands and privileges. Almost automatically, they became the centers of any local discontent. They need fear no severe reprisals from a father who was seeking a solution to the thorny problem of administering an extended realm. We may conclude that Henry's effort to secure the Angevin empire by dividing it in the hands of royal representatives was idealistic in concept. Would it prove practical in fact? In any case, no better plan was then available.

The time for testing the plan was not long delayed. At Christmas 1170, Becket, now archbishop of Canterbury, was murdered at the altar of his cathedral by four knights. So helpful as chancellor, Becket had become a fearful thorn in Henry's side. He insisted on the privileges of the Church, church courts, and churchmen in blunt defiance of the king's policies. At the last meeting of Henry and Becket, the king was reputed to have asked, "Will no one rid me of this troublesome prelate?" So Henry was almost universally held responsible for Becket's death. England was placed under an interdict until he should do penance for his crime. Disheartened but not ready to accept defeat, Henry launched an invasion of Ireland. It seemed that he was overreaching himself in attempting at such a critical time to expand his empire. At least, he was temporarily out of touch with affairs of state.

The three princes, each one estranged from his father, were still far from satisfied with their situation. Henry was handsome and charming—William Marshal called him "the beauty and flower of all Christian princes"—but irresolute, easily swayed from one opinion to another, and generous to the point of reckless extravagance. The Young King as he was called let his passions overrule his reason. He resented that even in his father's absence he had no real power to rule. Richard was at once the most athletic and artistic of the brothers. His boldness matched his strength; he had his family's propensity to violent rages. He loved his mother, but he too craved independent power. The precocious Geoffrey was attractive and quick-witted, but people were beginning to find him selfish and not to be relied on. He wanted freedom to enjoy the wealth of Brittany.

Shakespeare was to base his historical plays largely on Holinshed's *Chronicles*. Of Henry, Holinshed wrote: "Note how God stirreth up the wife of his own bosom and the sons of his own loins to be thorns in his eyes and goads in his sides." But it is hard to determine Eleanor's part in the family troubles that erupted after Henry returned from his inconclusive expedition to Ireland and did public penance for Becket's death. Eleanor and Henry were together for the joint coronation of Young Henry and Marguerite at Winchester and for their Christmas 1172 court at Chinon. No doubt she was thoroughly angry at Henry for virtually abandoning her save on such state occasions. She would welcome any weakening of his high-handed rule and any increase of her own influence. She had been giving a sympathetic ear to the complaints of her sons and urging them to go to Louis of France for help. Louis had advised young Henry to demand a specific territory in which he could be his own ruler. Even if Eleanor did not initiate a conspiracy against Henry, clearly she was aware of the mood of rebelliousness.

7. The Revolt of 1173 and relations with France

Early in 1173 Henry and Young Henry met with the count of Maurienne to discuss the future marriage of his daughter to young Prince John. As a token of good faith, Henry proposed that John

(Lackland) should be granted three Angevin castles. Young Henry was adamant in refusal: why should castles be taken from his territory to support John? With no agreement reached, he departed unceremoniously from his father's company one night and raced to Paris. Richard and Geoffrey followed Young Henry. Louis and his barons declared that "he who was once King of England is king no longer," and war broke out between Henry and Louis, between Henry and his sons. Henry protested vigorously to the pope "of the malice of his sons, so iniquitously turned against their own father that they regard it as a glory and a triumph to pursue him." In a pose of innocence, he grieved: "My friends have drawn away from me, my families entertain designs on my life." Then he acted with characteristic force, engaging 20,000 mercenaries from Brabant in Flanders to press the rebels hard.

Not surprisingly Henry laid much blame on Eleanor for encouraging the faithlessness of their sons. His archbishop of Rouen reprimanded her in a tone at once respectful but threatening:

> We all of us deplore that you, a prudent wife, if ever there was one, should have parted from your husband. . . .Still more terrible is the fact that you should have made the fruits of your union with our lord King rise up against their father. . . .We know that unless you return to your husband you will be the cause of general ruin. . . .Return then, O illustrious Queen, to your husband and our lord. . .or else, by canon law, we shall be obliged to bring the censure of the Church to bear on you.

Fearing for her safety, Eleanor dressed in men's clothes and with an escort of Poitevin knights fled toward Paris, but was captured by her husband's men and imprisoned at Chinon. By late 1174 Henry had put down the rebellion. Peace between the two kings was made at Montlouis.

Because he was deeply concerned for the property interests and future prospects of his sons, Henry made a generous settlement with them. They could hold castles and collect revenues in their assigned areas so long as Henry retained ultimate authority. He hoped that their presence would permit speedy response to local disturbances and give powerful effect to the policies of the royal government. He joined with his sons, particularly Richard, in punishing the nobles who had rebelled in 1173 and in affirming royal control over the counties of La Marche and Angoulême.

Eleanor was not involved in the peace settlement. She had been taken to England as a "distinguished prisoner." Despite his own infidelities, Henry was outraged by Eleanor's ability to deceive him. Reconciliation seemed impossible. Henry may have thought to divorce her, but what then would have become of her hereditary lands of

Aquitaine? She turned down the suggestion that she retire as abbess of Fontevrault. For the next dozen years she would remain a prisoner in what she considered a foreign land. Her career on the stage of political history seemed at an end. She accepted her separation from husband and children, her loss of power and prestige. But she remained alert to the affairs of the world, waiting for a time when she might be called back into the drama of events.

In 1177 Henry and Louis made a peace treaty and reaffirmed their intention that Richard and Alice should be married. When Louis decided that his son Philip should be crowned, Young Henry went to Reims to represent the Plantagenet family at the coronation. Philip succeeded to the throne in 1180. He was to prove a more difficult enemy than his father: more determined that French power should spread; more skillful in both war and diplomacy; free from any lingering sentimental attachment to Eleanor; and just as keen to take advantage of any dissension among the Plantagenets.

The key to the strength of the Angevin empire was the ability of its ruler to muster the men and resources of several lands to quell an uprising or repel a threat to any single domain. The princes must remain answerable to the head of the family. What might happen when eventually Henry's authority must be withdrawn? Although he made attempts to restore with his sons the trust and friendship that probably never existed between them in the first place, in his heart he recognized the fragility of his empire and dreaded the future. Legend has it that, showing a visitor to Winchester a painting of an eagle beset by four eaglets, Henry said: "Those eaglets are my sons who will go on persecuting me until I am dead. The cruelest of all, the one who will hurt me more than the other three, is the youngest, my favorite." Henry himself was tired, growing stout and lame, careless of his appearance, but unwilling to cease his restless activity. His commanding presence had imposed authority on his realm but had not made it orderly. He had been headstrong and impetuous. His personality dominated the Angevin empire; without him, it had no unifying structure.

Resentful of their father and suspicious of each other, Henry's sons caused spasmodic warfare in the 1180's. It was far easier to start than to settle a dispute over doing homage or building a castle. It was easiest to plot uprisings in Aquitaine, where the nobles were notoriously volatile and Richard could be denounced as "tyrannical." Irresponsible Young Henry, abetted by Geoffrey, organized such a rebellion, and the king had to intervene in support of Richard. Suddenly Young Henry fell sick. Before he died, he received a token of forgiveness for his treachery from his father, whose wary ruthlessness was mixed with wistful tenderness.

Thinking now of Richard as his main heir and anxious to provide a territory for his youngest son, Henry proposed that Richard turn over Aquitaine to John. Richard flatly refused to surrender lands for uncertain future promises. Probably with tongue in cheek, Henry suggested that John invade Aquitaine, and the always opportunistic Geoffrey sided with John.

Henry commanded the three sons to come to England for conferences at Winchester, in which Eleanor joined. Henry had released her from custody. Perhaps he was at last lonely for her company. Perhaps he thought she would be helpful in settling the family arguments, especially because of her influence with Richard, for whom she had always shown particular affection. Now planning for John to pacify Ireland and become its king, Henry ordered Geoffrey to go to Normandy as its custodian. Richard took offense and led his forces against Geoffrey. Henry went to Normandy to restore peace. Summoning Eleanor to join him, he persuaded Richard to restore Aquitaine to his mother. The longstanding agreement that Richard and Alice would be married, with the Vexin as her dowry, was renewed with Philip. Sensing his own ambitions being thwarted, Geoffrey went to Paris to plead his case with Philip, but he was unexpectedly removed from the acrimonious rivalry when he was trampled to death at a tournament.

In summer 1187 the issues dividing Henry and Philip—Alice's marriage, control of the Vexin, and now custody of Geoffrey's small children—reached a crisis, and a pitched battle between the kings seemed imminent. Because battles were so risky, they agreed instead on a two-year truce. When they separated, Henry was disturbed that Richard chose to depart in Philip's company, and it was soon reported that the two had become fast friends. Richard vowed to take the cross against the mighty Saladin, who had captured King Guy of Jerusalem at the disastrous battle of Hattin. Henry and Philip talked of going on crusade themselves, but the situation in France was so fraught with tension that armed conflict resumed in the spring.

Summer 1188 was consumed in marches and countermarches, Richard making gains in Toulouse, Philip in Berry, and Henry laying waste territory in western France. In October the three met to try to come to terms, but the conference broke up inconclusively. Richard, plagued by continuing rumors that Henry preferred John to him, was convinced that his father was a weak negotiator. So Richard went off once more with Philip to bargain for himself, recognizing Philip as the overlord of Aquitaine.

When the three reconvened in November, it was obvious that Richard and Philip had collaborated to present an ultimatum to Henry. Philip would give back all his gains in Berry if Richard and Alice were promptly married and if all the Angevin barons swore fealty to Richard as Henry's heir. This was the crucial question: would Henry commit himself to Richard as his successor? Henry refused. He must have recognized that the experienced soldier and skilled diplomat Richard was far more promising as a successor than the untested John, but he could not bring himself to take this decisive step. Apparently he feared that such a commitment for the future might irreparably weaken his authority in the present. Henry had lost touch with reality, failing to measure the acuteness of the crisis or the strength of his opponents.

Uncertain of his father's intentions, Richard said: "I must believe what I thought was impossible." He went on his knees to Philip and did homage for all the Angevin lands on the French side of the Channel. Richard had chosen to trust Philip, not Henry.

Henry, ill, could not attend the meeting scheduled for January; so fighting resumed. At La Ferté the papal legate confessed his inability to bring the contenders to agreement. When Henry retired to Le Mans, Richard and Philip followed in close pursuit. Hopelessly outmatched, Henry retreated northward. The faithful William Marshal held off Richard. When they confronted each other, Richard cried, "Do not kill me, Marshal, for I am unarmed." "No, let the Devil kill you," responded Marshal, as he ran his lance through Richard's horse.

Henry's road to escape was open. Unaccountably he turned back, with only a handful of supporters, to his favorite castle of Chinon. Was it blind courage that directed him? Or fatalism? Or simply realization that his stamina was running out? On 3 July Philip and Richard occupied Tours. The next day Henry rode out, in physical agony, to meet his young opponents. Grudgingly he accepted their demands, including a fine of 20,000 marks, and submitted all claims to Philip's judgment. But he whispered to Richard, "God grant that I may not die until I have had my revenge on you."

Henry was carried back to Chinon. The pathos of it all was his full awareness that he was a shamed and conquered monarch. Having promised to forgive all those who had trusted their futures to Richard and Philip, Henry requested William Marshal to read their names. When the first name was John, who had forsaken his father only weeks before, Henry said: "It is enough. . . . Let the rest go. . . . I care no more for myself nor for aught in this world." On 6 July 1189, Henry died.

8. Richard and Eleanor maintain the empire

So the experiment in family politics ended in wrangling and failure. Henry and Eleanor had not conceived a new form of government for their empire. Rather the scheme gradually took shape as they came to it step by step, using familiar means—family, influence, pressure, homage—and the people at hand. But all their sons, and Eleanor and

Henry as well, had failed to adapt themselves to the new situation and to meet the unexpected demands it put on them. In competition with selfish ambitions, the idea that a group of princes, faithful to the king and trusting each other, could successfully control the Angevin empire, had proved to be no more than an empty dream. When Richard inherited Henry's lands on both sides of the Channel, he was the sole ruler of the empire and he gave not a thought to dividing it amongst his relatives.

Would Richard be skillful enough in the arts of foreign policy and domestic government to keep Philip at arm's length and maintain the integrity of his empire? To begin with, the Aquitaine he held and the England and Normandy he inherited were in sound political and economic condition. And he was favored with the devoted and far-seeing help of his mother. Richard met William Marshal at Fontevrault where his father's body lay. He did not chide the famous knight for his recent effrontery; rather, he admired his loyalty to the old king, bestowing on William the hand of the youthful countess of Pembroke—probably the richest heiress in England—and sending him post haste to celebrate his marriage and to release Eleanor, whom Henry had left imprisoned.

William found Eleanor at Winchester, acting like the queen she was. She had already set herself and other prisoners free, knowing from experience that it is "a most delightful refreshment to the spirits to be liberated from hateful prisons." On her own initiative, she rode from town to town restoring estates, listening to complaints against sheriffs, inspecting royal castles, founding a hospital, and spreading a spirit of release from oppression and of enthusiasm for the new reign.

In 1189 Eleanor was in her late sixties. One might have expected her to be exhausted by concern for ten children, embittered by fifteen years of confinement, out of touch with current affairs, ready for permanent retirement. Instead, she was alert, her mind sharpened by close observation of fallible humanity and by reflection on the experiences of an interesting life. She was filled with long-suppressed energy, anxious to give rein to her desire for action and urge to rule. She must indeed have seemed "a formidable figure" to her contemporaries.

When Richard reached England in late summer he was impatient to start his crusade. His wish to follow the highest calling of a Christian knight was sincere. Also, success on crusade would bring him unmeasurable honor. He would be the hero of Christendom, his exploits the proper subject for the most famous troubadours. To marshal resources required wealth way beyond what Henry had accumulated in the royal treasury. So Richard put up for sale lands and castles, offices and appointments, privileges, whatever he possessed, and found willing purchasers among his lords and churchmen.

But first Richard must be truly king. With pride and joy Eleanor had prepared a brilliant coronation ceremony, which took place at Westminster in September. By mid-December Richard had gone to the continent to oversee further preparations for the crusade. He had appointed Eleanor and his trusted chancellor, William Longchamps, to exercise royal authority in his absence.

Although he had provided John with lands and wealth, Eleanor had counseled Richard not to give his heir-apparent a major role in the government of England. She saw the impulsive Richard's problems more clearly than he and measured his potential enemies—the underhanded John and the pertinacious Philip—with a practiced and perceptive eye.

Eleanor and Richard parted at Chinon in June 1190. Richard and Philip were to combine their crusading forces in Sicily. Eleanor had, of course, been thinking of the succession and of a proper wife for the still-unmarried Richard, who had long before discarded the idea of a marriage to Alice. With no thought for the perils of a long mountainous journey, Eleanor went to Navarre to find the Princess Berengaria, "virtuous and fair, prudent and gentle," and take her to meet Richard in Sicily in spring 1191. Then Eleanor headed home. Richard and Berengaria were married in Cyprus, en route to the Holy Land.

On crusade Richard became a legend. A valorous and dynamic leader, he quickly captured Acre, which had baffled all earlier attacks. Richard far outshone Philip, who at once planned his return to France. Richard won two victories over the previously invincible Saladin. To his chagrin he was unable to recapture Jerusalem, but he concluded a three-year peace with Saladin which promised pilgrims unhindered access to the holy places. By the time Richard was ready to leave the Holy Land in October 1192, he had long since heard from Eleanor of plots taking shape against him.

With Richard away, Eleanor was in effect regent, overseeing the defense and the government of the realm. She arranged to replace the blundering William Longchamps as chancellor and she used Hubert Walter of Salisbury as treasurer, who let "the pressure of the royal hand lie as lightly as possible upon the people." At Christmas 1191 Eleanor learned that Philip, already at home after release from his crusader's vows, was planning an invasion of Normandy and inviting John to join him. Eleanor warned the Angevin garrisons to repel Philip at the frontier, meanwhile reminding him that the Truce of God prohibited seizure of property from crusading lords. Aware of John's fickleness, she forestalled his departure by calling a meeting of the Great Council, which forbade him to leave on penalty of losing all his possessions in England.

Advised that Richard would be home before Christmas 1192, Eleanor worried when there was no further word from him. It seemed that he had disappeared from the map. After weeks of anxious waiting, reports came that Richard had been arrested by imperial soldiers in northern Italy and was in the hands of Duke Leopold of Austria, whom he had humiliated during the assault on Acre. Soon the crafty John was spreading the rumor that Richard had indeed been killed. John hired mercenaries from Flanders and strengthened the defenses of the royal castles of Windsor and Wallingford where he had placed commanders sympathetic to him.

Philip's forces seized the castle at Gisors but Rouen held out against them. Finally it became known that Richard was the prisoner of Emperor Henry VI. Eleanor protested vigorously to the pope that the Truce of God had been violated, that he had sent no legate — not even an acolyte. In fact, Celestine had excommunicated Duke Leopold and threatened France with an interdict, but he hesitated to excommunicate the Emperor. Eleanor threatened to split Christendom. "The kings and princes of this earth have conspired against my son [who] is kept in chains while others ravage his lands. . .and the sword of St. Peter remains in its scabbard. . . . Alas! I know now that cardinals' promises are empty words. . . . I have lost the staff of my age, the light of my eyes," and she signed herself "Eleanor, by the wrath of God, Queen of England."

Negotiations with Henry VI produced a bargain: Richard would be released on payment of a stupendous ransom. Eleanor formed a ransom committee of notables of Church and State, including a representative of London, now a self-governing commune. To raise the 100,000 marks, each landlord was to contribute one-fourth of his annual income, each knight to pay a fee of 20 shillings, each sheep raiser the value of a year's wool-clip, and churches would give their plate. The payment of ransom was customary in feudal society; so there was little complaint. Wisely she kept all ransom contributions under her personal control — 35 tons of pure silver. The Great Council confiscated all John's lands in England and besieged Windsor and Wallingford.

In late December 1193 Eleanor set sail with half the ransom and hostages for payment of the rest. In January she reached Cologne; in February at Mainz Richard was released to his mother and to freedom, and they sailed down the Rhine River in triumph. In mid-March they landed at Sandwich and proceeded to give thanks at Becket's shrine. The people greeted Richard everywhere with great joy. He summoned his treacherous brother to court but John remained in hiding. In April Richard was recrowned at Winchester, with Eleanor present. As Stubbs wrote: "Had it not been for her governing skill when Richard was in Palestine, and her influence on the continent, England would have been a prey to anarchy and Normandy lost to the house of Anjou."

Richard and Eleanor then sailed together from Portsmouth and Richard carried out his intention of punishing Philip for his depradations in Normandy and Berry. John, desperate, approached Richard to beg forgiveness. Richard, perhaps at Eleanor's urging, said: "Let him come without fear. He is my brother. It may be true that he has acted rashly, but I shall not hold it against him." His reprimand to John was mild but contemptuous: "You are a mere child; you have been ill-advised and your counselors shall pay for it."

Eleanor was now free to spend a few comparatively restful years at Fontevrault. Although she was distressed that Richard and Berengaria were childless and lived apart, other dynastic matters were concluded favorably. Her daughter Joanna, the widowed queen of Sicily, married Raymond VII of Toulouse. Eleanor's grandson, Otto of Brunswick, was elected Holy Roman Emperor. Such family arrangements strengthened Richard in his opposition to Philip.

One evening in March 1199 the brave but rash Richard, as Saladin had described him, was watching his troops besieging the castle of Chalus, held by a defiant vassal. An arrow from a cross-bow struck him. After it was extracted, gangrene set in, and Richard lay dying. He sent word to his mother, who came "faster than the wind." On 6 April he died in her arms. The loss of this beloved son has been called the most terrible event in Eleanor's life. But, after making a munificent contribution to Fontevrault for Richard's burial, she had no time to mourn. More than ever she felt that the peace and order of the empire depended on her.

9. The failure of John

The death of Richard was so sudden that no preparations had been made for it. Unfortunately, it opened up again the difficult question of succession. For many years his only surviving brother had been generally acknowledged as heir-apparent; Richard is said to have confirmed on his deathbed his choice of John as successor. And John had dashed to Chinon to lay hold of the royal treasure. But there was another candidate, Arthur, the son born to Constance of Brittany after the death of Geoffrey, who had been older than John. The laws of inheritance were not yet firmly fixed. Equal division of an estate was giving way to the more practicable custom of favoring the oldest son, but the principle of primogeniture was not universally accepted. Neither William the Conqueror nor Henry II had felt bound to it. Consideration could still be given to the fitness of the heirs or to local circumstances or popularity. Strict primogeniture would have made Arthur king, but he was a youth of thirteen who had spent much of his life at the French court. His uncle John was in his early thirties, with experience in warfare and political dealings, rich and potentially powerful—with his own lands and those of his wife Isabella of Gloucester—but widely unpopular, with a reputation for cunning and cruelty. In other words, there was scope for a difference of opinion among great lords who felt their futures were at stake.

William Marshal, Earl of Pembroke, and Hubert Walter, Archbishop of Canterbury, discussed the succession. The archbishop supported Arthur, who had the clearer claim. William disagreed: "Arthur has dangerous advisers; he is overproud, irascible; he dislikes the English. Let us consider John, his father's and brother's nearest heir, as having the better claim." The archbishope conceded: "It shall be as you desire," but he warned: "You will regret it more than anything you've ever done." Eleanor approved of this choice; in fact, she may have inspired it. She preferred the son she knew to the grandson she had scarcely seen; she did not like Arthur's mother, Constance of Brittany. But Eleanor was not fond of John; she could not trust him. He was shrewd and tenacious but unstable. He had a capacity for charm but little for honesty. His talents were vitiated by gluttonous tastes, lack of scruple, ferocity, and cowardice, so that most people thought him "a thoroughly wicked man." His best recent biographer writes that John "had the mental abilities of a great king but the inclinations of a petty tyrant...light, profligate, perfidious."

Eleanor needed a strong protector; she feared for Aquitaine; so she acted forthrightly in support of John. She toured all of her own domains, reminding everyone that she was still powerful in her own right, with influence over the new king, and discouraging dissension. She paid particular attention to the towns, which had been growing in population and flourishing as trade expanded within the empire and with Flemish weavers and Italian merchants. Royal patronage of towns was a modern policy. To five towns she granted charters, giving a measure of self-government, freeing them from dependence on a feudal lord but imposing on them collectively feudal obligations to the king. Typical is her treatment of the thriving port of La Rochelle:

> We grant to all the men of La Rochelle and to their heirs, a corporation...which shall enable them to defend and preserve their own rights more effectively....and we desire that their free customs...shall be inviolably observed and that, in order that they may maintain them and defend their rights and ours and those of our heirs, they shall exert and employ the strength and power of the commune, whenever necessary, against any man.

Privileges and responsibilities, alike, derived from the crown. Henceforth no fractious baron should carry the people and resources of such towns into rebellion.

Finally, responding to the uncertainties of the times, Eleanor went to Tours and did homage directly to Philip for Poitou and Aquitaine. This action kept her hereditary lands under her own control. Neither John nor Arthur could seize or use them, nor could Philip dispose of them, without her permission.

Eleanor and John met at Rouen on 30 July. Somewhat in awe of her, John was wise enough to realize that her cooperation could be of critical value to him. He affirmed Eleanor's power: "We desire that she shall have Poitou throughout her life and shall be lady not only of all the territories which are ours, but also of ourself and of all our posessions." With Eleanor's approval John and Philip signed a truce. To seal the agreement a marriage should take place between Philip's heir, Louis, and a daughter of Eleanor's daughter, Eleanor of Castile. Delighted at the prospect of another family alliance to bolster the Angevin empire, Eleanor herself made the long journey across the Pyrenees and selected her granddaughter Blanche as the likeliest bride. In May Louis and Blanche were married in Normandy.

So far lacking children, John put aside his first wife and, in August, married Isabella of Angoulême. She was a young and lovely bride, but she had already been engaged to a member of the always belligerent Lusignan family. So the marriage was a political blunder. The Lusignans protested to Philip, who summoned John to answer their charges. John refused to heed his overlord and was condemned by default. So war again broke out in summer 1202 between France and the Angevins. Philip declared his support of Arthur by knighting him, and Arhur swore fealty to Philip for all Angevin lands.

Seeking safety by journeying from Fontevrault to Poitiers, Eleanor was captured at Mirebeau by Arthur and his Lusignan allies. A desperate plea for her rescue reached John at Le Mans. For once he acted with decision and gallantry. He made a forced march, attacked at dawn, freed his mother, humiliated the captured knights, and led Arthur off a prisoner.

It was Arthur's misfortune that he was the logical center of opposition to John. If Arthur was Richard's rightful successor, John had usurped the throne. The barons would be free from John's harsh treatment if only Arthur were their overlord. And Philip, of course, would be far more secure if John were deposed. But it was the inexperience of youth that betrayed Arthur. In prison he blustered about his rights, demanding his inheritance. John's fury mounted. Arthur disappeared. Conflicting stories circulated, but it is clear that Arthur was murdered, probably by John's own hand. On 16 April 1203, John sent a message to Eleanor: "God be thanked...things are going better for us than this [messenger] is able to tell you."

In fact, things were not going well for John. His cold-blooded murder of Arthur outraged feudal society and provided moral justification for all his enemies. With Arthur gone, all who had cast their lot with him owed homage to the redoubtable Philip. John appeared blithely unaware of the troubles he had created for himself. In Normandy he was menaced by French and Bretons and many Angevins. Even many Norman barons gave their preference to Philip as overlord. As his ill-defended castles fell into the hands of his opponents, John wallowed in inactivity, murmuring, "One day I shall recover all I have lost." Instead, in December 1203, he sailed for England, abandoning Normandy.

10. Death of Eleanor and end of the empire

Meanwhile, Eleanor lived on at Fontevrault. We do not know if she understood John's last message or even heard of his deepening losses. At the very end of March 1204, Eleanor died and was laid to rest beside her beloved Richard.

What should we say in the late 20th century of Eleanor of Aquitaine? In her own day she was both adored and reviled. The nuns at Fontevrault, pleased by her unaffected behavior and mindful of her unfailing charity, thought that "she surpassed all the queens of the world." The sainted Bishop Hugh of Lincoln, on the other hand, who was such a good friend of Henry II that he could poke fun at him, blamed all the woes and mischief that beset the Angevin empire on Eleanor, the wicked adulteress, irreverent, frivolous, luxury-loving, arrogant. Indeed he predicted the downfall of the Angevins: "The present King of France will avenge the memory of his father, King Louis, upon the children of the faithless wife who left him to be united with his enemy. . . . Philip of France shall entirely destroy this race."

As almost always, the truth about Eleanor lies somewhere between these conflicting characterizations, but the truth is hard to discern and even harder to document. The very long poem that was written about the life of William Marshal, the earliest biography in French that exists, demonstrates that the 12th century "is a masculine world, and in it only males count. . . . Very few feminine figures occur. . .and their appearances are fugitive. . .[they] remain shadows, barely glimpsed. . . . Nothing of what they might have said. . .seemed worthy of being reported; all the dialogues are among men." Because she was a woman, Eleanor is scarcely mentioned by the medieval chroniclers. To be sure of what she, individually, achieved is almost as hard as it was for her to achieve it. Because she was a woman—even though a queen—she was excluded from the main events of an era dominated by men and their military triumphs. Because she was a woman, she was from birth considered to be of little significance, save as the heiress of Aquitaine. Lacking military victories, lacking legal rights, she lacked the power independently to retain her property or govern her land. Because she was a woman, she could achieve her purposes only as a companion to men, influencing the policies of her husbands and enjoying their successes, or guiding the careers of her sons.

So it was that Eleanor's accomplishment derived from personality: her fierce determination, tireless resilience, resourceful initiative. The social grace she inherited eased her relations with people; her familiarity with the arts polished her taste; her charity increased as she practiced it. Her political acumen she developed until she could foresee the needs of her times and the consequences of ill-planned actions. In accounting for her extraordinary achievements over a very long life, we take note of her glamorous appearance, charming manner, thoughtful mind, firm heart, and indomitable courage.

Eleanor married two royal husbands and bore them ten children; three of her sons in turn became crowned kings. Her influence shaped the history of Europe for three generations, and she left grandchildren and greatgrandchildren who ruled throughout the continent and even to Jerusalem. So Eleanor's long career was unique in the Middle Ages in its circumstances and its distinction.

When he died in 1153, Bernard of Clairvaux could hardly have guessed that Eleanor was to become not only the most remarkable woman of her times but the key figure in the political history of the century—the "matriarch" of western Europe. He would have been relieved to know, at least, that there were no others like her.

Recording the year 1204, Matthew Paris stated simply: "In this year died the noble Queen Eleanor, a woman of admirable beauty and intelligence." Richard of Devizes was more eloquent but maintained his masculine bias: "Eleanor played a dominant role in politics and literature alike, and upon social and economic matters her influence was strong...[She] defied an emperor, threatened a pope, and ruled her twofold realm with the utmost lucidity and control....[She was] a woman beyond compare, towering above the age in which she lived, beautiful and chaste, powerful but modest, and meek yet eloquent, which is something rarely met with in a woman."

As Eleanor lay dying at Fontevrault, Château Gaillard, pinnacle of Angevin power and pride, fell to Philip's assault. There followed the surrender of Caen, Bayeux, and Rouen. These were the disasters that Eleanor had struggled to stave off. Since Richard's death she had stood alone as the symbol of loyalty and permanence of the Angevin empire. "Who," asked Richard of Devizes, "could be so savage that this woman could not bend him to her wishes?" But even her most ardent supporters, like William of Les Roches, had rejected John, in revulsion against the murder of Arthur. "Eleanor was the great source and prop of John's continental position," as Bishop Stubbs was to write. "His fortunes were not hopeless until he lost his mother."

Then, Normandy was gone and Anjou, Maine, and Touraine. At John's death in 1216, only a small area of Gascony still belonged to the king of England. In the following centuries the English might overwhelm the French at Crècy and Agincourt; not until the mid-16th century did they give up their last foothold across the Channel. But it was with the death of Eleanor of Aquitaine that the Angevin empire—and the dream of a supra-national state governed by the mutually supportive branches of a single royal family—came to its end.

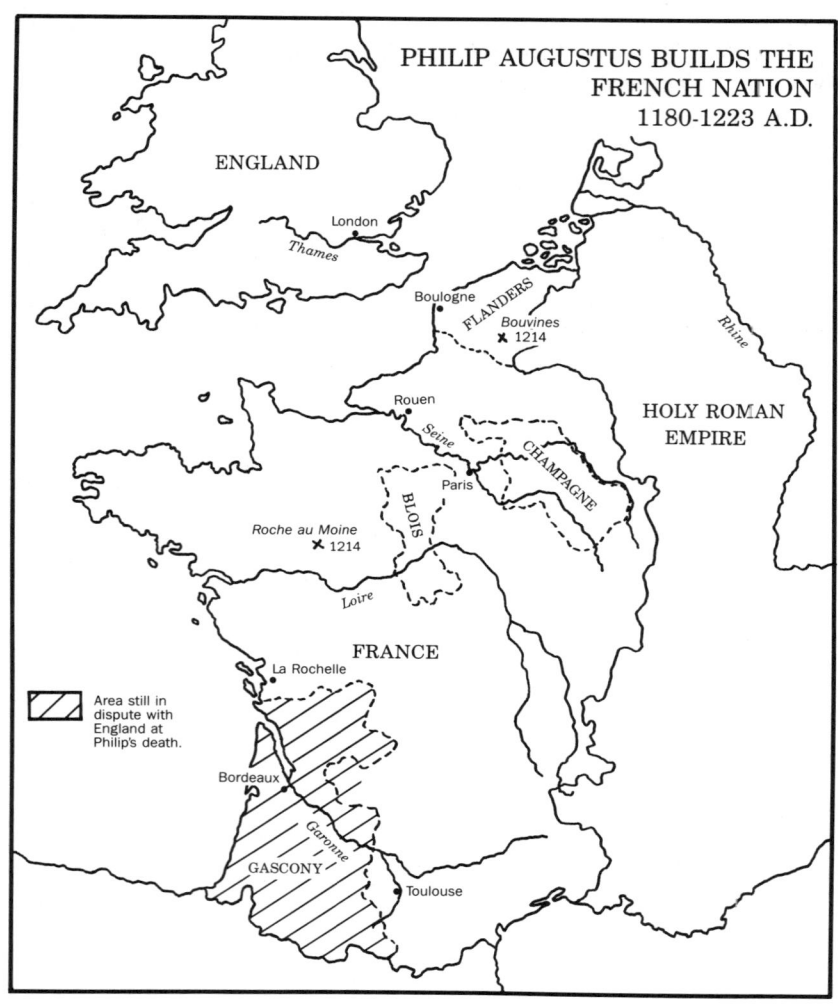

PHILIP AUGUSTUS BUILDS THE
FRENCH NATION
1180-1223 A.D.

ENGLAND

London

Thames

Boulogne

FLANDERS

Bouvines
✗ 1214

Rhine

Rouen

Seine

HOLY ROMAN
EMPIRE

CHAMPAGNE

Paris

BLOIS

Roche au Moine
✗ 1214

Loire

FRANCE

La Rochelle

Area still in
dispute with
England at
Philip's death.

Bordeaux

Garonne

GASCONY

Toulouse

Chapter Eight

NATION BUILDING: PHILIP AUGUSTUS (1165-1223)

1. Philip's youth

Gerald of Cambridge, a young English scholar visiting Paris in 1165, wrote in his memoirs:

> One night in the very beginning of autumn, shortly after the dead of night, it was said that by God's grace Philip had been born. This rumor was bruited through the city and received with inexpressible delight. At once...on every side there burst forth such a clamorous pealing of bells and so great were the waxen lights kindled in every street, that those who knew not the cause of the unwonted tumult, the deafening sounds, and the universal illumination, imagined that some conflagration was even then threatening the city.

To us moderns, accustomed to bullhorns and floodlights and fireworks, medieval methods of celebration may seem ineffective, but the excitement was not. Here in the center of his realm, amid his most loyal subjects, a son was born to a king who had already ruled nearly thirty years without a male heir. His people had been deeply alarmed, for if a king should die without an undisputed heir his country could be exposed to grave danger. Now at last God was looking with favor on the distracted land of France.

Gerald wrote further:

> Looking out, I saw in the street two poor and miserable old crones carrying waxen candles before them; their countenances, their words, their gestures, all alike expressed exultation as they hastened along with rapid steps. I inquired of them what might be the cause of all this excitement and delight, whereupon one of them looked back and replied, "Now we have a king given us by God, a mighty heir to the kingdom through God's bounty; through him shall fall on your king loss and disgrace, shame and heavy punishment, rich in confusion and distress."

Surely not the "old crones," and probably not many citizens of Paris, realized the magnitude of the task which faced the "mighty heir." The kingdom he would one day rule was far from mighty. True, it was the old Frankish kingdom which Clovis had created from the remnants of Roman Gaul and on which Charlemagne had based his empire. But France had shrunk woefully in size. By the 12th century, as we have seen, the royal domain was reduced to the area around Paris, and only the nearby provinces made even perfunctory acknowledgement of the overlordship of the kings of France. The lords of other districts — Toulouse, Burgundy, Flanders — could afford to disregard the king, for they were as rich in land and manpower as he. Ruler by divine right, successor to Charlemagne and the Caesars, Louis VII might claim to be. In theory, he might hold absolute sway over his subjects; in practice, he was a feudal king whose strength depended on the good will of his great vassals.

Indeed, the king of France was scarcely "one among equals." Why should the feudal potentates accept his sovereignty, or right to rule, when they were powerful enough to ignore his demand even for their pledge of fealty? Among them, of course, was his strongest "vassal," Henry II. To bring down this mighty ruler must seem a hopeless undertaking for the baby Philip. If he could accomplish it, he would make France a great nation.

Philip's education was conventional for a young noble of his time. The prince grew to be bright and active as well as pious. We are told one interesting story of his childhood. The four-year-old boy was present at a meeting at Montmartre of his father and the English king. Henry drew Philip to his side and surveyed him carefully, then "thrust him aside with a melancholy air, as if he read there some dreadful portent." No doubt the meeting took place, but the "dreadful portent" may have been the product of the imagination of a chronicler writing long after the event. Thomas Becket, however, was an eyewitness of this occasion and reported the singular courtesy of Philip in begging the irritable Henry to "love his father and himself and so obtain the good grace of God and men." "It seemed," Becket added, "that God had inspired the mind and tongue of that chosen child."

For Philip's amusement a menagerie of wild beasts was collected. The real love of the young man's life was hunting. On one expedition in 1179, hunting wild boar in the forest of Compiègne, the fourteen-year-old Philip outdistanced his retinue and lost his way. He was finally found and brought home by a friendly woodsman, but he fell ill from exposure and shock. The prince lay so near to death that his father vowed he would go on a pilgrimage if his son's life was spared.

On Philip's recovery, Louis prepared to fulfill his vow. It was to Becket's tomb that he proposed to go, and Henry graciously granted him safe-conduct. A pilgrimage was accorded the utmost respect. That Louis could go peacefully with a small retinue to Canterbury and be welcomed there by Henry—that these two bitter rivals could meet in amity—indicates the prestige attached to the performance of religious duties. Moreover it indicates that the two hostile monarchs, although unwilling to establish a real peace, could work out an agreement to suspend conflict between their nations.

When Louis returned from his pilgrimage he was old and ill. Philip was still a youth, but education in those days was not the lengthy and complex project it is today. Accordingly it seemed wise for the son to assume some of the royal duties. In feudal monarchies the heir was often crowned in his father's lifetime, thereby reducing the chances of a disputed succession leading to civil war. So on 1 November 1179, at Reims, Philip was crowned joint-king with his father. In less than a year, Louis VII was dead, and Philip ruled alone in France.

2. Philip as king: policy and early success

As we have seen, Philip had not acceded to an easy position of "pomp and circumstance." He faced arduous tasks of defense and government that would require of him both military and political virtues. First, he must maintain the independence of France, threatened with extinction by the Angevin empire. Second, he must keep in subjection those unruly barons who would prefer their feudal obligations to be formal rather than actual. Third, he must be sure to keep the ecclesiastical fiefs and the new commercial towns in alliance with the Crown by preserving them from the grasping hands of ambitious barons. As a basis for fulfilling these objectives, Philip had inherited from his father firm control of a well-ordered royal domain. But his resources were limited, and his dream of restoring France to the dominant position it had occupied under Charlemagne could not quickly be achieved.

Continuance of the truce with England was the prime essential.

With nothing immediate to fear from his chief foreign enemy, Philip could attend to consolidating his power at home. Seeking to benefit from any uncertainty caused by a change in central administration, many of the nobles had taken arms in the effort to increase their own domains. Easiest targets were the properties of the Church, lacking armed defenders, and often subject to dispute of titles and boundaries. Philip was prompt to use royal power to protect bishops and abbots from the ravaging barons. Thereby he gained the grateful friendship of the Church, with all its influence over the minds of his subjects, and the renewed fealty of the barons, respectful of an overlord who could compel their obedience. Both lay and clerical lords were brought to recognize their dependence on the king, whose reputation for just dealing and decisive action was enhanced.

The isolated foray of a petty lord was comparatively easy to put down. The quarrels of the great lords, contending for the rewards to be gained from positions of authority near the throne, were more difficult to settle, as well as more dangerous to the royal power. The defection of a powerful family, with its supporters attached to it by the strength of the feudal code, might well destroy the unity of the realm and leave the king the pawn of the contending factions. Philip's mother, Adela, was of the family of the counts of Blois and Champagne, whom Louis VII had so favored that they had become the chief bulwarks of the royal prerogative. Philip, however, had come much under the influence of his namesake Philip, Count of Flanders.

Champagne and Flanders could not bask equally in the royal sunshine. When it appeared that Philip was strong enough to follow an independent course, using them but not relying exclusively upon either one, the two counts decided on a joint revolt. This unnatural alliance was defeated by the king, with aid from Henry II, who shuddered at any prospect of rebellious barons successfully defying a monarch. Champagne reaffirmed his loyalty. Flanders remained stubborn until Philip forced his submission in 1185. Then he surrendered the districts of Vermandois and Amiens as fiefs to the crown and promised the whole county of Artois on his death. Philip had made clear the price of revolt. He had taken the first major step in the extension of the boundaries of France. Philip the overlord had begun to establish himself as Philip the sovereign.

We need now to look at the Angevin empire from Philip's standpoint. What would its disintegration mean to France? Real friendship with Henry II could not be permanent. The frontier between French and English territory was so long and poorly-defined that border incidents were the rule rather than the exception. The frontier separated not two nationalities but two French-speaking groups who differed from each other only in owing allegiance to different lords. Interests were local; national policies could scarcely be said to exist. A change in the loyalty of a single jealous or avaricious vassal could ultimately embroil the two kings.

We have seen that Henry, seeking firm government, had assigned special titles and territorial responsibilities to his several sons. They repaid his indulgence with ingratitude. If they were to act for the king, should they not be independent? If the vassals in France paid homage to them instead of to their father, was it not their right to command feudal services? So Henry had sown seeds of the dissolution of his empire by granting favors to his ambitious sons, who complained that he had not granted them more.

Philip was well aware of this family friction, and he was one to bend an opponent's weakness to his own use. For Anjou and Maine, Henry himself should be Philip's vassal; for Brittany, Geoffrey; for Aquitaine, Richard. If he was powerless to entice the Old King, Philip could cultivate the friendship of the sons and induce them to transfer their allegiance from their imperious father to him. In working on their vanity, Philip would be undermining the cause of England and advancing the cause of France. Philip first encouraged Geoffrey to oppose his father and, then, Richard. So friendly did Philip and Richard become that they were said "to eat at one table, off one dish, and at night sleep in one bed." Richard gladly did homage to Philip for Aquitaine, forgetful that he was in Aquitaine only as his father's representative.

Alarmed that Henry, Richard, and Philip were quarreling amongst themselves instead of preparing to fight the infidels, the pope sent his legate to arbitrate their conflict. At once the French king adopted a high-handed attitude. "It did not belong to the Roman Church," he said boldly, "to lay censures on the realm of France if the king avenged his wrongs and the honor of his crown on his rebellious vassals." With Richard won to his side, Philip was confident he could outface his "rebellious vassal," the aging Henry. Reluctant to admit the collapse of his dream of empire, and still relying on his youngest and favorite son John, Henry took up the challenge of war. But John deserted him, as we know, and just before his death Henry had to give in to Philip and Richard.

In the ten years since his coronation Philip had made clear his intention of being a real king of France. He had made an ally of the Church by defending its property. He had suppressed outbreaks and had humbled the vassals who would have domineered over him. He had checked the Angevin effort to engulf his realm and reduce France to an insignificant dukedom. The death of Henry II removed from his lists his most astute, far-seeing, and firm-willed opponent.

But the future was not all clear, nor was it to be easy. Richard, King of England, might not prove so amenable an accomplice in the dismembering of the Angevin empire as Richard, Duke of Aquitaine. Philip had made no startling advances. He had been collecting and ordering his strength, testing his vassals, halting the march of his enemies. The direct power of the king had been only slightly extended, at the expense of Philip of Flanders. By comparison with the rapid progress of a Charlemagne, Philip had merely been marking time. The real job of creating a national power remained to be done. And now the crusade delayed Philip's state-building.

3. The Crusade of Romance

No good man would willfully resist the call to a crusade. The first concern of a male Christian was to prove himself worthy of heaven; his first duty, if necessary, to fight for the cross. In the face of this obligation and opportunity, all business at home, however urgent, seemed petty. It was reasonable and proper to postpone lawsuits, marriages, financial transactions, even wars, for the two, three, or five years that one spent on a crusade. The voyage to the Holy Land held magic appeal for these men. Their devotion to the Church, their devotion to the welfare of their own souls, drove them forward. If the call came and they were found timid, a fatal stain besmirched their honor. For a medieval monarch, especially, one of the essential attributes of greatness was to have gone on a crusade. His reputation as a knight, his moral stature, was affected deeply by the fame he won in the service of the Church.

The year 1187 was fateful in the history of the crusades. Saladin, the greatest of all the Turkish leaders, swept over the Holy Land and recaptured Jerusalem. Gloom spread through Europe at the report that the Holy Sepulchre was once more in the hands of the Mohammedans. No longer could faithful Christians journey safely to their central shrine to do penance for their sins. When Pope Clement III urged a holy war against the Turk, the response from the chivalric orders was automatic. For the ordinary man, added inducements were the declaration of a debt moratorium and the imposition of a special tax, the "Saladin tithe," the payment of which he could avoid by taking the cross.

On the Third Crusade, known as the Crusade of Romance, would go the most powerful monarchs of Europe. Philip alone did not dare hold back: he would be the object of ridicule and slander, he could never truly be king. But he prepared for crusading only because it was indispensable to his fame as a Christian. He was not ardent for the cause of religion; he would rather stay at home, administering his government, laying plans for the expulsion of the Angevin power from France. Then came the news that Frederick Barbarossa of Germany would march his forces overland toward Constantinople. Lest the emperor put them to shame, Philip and Richard, after Henry's death, made peace between France and England. They would take their forces to the east by sea and unite to chastise the impudent Turk.

The star of a monarch shines brightest alone. In his own court he is supreme. Put another monarch near him, and he perforce is jealous lest his own star be dimmed by the brilliance of his rival's. Philip and Richard both chose to winter their armies in Sicily, and there appeared the first cracks in the friendship between them, which Philip had cultivated so assiduously. Philip was outraged by Richard's extravagant impetuosity; Richard sneered at Philip's cautious craftiness. Differences in temperament, in appearance, in policy, were exaggerated by their followers, until there was undisguised hostility between the French and English.

Philip sailed away first in April 1191. He made substantial progress in investing the stronghold of Acre, but his was not the flamboyant spirit to inspire great feats of daring. When Richard landed in June, Philip fell into the background. The hot-headed and open-handed Richard was the model knight-errant, devoted to the task at hand, thinking little of affairs at home. Richard of Devizes says that Richard "was burdened with the King of France, and hindered by him, like a cat with a hammer tied to its tail." This chronicler, we must realize, was highly prejudiced, but many even of the French knights preferred Richard's dashing leadership. The honor of the capture of Acre in July fell almost exclusively to him.

Philip had had enough of crusading. The count of Flanders had died, and Artois must be secured to the crown. Letters came calling Philip back to his kingly duties—some accused him of having them forged—and Philip, with the added claim of illness, chose to go. On 31 July, he left Acre "amidst the wonder, disapproval, and execrations of all."

4. Statecraft in the contest with England

Philip's abrupt departure, before even an attempt to recover Jerusalem, might well occasion criticism, but to us it does not occasion surprise. Philip had only left France because it was "the thing to do." Crusading was out of character for him, for it meant submerging his own projects in a joint undertaking from which he could reap no material rewards. Philip was a realist when most people were still idealists. The crusades could never in the long run succeed, for the forces of geography and economics and sociology were against them; so Philip wanted to waste no more time on them than was absolutely necessary. A poor because unconvinced crusader, Philip was an astute statesman. Uppermost in his mind was the ambition to win back the Angevin lands for France. What more opportune moment to choose than when Richard was still seeking elusive glory before Jerusalem and his brother John might be bribed into acquiescence with Philip's schemes?

Using the arts of diplomacy in the service of his country, he was frankly shrewd and unscrupulous. Peace with England was not now advantageous for France. So Philip begged papal absolution from the oath he had sworn not to attack Richard's lands while the crusade was in progress. Philip planned to keep on good terms with John. As long as Richard remained away, John might continue to enjoy the fruits and pleasures of playing the part of king. John Lackland had never been granted the rule over any of his father's French provinces, and so he should feel no particular loss if Philip wielded increasing authority over them. Thus Philip wound John into his web. It would collapse when Richard returned, enraged at Philip's faithlessness and John's unbrotherly selfishness. Both plotters were pleased, therefore, to hear that Richard's return was to be delayed. Philip in all probability urged the Emperor to set the ransom figure high and prolong Richard's captivity.

Philip was not to gain his ends without a contest. In 1194 he had to write to John: "Take heed to yourself, for the devil is loose." With Richard free at last, Philip must take heed to himself. For five years, war between Philip and Richard raged intermittently, the chief prize being Normandy. This border warfare was fierce, waged on the principle "first destroy the land, then the enemy." There was little field fighting; the attack and defense of fortified places was crucial. Castles and towns changed hands or were given to the flames. Gradually Richard gained the advantage, for he was the superior soldier. By early 1199, Philip had been expelled from Normandy save for a precarious hold on Gisors.

In 1197, as a symbol of the permanence of the Angevin power, Richard had constructed the gigantic Château Gaillard. This fortress had cost untold money and three years of labor. On a steep rock overlooking the Seine, sixty miles downstream from Paris, it controlled the river entrance to Normandy and blasted Philip's hopes that his capital might have an outlet to the sea. Its location was an eternal affront to the French king; its towering bastions made it seem impregnable.

"I shall take it, be its walls of iron," said Philip. "And I shall hold it, be they of butter," retorted Richard, who was willing to fight for anything—his honor, the love of the fight, the excitement of victory. He did not worry about the frightful drain his wars put on English resources. He seems not to have made a master-plan for the future. Philip had the longer vision. He never considered abandoning his objective of making France a compact and united nation. Despite reverses, he pursued his logical policy calmly and relentlessly. He preferred to leave the actual fighting to others. He would not make the foolish mistake of being killed by a chance arrow in a minor skirmish. "God visited the land of France, for King Richard was no more," wrote the chronicler. What advantage could Philip take of this fortuitous event?

Philip had used the Plantagenet family against itself to his own advantage. Against Henry II, Philip had played his sons Geoffrey and Richard; against Richard, his brother John; against John, whom should he play? John was outraged by the forces being raised against him under the banner of his nephew Arthur. Philip revived the question of inheritance so that Arthur could serve as a convenient puppet behind whom to conceal his own intentions. Finding John not a formidable antagonist, Philip at first maintained the truce with England. In 1202 he was ready to show his hand in a decisive break.

It was John, with his impolitic marriage to Isabella of Angoulême, who gave Philip the chance he had been waiting for. The Lusignan family had rallied many friends among John's vassals who were lukewarm in their support of a lord who disregarded their welfare. Following the letter of feudal law, the Lusignans carried their complaints of ill-treatment to John's nominal overlord Philip. Fully within his rights as the defender of justice, Philip called his barons together in Paris as a high court. John was accused specifically of injuries to Raoul de Lusignan, Count of Eu, and of failure at his accession to do homage to Philip for the feif of Normandy. Philip offered John a safe-conduct to Paris but promised nothing for the return journey.

The summons to Paris placed John in an extremely awkward position. If he went, he admitted in fact his status as Philip's vassal, and the Angevin empire degenerated from a unified state into a chance collection of fiefs. If he did not go, the court would be justified in harshly punishing his contempt. John chose to stand on his honor as a king. So Philip ordered the trial held despite the absence of the defendant, and John was sentenced to lose all the lands he held from the French Crown. Although unduly severe, this decision was legal. Philip had defended the weak against the over-mighty subject; precedent and public opinion were, in principle at least, on his side. The next legal step was for Philip, the overlord, to take back into his own possession the lands of the guilty John. This he did, assigning some of them to Arthur of Brittany, but retaining direct control of Normandy.

We already know that John, in an unexpected burst of activity, rescued his mother and captured Arthur. But the foul murder of Arthur was a horrifying violation of the code of chivalry, and John's vassals fell away from him.

Murderer or not, John was fatally indecisive. The vigorous Philip grabbed the initiative. "Philip harries your lands, your strongholds he captures, and their seneschals he ties to the tails of their horses and drags them to prison, and your property he uses as his own." John was warned but he took no action.

In autumn 1203, Philip laid seige to Château Gaillard. "He directed his engineers to destroy the outworks that secured access and controlled the waters. They breached the stockade of piles driven to obstruct river traffic below the fort and demolished the bridges that connected the Rock with the isles of the Seine and with the opposite bank. Pioneers working like ants threw up embankments to isolate the fortress from the landward side." His men destroyed the neighboring village and drove its inhabitants within the keep. The defenders saw their stores dwindling and drove the unhappy villagers out again, to starve and freeze on the sides of the great Rock. One expedition for the relief of the castle was repulsed in a furious combat.

Finally, in February 1204, Philip moved to direct assault. One by one the three circling walls were breached. On 6 March the fortress fell and its garrison was slaughtered. All Normandy was Philip's when Rouen opened its gates to him, returning to French ownership for the first time since the 9th century. The death of Eleanor left Aquitaine to John, but the terms of the court's judgment against him made it forfeit to the French crown. Philip did not delay invasion and John was unable to mobilize any resistance to him. The Angevin empire, which yesterday had seemed so strong, today had collapsed. With the exception of Gascony, Philip had gained possession of all the Angevin provinces on the continent.

5. Government of France and public works

Winning battles and seizing lands was a common enough occupation for medieval rulers. Welding conquered lands into a political unit under an effective government was a much more rare accomplishment. It involved the imposition of uniform laws and taxes on different districts habituated by long tradition to the local and informal jurisdiction summed up in the "custom of the manor." It was in this task that Philip exhibited his genius. Richard, for instance, pursued the will-o-the-wisp which was a crusader's glory, won the title of Lion-Heart by his gallant exploits, but did nothing for England. Philip, on the other hand, took the lands that had been Richard's, added them to his own domain, and formed of them all the unified kingdom, France.

For the nobles of Anjou, Normandy, or Aquitaine, Philip's victory was to be not merely a matter of a change in their overlord. Nor did Philip limit himself to disposing of the more rebellious vassals and replacing them with others more submissive to himself. He could not, of course, dispense with the feudal system, even had he wanted to, for on it the whole structure of society rested. What Philip did was to make the active role of the king the central element in the system. His decrees were to be given universal respect; he was to have knowledge of, and control over, the administration of all the districts in his realm. The rights he had previously enjoyed only in the royal domain—his personal estates—he now was to enjoy throughout the kingdom. He began the transformation of the feudal monarchy into the absolute monarchy by which, 500 years later, Louis XIV was to rule France.

It is interesting to note that in this process of governmental reform Philip had the benefit of the example set by his old rival, Henry II. Even while distracted by the problems of his unruly family and their continental possessions, Henry had vastly strengthened the English crown. He appointed competent sheriffs and enforced their obedience to the monarch. He increased tax revenues and established the exchequer for annual accounting of royal finances. He kept traveling justices constantly on circuit and maintained at Westminster a permanent royal court to handle affairs and settle disputes even in his own absence.

First, Philip retained under his own control the lands he appropriated from John. He would have no more such princely vassals as Philip of Flanders, with an arrogance equal to the width of their estates. The new provinces, then, remained under the crown. Into them Philip sent the customary local officials, provosts. Within a circumscribed area, each provost represented the king, acting as judge in minor disputes, as administrator of royal ordinances, as tax collector. A smaller number of more important officials, bailiffs, checked up on the honesty and efficiency of the provosts. Periodically the bailiffs traveled through larger districts, counties we would call them, hearing complaints against the provosts, investigating local conditions, and holding monthly courts.

This machinery of administration Philip inherited, but he made a significant change in it. For generations local magnates had monopolized the position of bailiff, coming almost to treat it as a private possession. They had too often neglected the king's interests in order to forward their personal interests. With the prestige of royal authority, they acted as local dictators and built a center of power which they might use to defy the king. Philip prevented this mischief by rotating men in the office of bailiff and by moving them frequently from one district to another. The king did not choose the highest-ranking man and make him bailiff as a badge of honor; he chose the best man he could find, employed him as a civil servant, and paid him a fixed salary from the royal treasury. The bailiff was thus rendered independent of local politicking but dependent on the king.

Outside his own domain, Philip employed other means to make his influence felt and his power effective. For those lords who disregarded his overlordship, the ultimate resort was confiscation and the establishment of new vassals on their lands. But most nobles recognized the futility of opposition to the increasing weight of royal authority. Many of them, voluntarily as well as involuntarily, surrendered to the crown a share in their estates. Under this system of sharing they were assured of half their revenues, secure behind the protecting arm of the king, while the other half went to swell his treasury.

Also, the policy of granting safeguard was widely extended. By submitting themselves directly to the will of the king, abbots and lords gained immunity for their abbeys and fiefs. That is, they were released from service to their immediate feudal overlord and became subject only to the crown. Scattered throughout France, their lands were centers in which the royal interest was paramount and the effectiveness of royal protection was exhibited. With every instance of sharing or safeguard, the king made himself stronger in fighting men, resources, and influence. The stronger he became, the better able he was to provide the security he promised. More vassals, therefore, hastened to accept the protection the king offered, and the power of the local barons declined.

Even the great barons were increasingly hesitant to offend the king. Before them they had the fearful precedent of the punishment meted out to John by the king's court. In thus defending sub-vassals against their lord, no matter how proud and mighty he was, Philip had gained valuable popularity. The barons saw the wisdom of being circumspect both in their treatment of inferiors and in their loyalty to the king. Before, the barons had been able brazenly to ignore the king in his shadowy position at the top of the feudal hierarchy; now he was able to make his presence promptly and sternly felt anywhere in his kingdom. Before, a baron in revolt had been able to command his vassals and enlist the sympathy of his fellow barons. Now, especially in the Angevin provinces, Philip bound the barons in a mutual contract of fidelity, so that they were obligated to suppress the insurrection of any one of their number.

So Philip overawed his great subjects, destroying their petty tyrannies as he extended his own absolutism; but he did not wholly ignore their welfare. He continued the process by which the old feudal services the barons owed the king could be converted into money payments, thereby relieving them of much personal inconvenience.

Money was becoming an increasingly abundant, important, and

desirable commodity. Adventurous individuals were leaving the manors and seeking a better livelihood in some trade or craft. The risks of a new business were too great for them as individuals, and so they tended to congregate in groups, build towns, and form associations for their mutual protection. The traders and craftspeople were a new class in society, without traditional rights; their organizations, or communes, were formed without the well-defined rules that regulated, say, an order of knights or a brotherhood of monks. How were this new class and its communes to fare at the hands of longer-established elements in society? Would they win a secure place for themselves, or would they be exploited by the powerful?

Foremost among the people of his time, Philip perceived the value to France of commerce and crafts, and the benefit to the crown from fostering their growth. He decided to promote the new commercial enterprise. He would regulate the formation of communes; no new ones would be established without his consent. He would grant them letters of protection, freeing them from tribute to individual barons in whose territory they might have grown up. In return, he would share in their selection of local governors and in the fruits of their trading. Earlier kings, notably Louis VI, had favored the growth of communes outside the royal domain, hoping the townspeople would be their allies in conflicts with too-powerful subjects. Philip continued the practice, with the same aim, but he went further and permitted the establishment of communes within his domain.

It might seem that he was reducing his own power by granting these communes large privileges of self-government. In reality, Philip bound the townspeople to himself by his favor. Each commune was treated as a corporate vassal, and its contract with the king worked both ways. The town was given certain liberties and often was granted safeguard. But as a vassal, it was bound to supply fighting men to the king, men troubled by loyalty to no other individual lord, a militia which might become the basis of a national army. In case of war or feudal disorder, each town chartered by the king was a ready-garrisoned stronghold in his cause. The fortifications of the towns were even harder to overthrow than the walls of castles.

More important still, the communes paid for what the king gave them. Since a commune could not perform personal service, it paid its rents in money. So, in exchange for lands often not his own and a promise of protection he would seldom need to provide, the king gained an annual income in money he could use as he pleased. Philip, then, "took the bourgeoisie into partnership." This new commercial class would grow in size and wealth through the years. Its opportunities for expansion and prosperity and independence from feudal obligations would rest in its close alliance with the crown. As supporters of royal absolutism, their moral and financial strength would make the communes valuable.

To manage the affairs of the widely extended royal domain, the communes, and the scattered fiefs over which the crown had assumed control, a considerable expansion of the size and functions of the king's government in Paris was necessary. This expansion was not merely quantitative but was accompanied by three changes in the make-up of the central authority: a change in the type of personnel and their tasks; a shift in the relative importance of the king's advisory bodies; a more widespread use of money.

The king's government had developed originally from his household. His personal assistants, whom he needed in his capacity of feudal lord to take care of his private business, had simply been available for use as managers of his increasing public business as well. Such officials were his butler, constable, and chamberlain. Of the same type as these, but vastly more important, were the chancellor, who handled all written letters, records, and decrees, and the seneschal who as military commander-in-chief was guardian and overseer of all the king's domain. As they were close to the king, these officials were usually of the high nobility, and it was natural, considering the customs of the day, that they should begin to look upon their offices as hereditary, as possessions which they should enjoy like fiefs. In the course of time, then, they had come to exert strong influence over the king and to possess so much power that it was impossible even for the king to limit them. Philip would permit no such overshadowing of his own authority. He purposely left the great offices of seneschal and chancellor vacant. To the other positions he made appointments of lesser men as a reward for services done him. These appointments to the traditional household offices accorded dignity rather than real executive power.

Practical control of administration and justice was in the hands of the bailiffs and provosts, who carried out the king's decrees as they were instructed by the king's inner council. This council was advisory; the active executive was the king himself. In the council were collected hardworking efficient men to serve as agents of the king's will. They were to be found, not among the *haute noblesse*, but among the classes working to raise their status in the world—lower clergy, lesser nobility, an occasional rich burgher. Such men had no personal power to augment; they "owed all to their master." These new "career men" were the permanent core of the council, or as it was called then, the *curia regis*. Unburdened with private estates to manage, they were in reasonably constant attendance on the king as he traveled over his country; they met at his command. It was a simple matter to convene them to advise on some state policy or to sit as a court of law. It was easy to despatch a member of the *curia regis* to make an investigation of some complaint, to hold court in a commune, to check up on tax-collection or law enforcement. The members were available to carry out the king's orders; they were trained in the new procedures of government—for instance, in the use of sworn statements and written evidence in a legal inquest; experience made them increasingly able and effective. The final authority was the king's—he was the judge—but inevitably he grew to depend on his expert councilors and to grant them some authority to make decisions in his name.

The *curia regis* was a workable body. Important matters more and more came to be handled by it rather than by the unwieldy and stubborn great council of barons. This body was too venerable to abolish, and Philip found it of some use to him. It was primarily a military gathering (every baron being, of course, a military chieftain) and was always assembled in a time of decision as to peace or war. Then it served as a barometer of feudal opinion: by the enthusiasm of those present Philip could gauge the strength of his cause; those absent he could account as enemies. In addition, the great council normally heard certain judicial cases involving prominent people. Here Philip found its size a real detriment, and so in 1216 he handed this function over to a smaller body, the court of peers, which he established by nominating to it twelve of his strongest direct vassals. The great council did not make laws; its participation in the government was based on no constitutional guarantee; it met at no legally fixed intervals. The king summoned it when he needed it; he restricted its activity to talking and giving advice. He had the *curia regis* to do the real work of administration.

His just and efficient government won respect for Philip, and his success against John filled French citizens with pride, but he could not be called a popular ruler. He lacked Richard's flair for the spectacular; he never seemed to act spontaneously. The combination of sternness, subtlety, and self-sufficiency in his character kept him from capturing the hearts or the imaginations of his subjects. Nevertheless, they recognized the favorable effects of his rule. The expanding towns prospered. Water power drove the mills; machinery was put to wider use; new "scientific" ideas improved the breeding of livestock and the exploitation of forest resources. Royal revenues increased and expenses were kept in check. In 1202, for example, revenues were more than double expenses. And Philip was a modern-enough ruler to appreciate the desirability of putting on a good show, impressing the crowd with the royal magnificence. He devoted his chief effort in this regard to the glorification of his capital city.

An overgrown town of nearly 100,000 people, Paris lay on both sides of the Seine. On the north side, or Right Bank, lay the buildings that served as the commercial center of the kingdom, newly expanded and totally lacking in defenses. As early as his departure for the Third Crusade, Philip ordered this area to be surrounded with a perimeter wall, strengthened every hundred yards or so by towers and pierced here and there by impressive gates. To protect the western end of the wall was to rise a new castle, the Louvre. A moat circumscribed this massive square structure, seventy-five yards on a side, with eight towers of its own. Within, another moat protected the central round tower whose walls, thirteen feet thick at the bottom, rose over a hundred feet into the sky. For Philip the Louvre was a vital defense work, facing towards his enemies downstream. Only later did it become the chief royal residence.

The construction of the fortified walls was completed by about 1200. Meanwhile, the city streets were dirt tracks which turned to mud after every rain. As he leaned out of his window one day, Philip's nostrils were assailed by a loathesome stench emanating from the mud. He forthwith gave orders for the paving of all the streets in Paris. The Ile de la Cité, in the middle of the Seine, was the political and religious heart of the capital. The old fortress of the Capets was increased in size, airiness, and comfort, to be a fitting residence for a king.

Life in his capital, Philip thought, should be attended with a maximum of safety, luxury, and convenience. Because public works were a severe strain on even careful Philip's treasury, he bargained with the guilds in Paris for the labor. They did the work on his streets and bridges, palaces and hospitals, and were repaid with special privileges. The corporation of the watermen, for instance, gained the right to fix weights and measures and to collect a fee from every boat touching at the bridge over the Seine. Philip honored the citizens by asking their advice; a council of six leading burghers assisted his provost in ruling Paris.

The king concerned himself with other work that was being undertaken in his capital. Bishop Maurice de Sully had commenced building the glorious Cathedral of Notre-Dame on the site of the earlier Carolingian cathedral, at the eastern end of the Ile. Philip took an intense, indeed almost a professional, interest in the construction, which was characterized by a magnificence of scale and decoration new in Gothic building, and he made handsome contributions of money and of holy relics. He also gave his royal consent to the erection of a stronghold for the Knights Templar.

To the masters and students of the young university, Philip gave a charter and decreed that all scholars should have the "privilege of clergy." At that time, all men in clerical orders were exempt from certain civic duties. They were subject to canon, or church, law and, if accused of wrongdoing, were tried in church courts. By granting this right to young scholars, Philip assured them of fairer trials and less severe penalties than civil, or feudal, courts would have provided. He hoped the university would teach the virtue of obedience to the king, who was the source of all power in the state. So Philip with his manifold enterprises called his citizens' attention to royal authority, and to posterity he left monuments of royal grandeur.

6. Philip and the Church

Philip had taken advantage of his victory over John to consolidate his domain and to bind his people in ever closer dependence on himself. Meanwhile the profligate John was plunging into deeper trouble. Having shamed himself in the eyes of his barons by his inactivity in France, he continued to quarrel with them over money and his method of government. Then he alienated himself from the pope by refusing to accept Stephen Langton, whom Innocent III had nominated as archbishop of Canterbury. The pope placed England under an interdict, and, in 1212, called for a crusade to depose the disobedient John. He appealed to Philip to organize the invasion force. The king accepted the papal command, ordering his power to assemble at Rouen. Before we follow the course of events, however, we should look back over Philip's relations with the papacy, which led to Innocent's choice of him as leader.

Every medieval monarch was faced with the problem of the power of the universal Church. For some generations, we know, the papacy had been maintaining that its spiritual power made it superior to any temporal power, that it could sit in final judgement on the acts of any king. Of all the proponents of papal supremacy, Innocent III was the most determined. He demanded that all European kings should recognize him as their overlord, from whom they held their kingdoms in fief. He defined his position in terms familiar to us:

> God has set two great lights on the firmament, the sun to rule the day, the moon to rule the night. So, in the firmament of the universal Church, He has instituted two high dignities: the Papacy, which reigns over the souls of men; and the Monarchy, which reigns over their bodies. But the first is far above the second. As the moon receives light from the sun, so does the royal power derive all its glory and dignity from the papal power.

There were occasions when it was necessary for kings to deal, however unwillingly, with this imperious representative of God on earth because for all Christians the pope's authority in spiritual matters was unquestioned.

After the death of his first wife, Philip had married a Danish princess named Ingeborg. It was not a happy marriage. Philip had sent her away and in 1196 he had married again. Violent criticism of his ill-use of Ingeborg burst from the lips of all those unfriendly to France or to Philip. The king of Denmark complained of the insult to his country and appealed to the pope for justice. Innocent was glad of this chance to assert his authority over a king and insisted that Philip take Ingeborg back, nullifying his third marriage. After Philip persisted in ignoring the pope's wishes, he was declared guilty of adultery and was excommunicated. When this drastic punishment failed to move Philip, the pope took the final step and imposed an interdict on France.

The words of the papal order are still impressive:

> Let all the churches be closed; let no one be admitted to them except to baptize infants; let them not be otherwise opened except for the purpose of lighting the lamps, or when the priest shall come for the Eucharist and holy water for the use of the sick.... Let the clergy recite the canonical hours outside the churches where the people do not hear them; if they recite an epistle or a gospel, let them beware lest the laity hear them. And let them not permit the dead to be interred, nor their bodies to be placed unburied in the cemeteries.... Let no vessels of holy water be placed outside of the church, nor shall the priests carry them anywhere, for all the sacraments of the Church beyond these two which were reserved are absolutely prohibited. Extreme unction, which is a holy sacrament, may not be given.

We must remember that the services of the Church were the sole means by which humans could be assured of eternal bliss in heaven. These services the interdict forbade. It was, therefore, the most fearful of all penalties, depriving the entire population of the customary satisfactions of church attendance and of hopes for the future. Because of Philip's refusal to mend his sinful ways, "a whole nation thought itself in danger of eternal damnation." The Church's moral power over his own people convinced Philip that submission was his wisest course. He bowed to Innocent's judgment and the interdict was lifted.

Although the pope's claim of superiority over kings appeared to have been vindicated, Philip's submission was really little more than a formality. He did put aside his third wife and promise to take Ingeborg back. But he kept her living in seclusion, deprived of all queenly honors, and the pope was powerless to interfere. Furthermore, Philip's submission had been in a matter of private sin, not of public policy. When his obstinacy threatened to jeopardize the national welfare, Philip gave in. But he did not relax his efforts to substitute royal for papal control of the Church in France. The king refused to be a vassal to anyone, even to the pope.

The two crucial issues at stake were the power of appointment to church offices and the use of church revenue. To begin with, Philip asserted his legal rights. When a bishop's see was vacant, the king was entitled to collect and enjoy the revenue. Clearly it was not always to the advantage of the king to be too hasty in filling the vacancy. Using this right as a lever, Philip could exert particular influence over the choice of a candidate for the bishopric. The Church could accept the royal nominee or could watch its revenue filling up the royal coffers. Pressing his legal right, Philip actually expanded the scope of his authority over church affairs. An appointment to a bishopric frequently came to a political official as a reward for faithful service. Philip's "most useful clerks became bishops at his will." So Philip's admission of the supremacy of the pope was nominal only. In practical matters he maintained, and even increased, the independence of the French Church from papal interference. He was the champion of nationalism in religious policy.

Innocent realized that in the affair of Ingeborg he had won an empty victory. It was important for him to keep up a proud front of church unity, and so he was careful that his further relations with Philip should be thoroughly cordial. The Albigensian heresy gave him an opportunity to show off his friendliness toward the French king. Most of the inhabitants of Toulouse in southern France had broken away from the moral code and the sacraments which were central in the Roman faith. Innocent was keenly anxious to bring them back to their ancient loyalty, at the same time saving France from unnecessary bloodshed. But when the Count of Toulouse gave armed support to the heretics, seized churches, and connived at the murder of the papal legate, the heresy became a revolution.

Innocent preached a crusade against the Albigensians in 1207 and urged Philip to undertake the command. The king desired to bring Toulouse into closer dependency on the crown, but he saw some dangers in Innocent's polite offer. He should not look too grasping. He was not yet free of trouble with John in the north and a new campaign in the south might overtax his resources. Always hitherto his actions had aimed at the unification of France. Would it be wise to wage war against French citizens on behalf of a foreign potentate? Philip preferred to remain on the sidelines. He watched the crusade degenerate into a feudal war for control of territory, engendering bitterness and hatred. When both sides were weakened and sick of futile bloodshed, it would be time for the crown to assume the role of protector and reap its reward in the form of direct control over the exhausted countryside. The pope's offer, then, had seemed to promise to Philip no material advantage which could not be gained by doing nothing. But the pope had not been able to act without first consulting the king. If Innocent should again approach Philip, with a suggestion of more practical benefit, king and pope might find it advisable to work in partnership.

Such an opportunity Philip saw in the projected crusade against England. Innocent turned to him as the strongest available monarch. Philip was not interested in humbling John before Innocent, but he desired to crush the rival king who served as a center around whom had gathered all those opposed to Philip's achievement of absolute rule over a united France. As leader of Innocent's crusade, Philip could accomplish his end, with the moral influence of the papacy assuring him of support throughout Europe. So in 1213 Philip moved his forces to Boulogne and Gravelines, ready to embark, with the papal blessing, for the defeat of his arch-enemy, John.

Suddenly the bubble burst. Desperate at the prospect of losing his kingdom altogether, John surrendered to Innocent. He agreed to hold England as a fief from the pope, at an annual rent of 1000 silver marks. The crusade was unnecessary, and Innocent's legate ordered Philip to cease his preparations. But Philip would not turn back. His host was in readiness. His opponents had declared themselves. His greatest opportunity was at hand, and Philip had never yet failed to seize an opportunity. The pope might desist or even change sides, but the king would persist in his favorite scheme. For the moment John was saved, but his ally the count of Flanders, Philip's recalcitrant vassal, lay open to a French attack. Philip advanced into Flemish territory, but his accompanying fleet was defeated by English ships in the Channel, and he had to turn back. Although victory was eluding him, Philip remained attentive to his main chance.

7. Bouvines—1214

By spring 1214 an awesome alliance had raised itself against Philip. John was preparing to lead a descent on the coast of Poitou. He had dispatched a powerful contingent under his best soldier, William of Salisbury, to Flanders to join with the count and with Reginald of Boulogne. These represented the opposition of the great feudal lords to Philip's central government. Coming to aid them was Otto the Holy Roman Emperor—son of Henry of Saxony, nephew of Richard the Lion-Hearted, and now the avowed enemy of Innocent III. John and Otto planned to invade France simultaneously at two points. Philip would have to divide his forces, which then could be destroyed separately or crushed between the converging attackers.

The very magnitude of the threat to Philip's regime worked to his advantage. His enemies were a coalition in which the foreign element was predominant. Their purpose was once again to cut France up into little pieces, none strong enough to rank as a major power. Their victory could result only in a return to the constant warfare which feudal anarchy rendered inevitable. Philip, on the other hand, was defending France against a foreign invasion; his cause was national. He stood for the unity under which the nation had come to enjoy the prosperity bred by peace and order. His was the popular side.

While Philip marched north to parry the thrust from Flanders, his son Louis the Lion hurried westward to face John. Checked by Louis, John was irresolute as ever and drew back. The outcome of the war hinged on Philip's success. His army was comparatively small, perhaps 25,000 men, but it represented the nation. The loyal barons had brought in their retainers to fight side by side with the contingents of burghers from Philip's communes. Together they were defending their homeland. The invaders numbered more than 40,000. But their counsels were divided, their purposes confused, their support from home uncertain. Incidents in the two camps on the eve of battle are indicative. Reginald of Boulogne opposed risking all in a pitched battle and was accused of treachery by his jealous allies. Philip went on his knees and prayed with a good conscience, unconsciously mixing the ancient belief in the divinity of kings with the astuteness of a master-bargainer: "Lord, I am but a man, but I am a king. Thine it is to guard the king. Thou wilt lose nothing thereby. Wherever Thou wouldest go I will follow Thee."

The battle took place on an extremely hot Sunday, 27 July 1214. Philip drew up his army in line on a low plateau rising from marshy ground near the town of Bouvines. As they awaited attack, with their backs to the sun, the king addressed the troops:

> In God is all our hope, all our trust. King Otto and his army have been excommunicated by the Pope, for they are enemies and persecutors of Holy Church. The payroll for his soldiers comes from the tears of the poor, from the pillage of lands belonging to God and the clergy. As for us, we are Christians, in peace and communion with Holy Church. Sinners though we are, we are in accord with the servants of God.... Thus may we count on divine mercy. The Lord will give us means of triumphing over our enemies, who are ours!

The Germans advanced confidently and the struggle was fierce, especially in the center of the line where the two royal leaders had stationed themselves.

The German infantry overwhelmed the French, reached Philip, and pulled him from his saddle with the point of a pike stuck fast in the triple thickness of his neck armor. Only the excellence of his armor saved the king from death. Meanwhile, a picked force of five hundred French knights, the "Household Cavalry," had been seeking the Emperor.

Now they returned, rode over the infantry, and rescued Philip, who remounted to rejoin the fight. Once more the French chivalry charged, penetrated to Otto's position, and engaged him in hand-to-hand combat. The Emperor, in his turn, lost his horse, then found another. In the confused melee, Otto saw himself almost surrounded. He turned to flee, his chief lords with him.

"We won't see his face again today," said Philip grimly, and his prediction was correct. The fury of the French assault pressed backward the English bowmen on one flank and the Flemish chivalry on the other. Reginald of Boulogne valiantly kept up a "forlorn hope" defense in the center, only to be captured in the end and to discover that William of Salisbury and Ferrand of Flanders were prisoners too. The rest of the coalition army was in full retreat.

Philip's triumph was overwhelming. He had united the French people to repel a threat to the nation. They had rallied to his banner and gained a national victory. Philip's return to his capital over roads strewn with flowers was one continuous triumphal procession, as he received the plaudits of the entire population. He went to Notre-Dame to offer a Te Deum. The university students made merry for a week.

8. Character and achievement of Philip

Bouvines changed the course of European history. Otto gave up the imperial throne. Frederick II of Hohenstaufen became Emperor but, like Otto, proved to be an implacable enemy of the papal power. The successors of Innocent III never again could assert a prestige and influence equal to his. Defeated in his desperate enterprise, John was forced to make concessions to his barons in Magna Carta, and England took its first step on the road to constitutional government. The pretensions of the great French vassals to independence were shattered, and French unity was established beyond dispute. So did Philip's concentration on the task of creating a nation have decisive effect on the western world of his day.

Bouvines was Philip's final exploit, as well as his greatest. The remaining nine years of his reign were uneventful at home, as the government he had organized performed the routine tasks of ruling the kingdom. He permitted his son Louis to invade England in 1216, when John's perfidy outraged his barons to the point of armed rebellion. But Philip had no wish to be king of England; so he took no part in the expedition, probably foreseeing its ultimate failure when, after John died, the barons rallied to the boy-king, Henry III. Philip's lifetime work was done.

What was the extent of Philip's accomplishment? He does not present the romantic figure of the warrior-king. In his life there was little mad galloping into battle at the head of the French chivalry, no memorable generosity to a fallen foe, no ardent wooing of a beautiful princess. Although his own tastes ran to good living, his career was, in general, unglamorous. So he made small appeal to the medieval chroniclers and troubadours. They admit his greatness and call him "Conqueror," but they pass over him hurriedly, preferring to dwell on the exploits of the Lion-Hearted. When they describe Philip, it is usually to point out how far Richard exceeded him in valor or honesty or grace. Through a large part of Philip's reign there was not even a queen to brighten his court, to charm visitors with a smile, to lure the king away from business, to be the center of the songs and dances of a gracious society.

Instead, the court was the scene of incessant labors. Always in the background was the king, solitary, silent, inscrutable, taking no one fully into his confidence, not even trusting his oldest son. He worked constantly to shape France according to his plan—to establish unity of administration where there had been multiplicity. He preferred the arts of politics and diplomacy to the hazards of a war, however glorious. He was the practical statesman, who could subordinate his feelings to his commonsense. His grandson, Louis IX, remembered this advice from his grandfather: "No one can be a good governor of a land unless he knows how to refuse as boldly and vigorously as he knows how to give." Philip was a hard and close-fisted master. He had a grasp of realities— an understanding of his times and of the sources of a king's power— that would have amazed the carefree Richard. Driving him on to the achievement of his purpose was a single-minded, invincible will. Philip always thought before he acted, and then he acted firmly, deviously, ruthlessly, as the occasion demanded.

His extraordinary intelligence and determination explain Philip's success. The France he inherited was still a weak collection of scattered fiefs, eclipsed in strength by the Angevin and German empires. This France Philip tripled in size, wiping out the independent powers within the realm, making it a compact geographical unity. For this enlargement of the boundaries of the state, Rigord gave Philip the title Augustus, recalling the statemaking of the first Roman Emperor. Along with this physical consolidation, Philip gave France political unity, carrying the authority of the crown and establishing order even to the frontiers. He multiplied the extent of the royal domain and made his control over that domain absolute. Philip's *cura regis* became the center from which radiated the decrees and the justice that governed the whole kingdom. Philip increased the number of districts subject to the administration of a provost from 38 to 94, and he doubled the revenue of the state.

Philip's desire was to make his France as strong as Charlemagne's. Although not comparable in extent, his realm was more fully centralized and more strictly ruled than Charlemagne's had been. As Philip strengthened the internal organization of his kingdom, made it responsive to his will, undivided in its loyalty, so did he build the power that enabled France at Bouvines to repel the combined attack of England and Germany. The France that Philip created was a great state, the leading state and cultural center of Europe, as Charlemagne's had been.

The capstone of Philip's accomplishment was the change he effected in the personal position of the king. He gave truly royal grandeur and significance to what had often been an empty feudal dignity. His predecessors had trembled on their thrones at the murmured threats of the great barons and had relied on the capricious support of the communes or the Church. Philip demanded and received the loyal support of barons great and small, of townspeople, of churchmen. He was not their creature; he was their master. He raised the king to a position of supremacy above the baronage. There was no feudal election to determine who should have the crown after Philip's death. His son succeeded him naturally, and without any need of being honored with a coronation while his father was alive.

In Philip's day the old feudal system which had held society together for two hundred years was beginning to decay. The chivalric ideals of courage, loyalty, and service began to lose their hold on people's minds. Mounted knights might be defeated by mercenaries. New forces—money, trade, social mobility, independent thinking— disrupted the established order. Strong men took advantage of their strength to exploit the weak, who strove in turn to escape the bonds which held them down. Customs, which had served as laws, were disregarded; feudal warfare became little more than semi-legalized robbing and looting. All people, save a few of the strongest, looked fearfully and hopefully for a new source of authority and order to replace the broken contracts of feudalism. Peasants, merchants, priests, abbots, lesser nobles, all needed protection.

In France it was the king who could give them this protection, it was the king around whom they could rally as the source of all glory and honor. Philip, says the Grand Chronicle of Tours, "liked to make use of little people, to make himself the vanquisher of the great, the defender of the Church, and the nourisher of the poor." We cannot believe Philip fancied himself as the benefactor of his people. He aimed to be the absolute ruler of a strong kingdom. But he did grant privileges to the new communes in return for their money. He did uphold the Church as long as it supported him and consented to his wishes. He made use of the lesser nobility in his *curia regis*, to break the tyranny of the ancient barons. He provided prompt and free justice for all people in the royal courts, which not even the proudest vassal could ignore.

One day Philip watched a statue of himself as a boy king being placed on the great western front of Notre-Dame. When he died at Mantes, on 24 July 1223, the shape and appearance of the cathedral were far different from what they had been at the time of his accession. And the France he left to Louis VIII was far different from the France he had inherited from Louis VII. In creating a mighty nation, Philip had refused to float along with the prevailing lawlessness, pettiness, and localism of his times. Instead, he molded his times in the direction of a new age of centralized monarchy, of rising nationalism, of spreading commerce, of new thinkers and disturbing ideas.

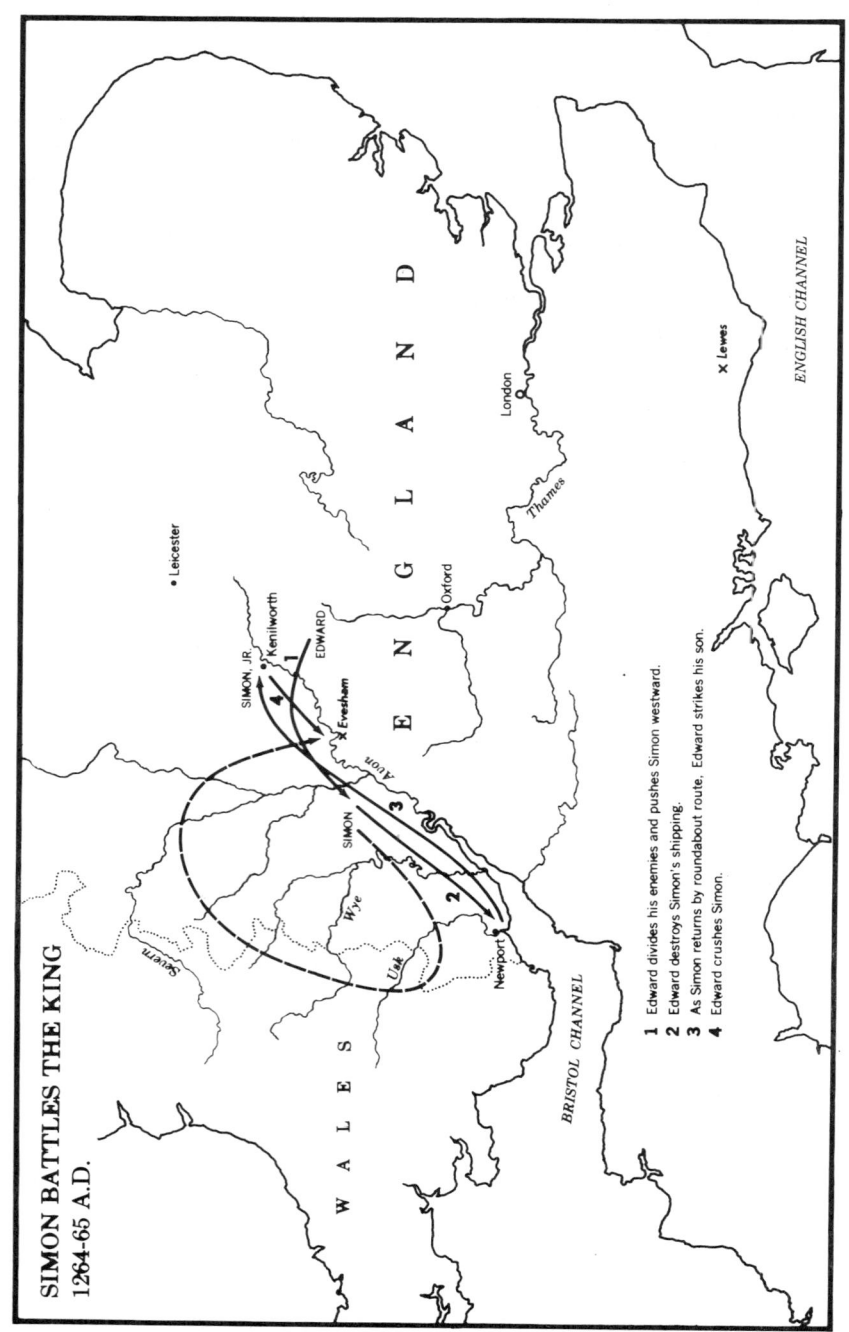

SIMON BATTLES THE KING
1264-65 A.D.

1 Edward divides his enemies and pushes Simon westward.
2 Edward destroys Simon's shipping.
3 As Simon returns by roundabout route, Edward strikes his son.
4 Edward crushes Simon.

244

Chapter Nine

CONSTITUTIONAL MONARCHY? SIMON DE MONTFORT (1208-1265)

It is not always the native son who becomes the national hero. Nor is it only the perennially successful person whose deeds we record in our history books. The man whose career we look at now was born a Frenchman but played his great role in England. He achieved some success, but only fourteen months intervened between his climactic victory and his crushing defeat and death. Then his body was mutilated, his widow and sons fled abroad to lead the unhappy lives of persecuted exiles, and within seventy-five years his family in the direct line had ceased to exist. Yet Simon de Montfort was an outstanding man of his time, and his impact on the history of England, at least, surpasses that of any of his contemporaries.

1. Simon de Montfort — typical medieval lord

At the opening of the 13th century Simon was born into the de Montfort family, long-established and powerful among the French nobility. That was an era when a person's rank in society was more significant than his or her nationality—the idea of nations being yet in its infancy—and when nobles of two countries had far more in common than either one had with the peasants of his or her own country. Society, at least the upper class of wealth and prestige, was international and Christian in membership and outlook, what we today would call cosmopolitan. The mixing of blood and name and language was commonplace. Especially, of course, was this true of England and France, as a result of 1066 and of the Angevin empire.

Typical of these old customs of feudalism, and in defiance of the rising sentiment of nationality, Simon's father held lands under both English and French overlords. Furthermore, he had married the sister of the English earl of Leicester, and the earl's death without direct heirs left his title and half his estates in the possession of the de Montforts. This inheritance seemed of doubtful value a few years later, however, when King John in his struggle with his barons confiscated the property. So it was that Simon's ambitious father sought wealth and fame in France rather than in England. As commander of the forces under the papal banner, de Montfort stamped out the Albigensian heresy and won for himself vast possessions from the forfeit lands of the heretics' protector, the count of Toulouse.

In southern France the good fortune of the de Montfort family again proved temporary. Their sudden rise to the very first rank among great lords had aroused the jealousy of their peers, the suspicion of kings, and the hostility of their new subjects. So Simon's older brother surrendered to Louis VIII the rights he could not defend, and by 1228 the de Montforts, apparently stripped of their lands in both Leicester and Toulouse, were no better off than at the time of Simon's birth.

Of Simon's early years and upbringing, meanwhile, we have heard nothing, because nothing is known. It is safe to say only that his education in both the practical and graceful accomplishments of knighthood was such as befitted his station in life and to surmise from his later concern for religion that he must have shown an unusually serious interest in his studies. In 1230 we meet Simon for the first time as an historical individual. In the confused period of the regency of Blanche of Castille which followed the death of Louis VIII, Simon, the younger of the two surviving sons of the Albigensian crusader, found it convenient to leave France. It was logical that he should go to England to pay court to the king in hopes of recovering the family possessions in Leicester. And it is not surprising that Henry III, looking for strong and vigorous supporters of his own throne, should have favored his suit. In 1231, Simon became Henry's man, doing homage for the earldom of Leicester.

Simon came into England a stranger and an alien. As he assumed the large lands and authority of the earl of Leicester, it is not hard to see that his peers must have looked upon this newcomer with some mistrust and envy. Simon owed his position, his estates, and his security to the good will of the king, and he spent his first years in England in loyal service that would keep him worthy of Henry's continuing kindness. So successful was the new earl that in 1238 he reached the pinnacle of royal favor and married Henry's sister Eleanor.

This marriage of a member of the royal family and an upstart foreigner was first kept secret. When the news was disclosed England was indignant. The clergy were incensed because Eleanor, a widow, had broken her vow never to remarry. The lords were infuriated that they, the guardians of the monarchy, had not been consulted in council before such a momentous marriage had been arranged. All true Englishmen and women felt it dangerous for a foreigner to have been placed so near to the throne, in a position second only to the king's own brother, Richard of Cornwall.

This danger seemed particularly acute at the time because relations with France were not good. Worse still, the king as yet had no son of his own to succeed him, and it did not seem inconceivable that Simon might one day seize the throne itself. But this last objection was reduced to insignificance the following year when the queen gave birth to a male heir. Despite all the criticism, Simon still stood in Henry's good graces; he had proudly served as hereditary steward at the queen's coronation; now he was chosen as one of the godfathers of the infant Prince Edward.

Simon soon learned, however, to "put not his faith in princes." The king was fickle; jealous perhaps of the firmness and strength of his brother-in-law, or perhaps listening at last to the chorus of protest that had accompanied Simon's advancement, Henry accused him of having plotted his marriage for his own unworthy advantage. Simon departed forthwith in fury for France. This was not his first return to the continent, for he had already begun to play the part of the great lord on the European stage. Traveling to Rome to obtain papal dispensation for his wife's broken vow of chastity, Simon had conferred with the Emperor Frederick II. On his return he had paused long enough to give Frederick soldierly assistance before Brescia, which the Emperor was besieging as part of his scheme to broaden his domain in Italy at the expense of the Italian cities and the pope.

Now in France, Simon began to consider going on a crusade, the customary resort of the noble discontented at home and anxious to exercise his warlike skills. The cloud of Henry's wrath hanging over his head seems soon to have dissipated, for in 1240 Simon was back in England raising money and men for the crusade on which he went with Richard of Cornwall. But crusading fervor had diminished by the mid-13th century, and their expedition was fruitless. Simon, nevertheless, so distinguished himself for valor and wisdom that the Christians in Palestine petitioned Frederick to appoint him their governor. The petition was ignored.

A war close to home next engaged Simon's attention. Henry III was anxious to establish his fame, and to replenish his treasury, by winning back from France the broad provinces which had been lost by his extravagant and careless father, King John. A large-scale military expedition to the continent would necessitate unusual expenditures. When Henry broached the proposal to the Great Council in 1242, the majority of the barons opposed it, aware of the costs and risks to which they would be exposed and sceptical of any permanent gain which would come to England from marauding expeditions abroad. It meant little to them that the French king refused to recognize Henry's brother's right to the title of count of Poitou, which Henry was using as the pretext for going to war. The barons in this case saw more clearly than the king what should be England's policy, and the Council prepared to refuse the grants of aid which he required. Unable to convince the barons in a body, Henry cajoled them with threats and promises as individuals, and secured enough support to undertake his war.

The actual campaign in France bore out the fears of those who had opposed the king's plan. The English army was too small to hold any territory; at Taillebourg it lost the one real battle that it fought. It was only Simon's bravery that saved Henry from capture. But Simon was heard to remark that the king might better have been shut up in his palace at Windsor, for which remark Henry never forgave him. Henry had to retreat constantly from the growing forces of the French and eventually to return to England with nothing accomplished. Simon de Montfort, however, had added to his own reputation. Once he was committed to the idea of the campaign, none had served the king with greater loyalty or energy. And Henry, at last realizing that in Simon he had an earl able and powerful and purposeful above the ordinary, rewarded his faithful services by giving him the castle of Kenilworth, in central England.

With the war over, Simon busied himself with the affairs of his earldom. He was an efficient lord, though harsh and uncompromising, and he enlarged and strengthened his new castle. But the England of those days was not an adventurous field for a restless nobleman and Simon thought again of fighting for the cross. Louis IX of France, called Saint Louis for his piety and devotion to the cause of the Church, projected a crusade against the Mohammedans in Egypt, and Simon's interest was aroused. While he was in the midst of preparations for the crusade, a summons from Henry changed his plans. The king had awakened to the folly of allowing one of his staunchest and most capable supporters to depart for an indefinite period of fighting in the East. His one remaining province in France, Gascony, was in a state of unrest, even of incipient rebellion, and he needed a fearless administrator to restore the order and prosperity without which Gascony was rather a burden than a benefit. For such a task the strong-willed and incorruptible Simon seemed clearly qualified, and the king's appointment of him as governor of Gascony sent him out of England to Bordeaux rather than to Damietta.

It was not as a mere seneschal or custodian of the royal property and interests that Simon went to Gascony. It was as a viceroy, empowered to act as a commander or judge in the king's name, standing in the minds of the provincials as the king himself. Here was room for the exercise of all Simon's talents and ambition. He had felt that it was "unbecoming to decline the danger of so great an exploit," but he soon found that he had underestimated its dangers and inconveniences. The Gascon nobles, he reported, "rode the country by night, like thieves, in parties of twenty, thirty, or forty." And the indecisive Henry sent his deputy no material support, leaving it to Simon to find the men and money which his task required. Faced with such difficulties, Simon wrote to a friend that he was finding patience in reading the Old Testament story of Job.

It was with patience and determination and perseverance that Simon set about to prove himself. Within a few months of his arrival, he had reduced the rebellious nobles to submission and to renewed oaths of allegiance as the king's vassals. The king's feudal dues were collected impartially and completely. The king's laws were obeyed. A chain of royal forts was constructed. Simon's rule was effective and thorough. The governor wasted no sympathy on the turbulent independence of the Gascon nobles. They, of course, aspired to a position in which their homage would be merely nominal and their own individual authority unchallenged. Simon found it necessary not to subdue them once but to overawe them into perpetual submissions. He promptly and sternly punished all offenders against his regime.

Such a sudden imposition of strict discipline did not please the Gascons. The strongest among the discontented plotted to free themselves from Simon's grip. Criticism of his iron-handed rule, complaints against his severity, his avarice, his haughtiness, multiplied in the hands of the king at Westminster. Those whom Simon had pacified protested their loyalty to Henry and filled the royal ears with suggestions that Simon was scheming to make himself an independent ruler. Such hints as these at length made some impression on the king, who was neither so clear of vision nor so firm of purpose as Simon, and it may well be that he had become somewhat suspicious of Simon's sweeping success. Anxious to maintain his popularity with the Gascon vassals, Henry does not appear to have realized that they complained of Simon in the hope only of regaining their license to make private war and to exploit Gascony for their own interests. Simon had shown a scornful disregard of them: "a man of such nobility as his should not be perturbed about 'foreigners'." Nor had he been at pains to explain his motives or justify his methods. He was a man of action, who had done the job he had been given to do. Far from the scene, however, rumors were spread of Simon's selfish ambitions.

Simon's policy was much stronger than Henry himself could have carried out, and the king wavered. At last, in 1252, he ordered a formal inquiry into Simon's administration and his accounts of revenue and expense. Indignant that his purpose should be misinterpreted and that his honesty should be questioned, Simon defended himself so ably that the Council could only clear him of all the charges. But the king's mind had been poisoned against him, and Henry was too petty in spirit to make gracious acknowledgement of Simon's services or generous provision for their continuance. Instead, he implied that Simon had been a swindler, even a *traitor*. "There is a lying word!" hotly retorted Simon. "If you were not my sovereign you would rue the day when you spoke it."

Simon could not conceal his wrathful indignation nor his contempt of the king's ingratitude. Although not a skillful politician, he remained a loyal lieutenant of the king. At his own expense and risk he returned to Gascony to chastise those who had sought the favorable opportunity to break loose from the royal authority. Then he retired into France. There Simon was now so famous that he was offered a place on the regency board which was to govern the kingdom in the absence of St. Louis. Simon declined this extraordinary honor on account, it is said, of the dying word of his old friend and adviser, the bishop of Lincoln, who urged that his first loyalty should be to England. And the chance to return to English service soon came. Simon, probably with some sense of self-satisfaction, went again to Gascony to aid Henry in making a settlement with his vassals there. And king and earl were, at least outwardly, reconciled.

Let us pause for a moment, in 1254, to review Simon's career. Starting in England as an unpopular alien, wholly dependent on the king, he had gained for himself a position of prominence in Europe. There had been an element of poor timing, however, in all his undertakings. He had been a crusader when the real crusading ardor was spent and Christendom was powerless to gain anything from fighting the Mohammedans in Palestine. He had stood in the forefront of Henry's most loyal vassals in the war with France, a war which was totally unsuccessful. He had served with competence as the governor of a large section of the king's domain, only to find his master jealous of his achievement and unwilling to support his well-chosen policy. He had become the brother-in-law of the king, but Henry had mistrusted and mistreated him. No irremediable break had been made with Henry, but in 1254 it did not seem as though either in England or in Europe there was an opening for the further development of Simon's career. Had he died then, his life would have been indistinguishable from that of numberless medieval barons.

2. Misrule and unpopularity of Henry III

Like everyone else, Simon was subject to changing circumstances. These now gave him a more important role than any he had played thus far. During Henry's reign Simon had not been the only man to suffer from the king's vacillation or to have occasion to find fault with his policies. As the years passed, bitter complaints against Henry's costly misrule could be heard on every side, and the king was losing friends throughout his realm.

Henry had come to the throne as the result of a wave of popular enthusiasm. We remember that in the last year of the reign of his father, the untrustworthy King John, many of the barons had despaired of the welfare of England. They had called for the aid of Louis, Dauphin of France, to dethrone their king. Delighted at the prospect of extending his own rule abroad, Louis was in England at the head of an army when King John died, of "a surfeit of cider and new peaches," after having, with the approval of the papal legate, repudiated Magna Carta. An immediate revulsion of popular feeling occurred. Although he was a mere child and the son of a well-hated father, the people preferred Henry to Louis because he was a native-born Englishman. Under the leadership of the regent, the aged but still redoubtable William Marshal, they compelled the foreign invader to make an ignominious departure from his nearly-won kingdom.

Unfortunately, this lesson of the increasing importance of nationality was lost on Henry. When he grew old enough to dispense with his tutors and take the reins of government into his own hands, he surrounded himself with a crowd of foreign favorites. He married Eleanor of Provence, sister-in-law of Louis IX of France, and allowed her to bring to England "an immense entourage of cooks, artists, jugglers, actors, and minstrels." Enormously expensive raiment and jewelry made Eleanor and Henry "glitter" at their marriage at Canterbury and her later coronation at Westminster. But before long, Eleanor was as cordially hated as she was acknowledged to be beautiful.

Henry placed her relatives of the prominent house of Savoy in positions of trust at his court, showering them with castles, titles, and grants of money. Although the king seemed blind to their selfishness and prodigality, the queen's friends were open to criticism from every point of view. As landlords, these foreigners carried out of England a large share of the income from their English estates. As a bloc at court, owing their offices to the royal will rather than to their importance as local magnates throughout the kingdom, they had no reason to oppose the exercise of absolute royal power. Among the English nobles they were suspect because of their elegant manners and their influence over the mind of the king. Above all, because the French supporters of the king split the barony, the English barons saw themselves in danger of losing their powers to hold the king in cheek, the very powers which they had forced King John to recognize in the Magna Carta of 1215. Time and again Henry promised to abide by the principles of Magna Carta—especially, that no tax should be levied without the consent of the Great Council of the barons. Time and again, abetted by his foreign advisers, the irresponsible Henry found it expedient, and possible, to break his promise.

For Henry was extravagant—as well in his way of living and in gifts to his friends as in his national policies. To be sure, his problem was difficult. In the 13th century an increase in population, improvements in agriculture, a wider variety of handicrafts, the expansion of trade which followed the Crusades to the East, and the growth of towns, combined to make prices go up. This rise in the cost of living was reflected, naturally, in a rise in the cost of government. Meanwhile, with the spread of the king's authority to the local districts through the sheriffs and itinerant justices, and with the elaboration of the machinery of the *curia regis*, government had expanded. Not only then had government become more expensive; there was more government to be expensive.

Although feudal theory still expected it, it had become impossible for "the king to live of his own." What had once been the cost of the king's private household had grown into the cost of his nation-wide government organization. The nation should defray such costs, but the requisite taxing machinery did not yet exist. So Henry was hard-pressed even for the routine expenses of his administration. Whenever he undertook any unusual policy—war, diplomatic negotiations, even his personal journey to Gascony—the king was compelled to call on his barons for aid.

From our modern vantage point, we can easily comprehend Henry's dilemma and identify his mistake. In a period filled with new problems, his thinking was old-fashioned and unimaginative. He failed to recognize the necessities of the economic situation, as he failed to appreciate the growing sentiment of nationalism. He wanted his funds to come from the nation but his policies to be his alone. Contrary to the spirit of his times, Henry persisted in thinking of England as his private domain in which "the command of the prince has the force of law," rather than as a nation composed of people with ideas and ambitions of their own. He looked upon his kingship as a personal privilege when, in reality, it was beginning to assume the characteristics of a public responsibility. His policies were still dynastic, designed for the benefit of himself and his family, when they should have been national, devoted to the security and prosperity of his kingdom.

When his barons refused him a grant of money unless they were given a part in the choice of officials to govern the country, Henry had only contempt for their desire. He clearly defined his own conception of the proper relation between king and people: "Servants do not judge their master. Vassals do not judge their prince or bind him by conditions. They should put themselves at his disposal and be submissive to his will." Henry was ambitious to use his private property, England, for the purpose of acquiring more private property. His abortive war with France, against the advice of the English barons, is a case in which his desire for glory led him into an error in policy. In his dynastic ambitions he accepted for his second son, Edmund, the pope's nomination as king of Sicily. But Edmund must first invade and conquer his kingdom. The army? The supplies? To be drawn from England, of course. For his brother, Richard of Cornwall, Henry moved heaven and earth to obtain election as Emperor. The extent of the bribes paid out of English funds may be inferred from the fact that Richard was the successful candidate.

This type of meddling in foreign affairs was costly. Were such policies effective? They met with failure on every side; the war with France gained nothing, Edmund never mounted the throne of Sicily, Richard never ruled Germany. Success might have redeemed these policies despite their cost; failure branded them as extravagant, and their originator as a foolish monarch.

Not only in politics did Henry's measures breed resentment, but in religious affairs also. Here again Henry misjudged the spirit of his times. The tragedy of the late medieval Church was that it chose to devote its resources and prestige to temporal rather than spiritual affairs. Innocent III had laid claim to be the overlord of all European sovereigns. But the Church's influence over the minds of people, and its claim to be an international arbiter, declined, and its enemies multiplied.

Alone among the rulers of Europe, Henry chose to support the pope in all his pretensions. While the other kings were trying to limit the church taxes which could be sent out of their countries and to prevent appeals from the national to the papal courts, Henry seemed determined to increase the influence of Rome over the English Church. He defended the pope's right of appointment to church benefices in England, to the misfortune of native churchmen and in opposition to the will of the English bishops. The Church decayed under absentee supervision or for lack of any supervision at all. In some cases the pope appointed his underlings at Rome to bishoprics in England before even the sees were vacant, and the incomes of the richest livings and monasteries were enjoyed by men who had never performed a single service within England's borders. In one year the English Church sent more money to Rome to support the pope in his continuing warfare with the Emperor than the English people paid in taxes to the crown. At other times there seemed to be a conspiracy between king and pope to defraud the English clergy; in support of their own selfish schemes. Henry protected a papal envoy like the archbishop of Messina, who traveled luxuriously among the English abbeys levying forced contributions for the papal treasury. In 1251 a papal mandate ordered one-tenth of all church revenues to be paid to Henry III for a crusade. The crusade could only have been aimed at the king's or the pope's political opponents.

This unnatural alliance, which prevented advancement of English clerics, taxed England to uphold the pope's temporal power in Italy, and caused a laxness in morals and discipline in the entire English Church, brought forth bitter protests from serious and patriotic churchmen like the learned Robert Grosseteste, bishop of Lincoln. He championed the rights of the English clergy; he criticized the corruption of the Church at Rome; he led the successful fight against Henry's demand for money for a crusade. In his position as chancellor of Oxford, he aroused among the university scholars strong opposition to the royal policy. His instructions deeply influenced the Franciscans, the order of begging and preaching friars whose good works among the poor made them so widely popular and respected. But the high-minded protests of patriots like the bishop of Lincoln were ineffective. While the king needed continued papal support for his personal ambitions, England must continue to pay for it.

There were few among the important native Englishmen, then, who were not embittered by Henry's sacrifice of English needs for the doubtful fruits of international politics and by the presence of foreigners in so many of the most influential and lucrative positions in both Church and State. "England for the English" might well have been the cry of both the discontented barons and the unbeneficed churchmen. In that age of rising nationalism Henry seemed bent on subjecting England to foreign domination. Baron and bishop and town merchant, newly rich from the risks of trade, hated to see their substance sent abroad, spent lavishly and apparently without tangible return, by a king who was forever demanding more funds. By mid-century Henry had alienated a majority of the important people in English society. A crisis was at hand.

3. The Loyal Opposition; political theory

At the meeting of the Great Council in 1254, opposition to the king's measures was widespread and outspoken. Henry was blamed for having "put mean men in the highest place and . . . cast down and humbled the great." He seemed aware of his predicament but helpless to escape it. He pleaded with the Council: "It is terrible to think of my debts. By God's head, I owe 300,000 marks. I am a mutilated and diminished King, but I must get money for I must live." In response to his request for a new subsidy, there were angry demands that he dismiss the French favorites, "who by deceitful words flatter and mislead the King and with double tongue lead him into error. . . . Full of all malice, fraud, and falsehood [they are seeking] to bend to their own ostentation the rights of the realm." The king, in addition, must live up to all the provisions of Magna Carta and cease bargaining with the pope for the acquisition of a worthless Sicily.

For this meeting of the Council Simon de Montfort was back in England, and from it dates his rise to preeminence among those who resisted the king's efforts to rule as he saw fit at the expense of his subjects. Simon was well-qualified for this leadership. His cheerfulness and affability had attracted friends, and his temperate habits and attention to religious duties had won him a high reputation. He had exhibited his ability to command and his iron-like strength of purpose on crusade and in Gascony. He had worn out his property in the king's service, but had been rewarded with anger and mistrust, so that there was little chance that he could be bought off. Men and women believed that Simon would prove a strong and steadfast rock on which the party in opposition could base itself.

By 1257 the king's need for money was no less than before, but conditions in the country made it far less likely that he could collect anything. Mathew Paris, the monastic chronicler of St. Alban's and our best and most vivid contemporary source of information, describes the troubles then facing England, and places the blame for them:

At this time the clerks of the king's chamber examined all the finance registers, and having made a strict calculation of the amount expended, it was proved by them that since the King had commenced plundering and wasting the wealth of his kingdom, he had expended 950,000 marks, which it was dreadful to think of.... The scarcity of money, caused by the spoliation practiced by the King and the pope, brought on unusual poverty. The land lay uncultivated and great numbers of people died from starvation.

The bad harvest and resulting high price of corn coincided with stirrings of unrest on the borders. The king's son Edward had been unable to overcome the independent-spirited Llewellyn of Wales, and the border lords on the English side complained of the weakness of the central government. Richard of Cornwall, often in the past the arbitrator of disputes between Henry and his lords, had departed for Germany in an effort to occupy the throne to which he had been elected. The king was left alone to face his aroused opponents. The threat of rebellion was in the air. No one dreamed of doing without a king. But more and more people had become convinced that his powers must be limited, that he must be required to adhere to his promises and to rule his English subjects in fairness and in accord with traditional usages.

The Great Council was summoned to meet at Oxford in 1258. Suspicious of Henry's intentions, expecting bloodshed, the barons assembled, accompanied by bands of armed men. "Am I then your prisoner?" the king asked in surprise and dismay. In truth he was, and hostilities were avoided only because he was powerless to withstand the concerted opposition.

The situation was confusing. Few trusted the king, but he remained the fount of all authority and honor. Advised by his council, the king made the laws. There were a few extreme political theorists who suggested:

> Each king is ruled by the laws he makes;
> A king may be dethroned if the laws he breaks.

But the king, some king, was indispensable. Without a king, thought the 13th century, there would be no government. So Henry was not dethroned, nor was the method of law-making changed. What the barons insisted upon was guarantees that the laws would be efficiently administered. What they demanded—and what they won by the Provisions of Oxford—was control of the executive machinery of the government.

From the great barons and churchmen a committee of fifteen was created. Without the consent of this committee the king could do nothing. The committee was to meet periodically with the *curia regis*, the king's immediate advisers. These ministers, in turn, were responsible to the committee. If their actions were unsatisfactory to the barons, they could be dismissed, regardless of the king's wishes. Thus it was established that the barons as a whole should not only have a voice in the making of the laws but that a select committee of barons should have control over the execution of the laws. Everything was to be done in the name of the king; nothing important to be done by the king alone. The ruling power lay in the hands of fifteen of the "best men" of the kingdom—the strongest, the richest, the wisest (at least in their own eyes). Monarchy in name; oligarchy in practice; democracy, of course, not even thought of.

Along with the earl of Gloucester and one or two others, Simon had played a leading part in the deliberations which had given birth to the Provisions of Oxford. Naturally he was among the great men chosen for the committee of fifteen. According to his French biographer, Charles Bemont, Simon was "born to rule, not to serve . . . he took his stand against arbitrary power . . . his enmity to Henry appeared at first to indicate immoderate pride and unsatisfied ambition, but it really took its rise in a nobler sentiment, a passion for the public good. Before the meeting at Oxford, his friends put all their trust in him; after 1258, the whole country looked to him as a leader of the revolution." Actually, Simon was not wholly pleased with the Provisions: he lamented the selfish class spirit which motivated the barons' desire to control the king. However, he called the Provisions a "charter made to the community of England." In reality, they were nothing of the kind. They were merely the items in a compact by which the king acknowledged the right of the highest classes in society to take a part in their own government. The "community" was not consulted.

To us of the 20th century the "revolution" does not seem very radical. But to those of the 13th century it did. They had considered the king absolute, the keystone of the social arch, the source of honor, the final judge, the ruler blessed by God. Now his authority was to be hedged in by restrictions, his power reduced to a formality. He was to be the creature of a committee of lords, men whose relationship to God was far less direct than his. The Provisions, then, were a shock to the social and religious traditions of the 13th century, as well as to the political. They necessitated changes in the thinking of the time from which many, even the more forward, began to recoil as soon as they realized what was being done.

The compact made in the Provisions would endure only so long as the barons could remain united in their aims and in possession of force superior to that of the king. Almost immediately, cracks opened in the wall with which the barons contained Henry. Some of them questioned the legality or the propriety of the new position to which they had relegated the king. Others grew envious of the vast powers of the committee of fifteen, wondering if they had not merely exchanged one form of tyranny for another. There were disputes as to policy among the leaders themselves, Simon and Gloucester in particular.

Gloucester, a very great landholder, felt that the "revolution" was now over. In the Provisions, the barons had gained everything desirable; their interests were now protected from royal despotism. Simon, more idealistic and perhaps more "democratic," felt that the "revolution" was as yet incomplete, and he "stood like a pillar" for what he thought was right. It was not enough to protect the barons from the king. It was now equally necessary and proper to protect the lesser people from the arbitrary rule of just such absolute landlords as Gloucester. Simon's prestige was sufficient to gain some acceptance of this idea from the Council. As a group, the great men of the kingdom had agreed to certain restrictions on their actions as individuals: they had acknowledged that their estates were not to be exempt from the royal authority and that their tenants should enjoy the same privileges they had wrested from the king. Now, said Simon, they must carry out their promises.

In adopting this policy, Simon put himself at the head of the new and growing force in England—the "community of bachelors," the middle class of knights and country gentry who had been serving, since the time of Henry II, as the local officials of the royal government and had been exposed to the selfishness and arrogance of the barons. Gaining the support of the knights, however, Simon was running the risk of losing the support of the barons, many of whom now grew frightened at the prospect of the invasion of their ancient rights by the national government. Simon seemed not to notice this risk, and he was openly scornful of the timid barons. "With such feeble and faithless men," he exclaimed, "I care not to have aught to do." This tactlessness might have unfortunate effects. By attempting the logical extension of the concept of the rights of Englishmen, Simon was placing the original revolutionary victory in jeopardy and undermining the solidarity of the party which had won it.

The king, meanwhile, was doing everything possible to squirm out of his agreement and regain his personal power. In 1260 he was strong enough to move into the Tower and control London with his soldiery. He summoned all the barons to meet with him, suggesting that they should cooperate with their king in ruling England rather than surrender their ancient privileges to a self-appointed committee of fifteen self-seekers. To the barons, assembled at Winchester in 1261, he presented a papal bull absolving him from his oath to the Provisions. This papal pronouncement of the illegality of what they had done was too much for the waverers who were already doubtful of the wisdom of their deeds. Gloucester led some of the moderates back to the king's side, satisfied now, they said, that the foreign favorites had been dismissed and that the king would govern less wastefully.

The staunchest barons remained in opposition, stating that the king was subordinate to the law and that the law included both Magna Carta and the Provisions. Their leader, of course, was Simon. Henry long since had recognized his chief adversary and the strength of his reforming cause. Boating on the Thames one day, the king was caught in a thunderstorm and disembarked at the palace of the bishop of Durham, where he met Simon. "What is there to be afraid of?" Simon asked the king. "The storm is almost gone." Said Henry to his earl: "The thunder and lightning I fear beyond measure, but by God's head, I fear thee more." Assured that his course was right, Simon replied, denying any personal antagonism: "My lord, it is unjust and incredible that you should fear me, your firm friend, who am ever faithful to you and yours, and to the kingdom of England." We may acknowledge that justice was on Simon's side, contending as he was for the welfare of England, but surely we may excuse Henry for fearing his masterful opponent. There could never again be agreement between Simon and Henry as to what should be done for the good of England.

Disgusted by the king's repudiation of the Provisions, Simon once more retired to France in despair. But he could not remain inactive for long when he observed conditions in England going from bad to worse. As a popular song of the day described it:

> The world's state in this our day is changing, changing ever,
> But for the better, much I fear, it changes never, never ...

> The rich men are so grasping, they snatch at all they see;
> The poor who hath but little, is robbed of his scant store,
> That to the rich, who hath enough, he may give riches more.

Although the original opposition to Henry may have been based on the self-interest of the barons desirous of keeping power in their own hands, Simon was conscientiously anxious to cure these evils in society, to effect a "moral reform in Church and State." The rich and mighty, including the king, have a responsibility—he thought—to those under their sway. In cases such as that of Henry III, where the king was misled by foreign counselors to disregard the welfare of England, it was necessary and proper for the barons to act to protect not only their own aristocratic party but the kingdom as a whole.

Let us examine the political theory of Simon and the reformers as they drew it up at this time:

> The party of the barons ... devises naught against the royal honor or seeks anything contrary to it [but] is zealous to reform and magnify the kingly state.... To the barons belongs the purging of errors.

To purge the king's errors, of course, they must legally restrict his prerogative, but the king should recognize that

> all constraint does not deprive of liberty, nor does all restriction take away power.

He will be left absolutely free to do good and thereby to demonstrate his royal virtue and increase his glory. He will be restrained only from doing evil, and for such restraint he should be grateful.

> Let the king like everything that is good, but let him not dare evil. . . . Whoever is truly king is truly free if he rule himself and his kingdom rightly; let him know that all things are lawful for him which are fitted for ruling the kingdom, but not for destroying it. It is one thing to rule, which is the duty of a king, another to destroy by resisting the law. . . . Nor ought that properly to be named liberty which unwisely permits the foolish to have dominion; but let liberty be limited by the bounds of right; and when those limits are despised, let it be deemed error.

Here are two ideas new in 13th-century England. Liberty does not include the right to do wrong. And not even the king is free to disregard the law. The barons continue:

> We say also that law rules the dignity of a king, for we believe that law is a light. . . . If the king be without this light, he will go astray. . . . That stable law shall no king alter.

The barons realized that theirs was not the traditional theory, and they were prepared for argument.

> It is commonly said, "As the king wills, the law goes." Truth wills otherwise, for the law stands, the king falls. Truth and charity and the zeal of salvation are the integrity of law, the rule of virtue. . . . Whatever the king determines, let it be consonant with these; for if he do otherwise, the commons will be rendered sorrowful. The people will be confounded, if either the king's eye lacks truth, or if his heart lacks charity, or does not always moderately fulfill its zeal with severity. These three being in support, let whatever pleases the king be done; but when they are in opposition, the king is resisting the law.

Here, in their concern for popular well-being, the barons introduce a practical argument to bolster their theory. They affirm:

> We give the first place to the commonalty. Let every king understand that he is the servant of God. . . . Again, let him know that the people is not his own, but God's, and let him be profitable to the people as a help.

To accomplish this, the king must be ready and willing to submerge his own desires to his sacred duty.

> Let the king prefer nothing of his own to the common weal, for he is not set over all to live for himself, but so that this people which is under him may be secure.... The name of king is relative, his name is protective.... It is the glory of a king to save very many, with trouble to himself to relieve many. Let him not therefore allege his own profit, but his regard for his subjects by whom he is trusted. If he shall have saved the kingdom, he has done what is the duty of a king; whatever he shall have done otherwise, in that he has failed.

The king, then, must be willing to depend on his loyal people and arrange his policies to carry out their general will.

One weakness in this line of reasoning is that the general will of the loyal subjects is not always clear, even supposing that all are agreed as to who the loyal subjects are. In 1263 both of these matters were in dispute. The barons assembled in Oxford under arms, marched toward Wales plundering alien residents, and returned to occupy Dover, cutting Henry off from overseas aid. In July, Simon marched against the king in London in overwhelming force, and Henry once more solemnly promised to obey the Provisions of Oxford. But the general will was not clear. The conservative north was outraged at the mistreatment of the king by his "disloyal" subjects. Edward, the heir to the throne, fortified himself at Windsor as a center of opposition to Simon. Even among the "loyal" barons there were jealous murmurs against Simon's arrogance, and no efforts were made to legalize or perpetuate the powers won from the king. Who could say for sure what was for the welfare of England? The country was not united behind any one leader or plan. The deterioration of the situation into chronic civil war appeared likely.

Then a possible solution presented itself. Because neither side was strong enough to dictate a policy for the whole country, both sides agreed to submit their differences to arbitration. Here is evidence that Simon must have been activated by patriotism rather than personal ambition, for he directed the barons to accept as arbitrator – another king! Louis IX of France sat at Amiens in January 1264 to judge the disputes between Henry III and his barons. To be sure, there were not many available judges in such a cause. The natural choice would have been the pope, but he was disqualified by his close alliance with Henry. And Louis was world-renowned for his wisdom and justice. But there can have been little doubt as to how Louis would decide. Only at grave risk to his own power could he desert his fellow-monarch. Louis' decision was wholly favorable to Henry: the Provisions of Oxford were condemned, the king's absolute power upheld, and all that the barons had done since 1258 was undone.

The situation was intolerable. The king, the pope, and Louis were leagued against the English people, many of whom seemed willing to acquiesce in the loss of their native liberties. Who would dare dispute the judgment of Saint Louis? Who would oppose the will of an anointed king? Most of the older barons, bound by traditional thoughts and manners, would not. After Amiens, Simon said: "I have been in many lands, and nowhere have I found men so faithless as in England. But, though all forsake me, I and my four sons will stand for the just cause." And so he would have stood alone, in defiance of Henry, but a handful of ardent, youthful barons were ready to stand firmly with him. Civil war was inevitable—a war in which the conflict of ideas would split the old feudal nobility.

4. Between Lewes and Evesham: the Parliament of 1265

The king summoned his followers to Oxford, where he dismissed the scholars who favored the cause of reform. His army captured Northampton. Then Henry heard of a riot in London, where the merchants and artisans were showing their hatred of his heavy taxation. Many of the ill-armed London burgesses, like many of the enthusiastic Oxford students, flocked to Simon's banner, and the oddly-assorted army of the barons marched out to face the king.

The two forces met near Lewes. Simon was sleepless on the eve of the battle, "reserving it for divine duties and for urging his men to make serious confessions." But he had not allowed his religious earnestness to lead him into neglect of his tactical responsibilities. His varied military experience abroad had made Simon a good general. His soldiers wore white crosses, as the mark of their crusading devotion to an ideal, but also as a means of identification. He drew up his army in the customary three divisions: the Londoners and students on the left, a force of Welsh archers and young nobles under command of his sons on the right, his main force in the center. To this formation he added a clever ruse. On a rise behind his center he located a large litter, plainly marked with his personal standard. Simon had broken his leg some months before. The injury had prevented his attendance at Amiens. Although he was now well enough to mount his horse and go into battle, the litter appeared to be his post.

When the battle commenced on 14 May 1264, Prince Edward, commanding his father's right, quickly routed Simon's city dwellers, ill-equipped as they were to withstand armored horsemen. Their flight was rapid, and the youthful Edward pursued them headlong for four miles.

Meanwhile the king's left, under Richard of Cornwall, had been pushed back until its commander was reduced to finding temporary safety in a windmill, where the "Emperor's" ears were rudely assailed by the jeers of his foes. Simon's right and center could then combine their pressure on the enemy main force where the king himself fought. Henry's men gave ground and the king took refuge in the priory of Lewes. Only Edward could save his father now. Returning flushed with confidence from his rout of the Londoners, Edward led his men against Simon's litter. Their impetuous charge overturned the litter and killed its occupants—four hostages who had earlier tried to betray Simon and London into the power of the king. Simon's trick had worked; Edward's return was too late to reverse the barons' victory.

On the next day Henry surrendered to his earl. Edward was given as a hostage for "deliberate discussion as to what provisions and statutes ought to be established for the good of the kingdom." In this discussion as to the laws of the land, Henry would find himself a cipher, although his position would be accorded formal respect.

Now does fair England breathe again, hoping for liberty . . .
Earl Simon's faith and faithfulness all England's peace secure,
He smites the rebels, calms the realm, and drooping hearts makes
    sure.
And how does he keep down the proud? I trow 'tis not by praise,
But the red juice he squeezes out in battle's stubborn frays.

Lewes was an overwhelming victory. It crushed Henry's pretensions to irresponsible absolutism, and changed the relations of the king with his barons and with the laws. It was "a fact that could never be obliterated" from England's constitutional history. But it did not solve the immediate problem of the day-to-day administration of the realm. On what basis was the government to be carried on? What was to be the status of the king, who could no more be dispensed with than he could be trusted? A provisional government must be set up. To devise it, not the barons only, but also four representative men from each county, were called together. This council appointed three commissioners, who in turn would appoint nine more, and this commission would exercise the executive authority of which the king was stripped. Of the original three commissioners Simon was the chief.

The paradoxical result of the complete victory at Lewes was that it placed Simon in what was at one and the same time a very strong but a wholly untenable position. Lewes had made him the mightiest man in England. Before the battle he had been the champion of English liberties against royal encroachments. After the battle he was the only man strong enough to threaten those liberties and, indeed, to overthrow the political machinery by which England had been governed for hundreds of years. Simon alone, for instance, might have been able to get away with killing the king. But he was not strong enough to prevent the other barons from being keenly jealous of the powers which he had accumulated. And, assuming Henry dead, Simon could not have won much support for his own ascension to the throne.

There was, we can see, no provision for his position in the laws of the land, nor was there any precedent for it. "He was certainly a despot, with a king in his wallet and the forces of social revolution at his back," Churchill writes. A few of the barons, the emerging middle class, the university students, the honest national clergy, the Franciscans, and most of the townspeople, were his true supporters. But by now the vast majority of those of real wealth and influence were opposed to him. They realized that Simon, wielding the royal power and commanding popular support, might well upset their control of the kingdom. So they called him a threat to the nation, as he was indeed a threat to their class.

In short, the earl's position was impossible. He had grown stronger than the king, but in fact he was the king's subject. The king was his prisoner and must be kept in custody for fear of what he might otherwise attempt, but in fact he was the rightful king and the governing must be done in his name. Meanwhile, England's commerce languished, following an embargo imposed by papal order, and Queen Eleanor was negotiating for foreign aid to overthrow the upstart Simon.

The victory at Lewes needed to be consolidated; the new composition of the executive waited to be legalized. By themselves, as individuals, three, or nine, great lords had little political power and could not masquerade as petty kings, especially with the real king alive and their prisoner. What had been a makeshift must be transformed into a regularly constituted government, created by law, not by the compromises of the moment. Simon had the wisdom to recognize the one way out of the dilemma into which Lewes had thrown the country. In the king's name, he issued a call for a Parliament to meet in 1265.

What was this new thing to be known as a Parliament? Carlyle in the 19th century called it a "talking shop," and the name comes, of course, from the French verb *parler*, to talk. So far we have studiously avoided using the name, but in actuality Parliament was only the extension and expansion of the Great Council which had been meeting, talking, and advising the king since the time of the Conquest. To the Parliament of 1265 Simon proposed that four knights should come from each county. In 1254 similar representatives had come to the Council bearing information of the finances of their districts. To the Parliament of 1265, also, Simon called two burgesses from each of a certain number of towns. The writ calling them was sent direct to the towns, not to the sheriffs of the counties. Thus the towns were liberated from the dominating influence of the leading noble in the county, who normally held the office of sheriff. This was the first call in English history for representatives from towns. This new representation, and the direct method of securing it, were the only real differences between Simon's Parliament and the earlier Great Council.

The idea of Parliament did not then spring forth full-blown from Simon's brain. The name Parliament, in fact, had already been used for the Council. Nor was Simon's calling of Parliament done in an idealistic vacuum. It was a measure of practical politics. His government was not yet that of a united nation, as we have seen, but that of a faction only. It needed all the support and all the publicity it could get. The new men Simon called—the smaller gentry who had formerly been overawed by Henry's gorgeous favorites and the prospering townsmen who could not stomach an extravagant king—might be expected to favor his party. Calling them was excellent propaganda: "The general position of a party government could be strengthened by calling representatives of all the communities together and talking to them." Make them feel that Simon's government was their government. Simon summoned them to listen and to consult. How much actual voting, actual lawmaking, he would have allowed the new men to do must remain unknown. But it is probable that they would have done a large share. For of the barons, who by traditional right should have sat in any Parliament, Simon could trust only a very few. The majority, suspicious of his unabated zeal for reform, had deserted his side for the king's.

We must grant, then, that Simon's Parliament was dangerously imperfect. Without legal right he excluded many lords, calling only five earls and eighteen barons. He packed the House with his own partisans. Yet this Parliament of 1265 set a precedent of enormous importance in English history. After 1265, English laws would be made, not by the king with the advice of a Great Council representing the feudal nobility alone but by the king with the advice of a Parliament which, through the years, has come more and more fully to represent the whole nation. In the 13th century two new classes were entering society—the town merchants, or burgesses, with their wealth in ships and goods and money, and the substantial farming squires, or knights, who were landlords rather than mounted warriors. It was Simon who first gave these classes representation in national politics.

"This is the definite advent of the third estate as a political power." This is the beginning of the expansion of the Great Council into a Parliament representing *all* classes in society. At the same time, by calling them to sit in Parliament, Simon was extending the duties of these knights and burgesses. They had had experience in their own localities, assisting and conferring with the king's judges and commissioners. In the county courts they had shouldered most of the responsibility for enforcing the king's laws and collecting the king's taxes. Now they were called to Parliament to administer, not their own counties, but the kingdom. England had had long traditions of local self-government; Simon started the move toward national self-government.

Simon, the over-mighty subject, was unable alone to find a legal or satisfactory solution to the problems posed by the defeat of the king at Lewes. So he called a Parliament to bear the burden of finding the solution. This was a radical departure for a country in which, before, the king had always held the initiative. Simon based his move on the most advanced political thought of his day: "Those who are ruled by the laws [townspeople and small landlords as well as great barons] know those laws best, and since it is their own affairs which are at stake, they will take more care [to see those laws wisely made and justly executed]." These laws were to be sacred above the whims of any king. And Simon's move bore fruit perhaps even beyond his own imaginings. When next a Parliament was called in England, thirty years later, the royal summons read: "A most just law decrees that what affects all shall be approved by all." In calling his Parliament, Simon had "paved the way for the slow evolution of England toward political liberty."

But Simon's Parliament was not destined to be given the chance to reestablish orderly government. In the extremely precarious position of the king as Simon's prisoner, Henry's heir Edward recognized grave threats to himself. The relations of father and son had not been cordial; as a boy Edward had played games with Simon's sons and, since then, he had often sided with Simon against the foolish king. But seeing his own future power in danger, Edward resolved that he must treat his godfather Simon as a traitor and crush him. Being a hostage instead of a captive, Edward was guarded rather casually. It was an easy matter for him one day in May 1265 to challenge his guardians to a race and then, when their horses were exhausted, to mount a fresh horse held in readiness by an accomplice and flee to safety.

With Edward at large, a renewal of hostilities was assured. The prince, promising reforms, was a center around whom everyone displeased with Simon's autocratic conduct might rally. Simon, by contrast, was reduced to the status of an ambitious adventurer, rebelling against the lawful dynasty. In the masses who hurried to Edward's standard may be measured Simon's failure as a political manager. The same firmness of will and inflexibility of purpose that had stood him in such good stead in his earlier troubles with the king now lost him many followers less devoted than he.

Simon was entirely too zealous to be a good leader of a cause in which scarcely any two people of the time could be said to think exactly alike. Many customs, many loyalties, were involved in the delicate matter of restricting a king's authority, but Simon seems to have been blind to the shades of feeling and to have ignored the differences of opinion. His own mind made up, he would not listen to other's doubts; he disregarded tradition; he forgot the weaknesses of human nature. He did not see that most people lacked his unselfish singleness of purpose; he failed utterly to realize that they were jealous and suspicious of him. His keen sense of honor, his deep religious conviction, his fiery temper, all made him impatient of those who questioned or contradicted his will. He had neither the desire, nor the art, to compromise. His was a character to assert rather than to suggest, to demand rather than to request. The idol of the small person Simon may have been in 1265; but most of the great barons, incensed at his imperiousness, desired his downfall.

When the early summer hastened military preparations, Simon had only two forces on which he could rely. His son Simon commanded a force based on the nearly impregnable fortress of Kenilworth. He himself was in the west, having concluded an alliance with Llewellyn of Wales (another source of irritation for the *English* barons). Simon intended to unite his forces, but he grossly underestimated the size and the speed of the army gathering against him.

Edward was moving with a new energy and demonstrating a strategic skill remarkable in the annals of medieval warfare. Perceiving the fatal weakness in the division of Simon's forces, he interposed his own army between the two groups of his enemy. Capturing the bridges over the Severn River, across which Simon had moved into Wales, Edward effectively blocked his return to the east and broke the line of communication between him and his son. Advancing on Simon's rear, Edward pushed him across the Usk River, further west. Then he destroyed the shipping at Newport which Simon had collected to transport his army back by sea. Not strong enough to force the Severn crossing, Simon had to resort to a roundabout northerly march in an effort to join his son. But Edward, in his central position, had the advantages of superior mobility and of surprise. First he moved against young Simon, attacked him suddenly in the town of Kenilworth, destroyed his force, and sent the young man fleeing with a handful of followers to the castle.

Then Edward turned to face the tired army of the aging earl, who still carried Henry as his prisoner, and brought him to bay at Evesham early in August. There was little hope for Simon, surrounded by the far superior forces of Prince Edward, the young earl of Gloucester, and Roger Mortimer. He urged his supporters "to fly and save themselves for better times." When they refused to abandon him, Simon went out to survey Edward's advance. He recognized his own position to be desperate beyond remedy, and yet he had a word of praise for his antagonist, whose rashness at Lewes had been so disastrous. "By St. James!" Simon exclaimed, "they come on in good order, and it was from me they learned it. Let us commend our souls to God, for our bodies are theirs!"

There followed "a most severe conflict," but the outcome was never in question. Fighting to the last, Simon was killed. "At the time of his death," says William Rishanger who had succeeded Mathew Paris as chronicler of St. Alban's, "a storm of thunder and lightning occurred, and darkness prevailed to such an extent that all were struck with amazement. . . . Thus ended the labors of that noble man, who gave up not only his property, but also his person, to defend the poor from oppression, and for the maintenance of justice and the rights of the kingdom."

Simon's adversaries were less convinced of his nobility. Their treatment of the fallen Simon demonstrates the barbarism which persisted as the other side of the coin of chivalry. The pope had excommunicated him. Now that he was dead, his head, feet, and hands were cut off "contrary to all the laws of the knightly order, and his head was presented to the wife of Roger Mortimer." His body was rescued by some Franciscan friars, who had once been under the tutelage of the bishop of Lincoln, and disregarding the pope's decree, the monks gave it decent burial.

5. Simon — hero of the common people

It looked as though Simon had accomplished nothing permanent. Yet Simon's cause was triumphant, and he did not have to wait centuries for his vindication. In 1267 the Statute of Marlborough was passed, making the reforms of the Provisions of Oxford the law of the land. But Simon's real triumph was effected in the person of that very Edward who had vanquished him at Evesham. When Edward succeeded his father in 1272, he showed that he had learned valuable lessons from his observation of Simon's determined opposition to the king. Edward realized that it was not Henry, but Simon, whose thinking and policy were attuned to the spirit of the times. Government by despotic decree was beginning to go down before government by consent. The king could no longer neglect his people, who were emerging from the misery and ignorance of the Dark Ages into new prosperity and enlightenment and self-consciousness. If his rule was to be effective, he must first make it popular. The crown could not be powerful—indeed it probably could not continue to exist—unless it transformed its scornful disregard of the people into a close alliance with them.

The substance of Edward's heritage from Simon's "revolution" was that the king's role was that of leader. His policy must be designed for the benefit of the English nation as a whole. Simon had grasped the growing nationalism of his age. With the bishop of Lincoln he had stood for a national Church, freed from the exactions and interference of Rome. He had believed in a Church morally strong to supply the spiritual needs of the English people, not to abet the temporal schemes of a greedy papacy. Simon had issued a call for a national Parliament, representative of the various groups of people who comprised the nation, to replace the Great Council which was representative only of one class and insensitive to national origins. To the people's representatives assembled in Parliament Simon had been willing to entrust the working of England's governmental machinery.

Simon had not been a destructive anarchist but a constitutional reformer. He had planned not to overthrow, but to improve, the government. At no time had he attempted to exercise dictatorial power or to aggrandize himself at the expense of other citizens, great or small. He had aimed at capitalizing on traditional English virtues and institutions by transferring the customs of the county court to the larger arena of the national assembly. In Parliament would be united in a common cause both the hereditary members of the Great Council—the great lords and prelates—and the small but important new men of the day—knights of the shires and town burgesses. It was this sort of Parliament, representative of the people and endowed with the rights of law-making and tax-levying, that Edward I summoned in 1295. And his Parliament was the "Model Parliament," after which all later Parliaments were copied.

Simon stands forth in history as far more than just the leader of a group of discontented barons. We cannot claim for him the merit of having originated the political doctrine of responsible self-government, but we can praise him for recognizing and fostering it when it was endangered by a shortsighted king. The great movement in 13th-century England was the rise of new social classes to challenge the old feudal hierarchy and to win a voice in the governing of the nation. "To this, the work of a whole century," says Bemont again, "Simon de Montfort, 'that great and courageous party leader,' gave the decisive influence. . . . He served the cause of English liberty to the bitter end."

His savage enemies might mutilate Simon's body, but the commoner in England was grateful for his unflinching opposition to royal folly and tyranny. Here is an anonymous song of the day:

Sing must I now, my heart wills so,
   Although my tongue be rude.
With tearful thought this song was wrought,
   Of England's barons good,
Who for the peace made long ago,
   Went gladly to the grave,
Their bodies gashed and scarred and slashed,
   Our England land to save.

REFRAIN: Now low there lies, the flower of price,
            That knew so much of war,
            The Earl Montfort, whose luckless sort,
            The land shall long deplore.

On a Tuesday, as I heard say,
   The battle it was fought,
From horseback all they fight and fall,
   Of footmen they had naught.
Full cruelly they struck that day,
   All of the brandished brand,
But in the end Sir Edward's men
   They got the upper hand.

But by his death Earl Simon hath
   In sooth the victory won,
Like Canterbury's martyr he
   There to the death was done.
Thomas the good, that never would
   Let holy Church be tried,
Like him he fought, and flinching not,
   The good Earl like him died.

Death did they face to keep in place
   Both righteousness and peace,
Wherefore the saint from sin and taint
   Shall give their souls release;
They faced the grave that they might save
   The people of this land,
For so his will they did fulfill,
   As we do understand.

Next to the skin, when they stripped him,
   They found a shirt of hair,
Those felons strong that wrought the wrong
   And foully slew him there;
But worse their sin to mangle him,
   A man that was so good,
That how to fight and keep the right
   So truly understood.

This simple but sincere lament expresses the opinion of ordinary people. To them, Simon de Montfort was a saint, who had given his life in a sacred war. After Simon's efforts to reaffirm the principles of Magna Carta and to create a representative Parliament, the national government of England would never again be able wholly to disregard its responsibilities to the common people.

Conclusion

We have now thought enough about the Middle Ages to realize that a number of important and interesting things happened in the years 500-1300 A.D. that were once considered a period of unrelieved darkness and barbarism. Physical hardship, economic depression, political anarchy, intellectual stagnation were widespread. Creativity may have seemed a rare gift, but it had not lost its effectiveness. The human mind and spirit, ever venturesome, made efforts to solve the problems of political order and social organization, survival and happiness, improvement in the conditions of living, salvation for sinners. The movements thus originated seem to us somewhat slow and halting, sometimes misdirected and abortive. But they redrew the map of Europe, formed new centers of learning, reinvigorated the economy, established workable relationships between Church and State, people and government, people and religion, and widened the horizons of human endeavor.

Who would deny that there were elements of greatness in the people who conceived, shaped, and led these movements? They demonstrated vision and faith, strength and determination. We need only to recall the names in the chapter headings of this book to recognize the significant role of the individuals of clear mind and purposeful character who gave direction and meaning to medieval history.

But what of the people in general? In the Middle Ages their experience was narrowly limited by geographical and social barriers, illiteracy, scarcity of goods, inadequate means of communication and transportation. Inevitably the lives of most people, generation after generation, centered on the immediate, practical, mundane routine imposed by the struggle for existence. The average peasant in Toulouse, say, cared little who was his master's overlord or who appointed his bishop, even though he might tremble daily at their power over his destiny.

Essential activities occupied almost all of everyone's life. In the face of constant fear of natural calamities, disease, and destitution, self-preservation was an abiding concern and propagation of a family an obvious necessity. When the occasional breaks in routine permitted, people turned to simple, and usually communal, means of relaxation and amusement. They attended church services and enjoyed the stories depicted on the windows; they danced and laughed at street festivals on saints' days; they might even go on a pilgrimage to a nearby shrine.

The vast majority of medieval people were peasants, bound by the traditional relationships of parents and children and by the endless cycle of birth, childhood, maturity, death. The chief task of peasants was tilling the soil, augmented now by forestry or fishing, now by wine-making or sheep-raising, and interrupted by periodic outbursts of fighting. Existence for the masses must have been a drab and monotonous routine. But an ambitious individual peasant might change his or her fortune by gaining the favor of a local lord in his castle or of the abbot in the neighboring monastery. If he or she had the ability, he or she might even venture to seek a new livelihood in a trade or craft for the busy merchant in a growing town.

History — the combination and distillation of many human lives — presents a similar mix of the continuity of custom and the rare significant change. Often we are so much engrossed by our "normal" affairs that we fail to notice "big" events or accurately to gauge their "bigness." Often indeed the passage of time reduces the scale of changes we once thought decisive. In our own century, for example, the defeat of the Kaiser, or even of Hitler, did not destroy the industrial power and potential influence of Germany. The downfall of Nicholas II did not end Russia's expansionist policies. The depression after 1929 provided fertile ground for socialism, fascism, communism, but now we sense the revival of private enterprise, the profit motive, and international trade. Only on the rarest of occasions does an atom bomb, the exploration of space, the speed and range of electronic communication, change our whole way of life or outlook on humankind.

A look back

From our long-detached standpoint in the 20th century, and with the benefit of our familiarity with history, let us look back on the mixture of continuity and change that was medieval civilization. We can see that, time and circumstance having blunted the original stimulus for them, some of the major movements of the Middle Ages have by 1300 passed their peaks of momentum or significance.

Feudalism with its code of chivalry appears still to dominate western Europe. It is the economic and social system that had organized people when physical conditions prevented the operation of centralized government. But the feudal system is now being challenged from above by kings and from below by townspeople.

Joining a monastery has become commonplace and, frequently, comfortable. The earliest Benedictines have been followed by Cluniacs and Cistercians, Dominicans and Franciscans. There will be Jesuits and others. Monks are a major sector in the population, influential in commerce and education, health and welfare. But the original flowering of monastic zeal to take the vows to serve God and one's fellows has lost some of its fierce compulsiveness.

The Crusades are ending in failure. Military enterprise was not able to recover Jerusalem and attach the Middle East — in religion or politics — to western Europe. There is occurring some expansion of trade with Constantinople and some benefit from the westward spread of Arabic learning. Today's conflicts of Moslems, Christians, and Jews are sad testimony to the continuing divisions and turmoil in that part of the world.

In his papal bull, *Unam Sanctam*, Boniface VIII makes a sweeping claim to supremacy over all rulers, spiritual and temporal. Assaulted by external enemies and internal decay, however, the Church cannot maintain its universal power. Within a decade the pope will have moved to Avignon and become the captive agent of the French king. Although the pope's word has deep significance to this day, he has lost his secular power and most of his political influence.

In 1300 there exists the Holy Roman Empire of the German people, but western Europe is not to be united in a single state either copied after the ancient Roman Empire or based on the more recent effort by the Angevins to mix nationalities and languages and to leap over geographical barriers.

And a look forward

Probably we are inclined to think of the movements or institutions that declined in vitality as being especially "medieval." But if from our modern vantage point we look forward from 1300, we can see that much that we have found in the Middle Ages survived into later times, grew vigorously, continued to have great impact on history, and stimulated new developments.

The Norman Conquest of England and the expansion of the royal domain in France laid the foundations for the national governments that would dominate Europe in more modern times. In the new states power would be centered in the monarch and exercised by officials responsible to him. Within a century after Henry II and Philip Augustus the status of the monarch will be brought into question. Should his power be absolute? If not, what groups in the population should participate in making the laws and establishing the customary procedures under which power would pass from king to representative government?

Around 1300 kings are emphasizing their power by embellishing their capitals with palaces and cathedrals. At cities like Paris and Oxford groups of scholars, attracted by teachers as dynamic as Abelard, are forming the core of universities. Other walled cities stand at strategic locations throughout the countryside. More than military strongholds and government centers alone, these cities will be centers of art and learning, of trade and wealth. Skilled craftspeople will make desired objects by hand, and the import-export trade will flourish. Monarchs will borrow funds from international bankers in Pisa and Venice and Augsburg, and the Medici family will outshine royal dynasties in wealth and patronage of the arts. The shipping interests of Genoa will supply the knowledge and nurture the aspirations of a Christopher Columbus.

Already, by 1300, St. Thomas Aquinas had shaped a comprehensive definition of Catholic theology, seeking to synthesize natural perceptions and reason with revealed truths and faith. His scholasticism was intended to be the system of learning that would explain the single consistent system of the physical universe. St. Francis of Assisi, forming new groups of begging and preaching monks, had noticed the natural world around him and put forward the virtues of humility and love, compassion and forgiveness, as the equals of the conventional virtues of courage, strength, and honor. Roger Bacon, himself a Franciscan friar, had attempted to master all the scientific knowledge of his time. He advocated the observation of natural phenomena, the use of scientific instruments, and the value of experimentation. Although he himself understood the composition of gunpowder, he did not put his theoretical knowledge to the practical test.

In Italy, at the turn of the century, Dante, student of both classical and church writers, political activist, thinker and dreamer, master poet, is preparing to write the *Divine Comedy*, not in classical Latin but in his own Italian vernacular. In it, he describes the conditions and the inhabitants of Hell, Purgatory, and Paradise. The goal of life is blessedness and happiness. We seek it by combining classical wisdom with Christian virtue. And Giotto is the first painter to incorporate the sense of mass and movement in his realistic portrayals of the people he saw around him. He shows us the deepest emotions of human beings at the most dramatic moments in their lifetimes.

Giotto did some of his work in Florence, where he participated in the design of the magnificent Duomo. It was Florence, in the style of the city-states of ancient Greece, that was already proudly calling itself a "republic," where responsibility for public affairs is in the hands of more than one person, or even one particular group of people. Florence had minted its famous golden florin in 1252 and first elected a Medici to civil office in 1296.

In England, John Wyclif, priest and university scholar, will soon propose that Christian religion be based not on the sacraments and the teachings of sinful clergymen but on the words of the Bible itself, which must be printed in English. Further, Wyclif will attack the right of the Church to control property. His contemporary, Wat Tyler, will lead the Peasants' Revolt to improve the wages of farm laborers, in scarce supply after the ravages of the Black Death. *from scholasticism to*

As the Renaissance begins, Petrarch establishes humanism as the prevailing philosophy. Man in the image of God is the central figure in the world God has created. Developing all his skills, enriching his mind, sharpening his conscience, he is capable of achieving excellence and inner satisfaction. And so is woman. Unlike Guinevere of Arthurian legend and gentle, beautiful Beatrice who inspired Dante, a number of women of genius and fearless independence will soon appear and take a vital part in the affairs of the world. The visionary mystic, St. Catherine of Siena, will struggle to restore unity in the 14th-century Church. Christine de Pisan will write poetry and biography to support herself and her children and will champion the worth and capacity of women. Joan of Arc will embody the national spirit and valor of France defending itself from the invading English.

So we can see that 1300 is an arbitrary date, decreed by historians to divide the Renaissance from the Middle Ages. While for most people alive in that year life moved along in its continuing ebb and flow, a few extraordinary people were finding opportunities and pursuing ideas that would ultimately change the face of the world. The material and spiritual developments of the late Middle Ages herald the dawn of the Renaissance. In the decades to come, new kinds of people — diverse individuals from all walks of life — will achieve a prominence that had hitherto been within the reach only of cardinals and kings.

Alchemists turned scientists, sea-captains turned explorers, money-changers turned merchant-bankers, artists, sculptors, and architects, minor churchmen, clerks, and yeomen farmers, all these may become the "heroes" of their times. In originality of thought and action, in quality of achievement, in impact on humankind, some of them will outstrip the princes of Church and State. For the new era will be worldly and materialistic, open and cosmopolitan, rich in imagination and invention, demanding of personal success and satsfaction, responsive to the genius and ambition of the individual, heartless in rejection of the failure or the fool. These will be some of the characteristics of the Renaissance that were barely dreamed of in the Middle Ages.

Dynastic Tables

CAROLINGIAN DYNASTY

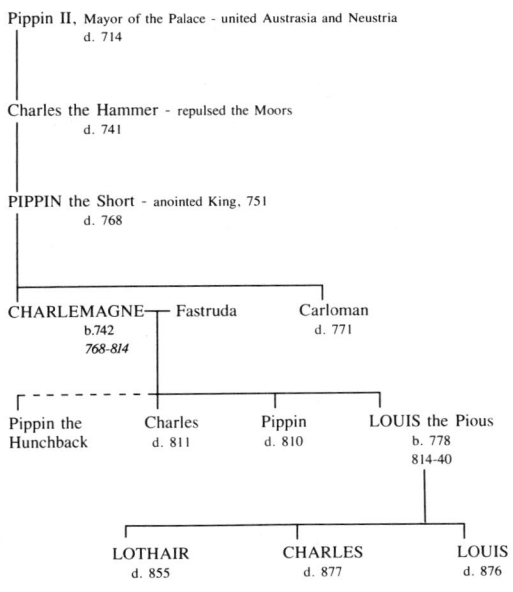

Pippin II, Mayor of the Palace - united Austrasia and Neustria
d. 714

Charles the Hammer - repulsed the Moors
d. 741

PIPPIN the Short - anointed King, 751
d. 768

CHARLEMAGNE — Fastruda   Carloman
b.742   d. 771
768-814

Pippin the   Charles   Pippin   LOUIS the Pious
Hunchback   d. 811   d. 810   b. 778
                                                                814-40

LOTHAIR   CHARLES   LOUIS
d. 855   d. 877   d. 876

(followed by creation of the "successor kingdoms")

NORMAN KINGS OF ENGLAND

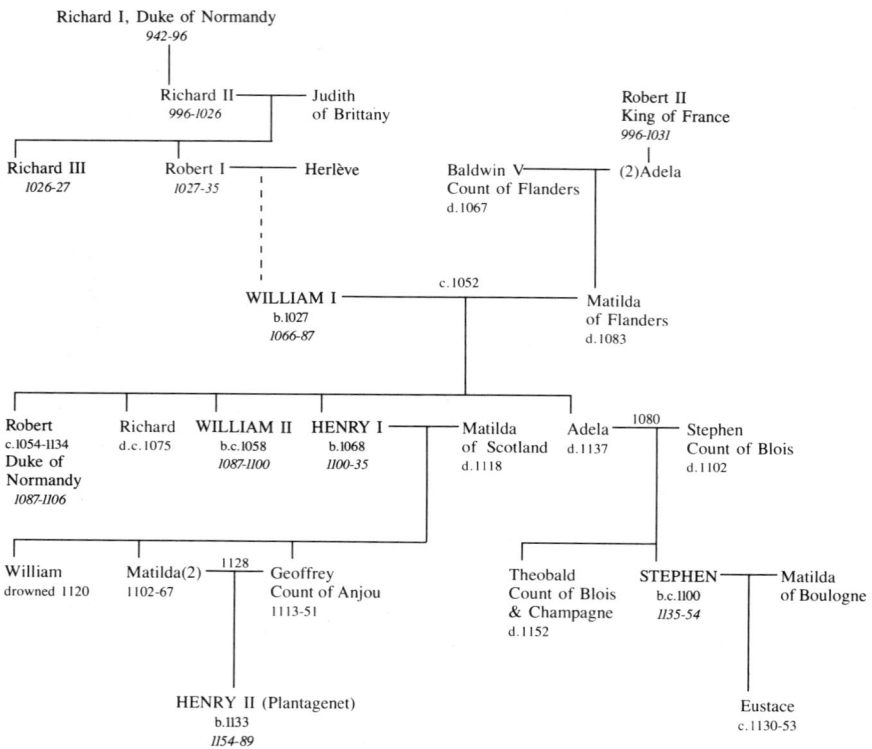

CAPET DYNASTY IN FRANCE

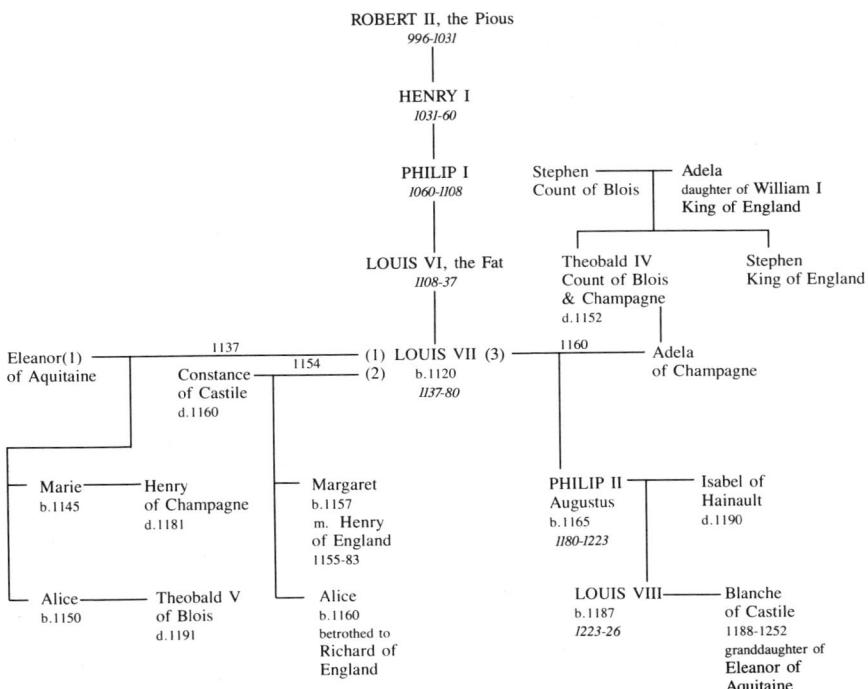

ROBERT II, the Pious
996-1031

HENRY I
1031-60

PHILIP I
1060-1108

Stephen ——— Adela
Count of Blois | daughter of **William I**
King of England

LOUIS VI, the Fat
1108-37

Theobald IV
Count of Blois
& Champagne
d.1152

Stephen
King of England

Eleanor(1)
of Aquitaine

1137

1154

(1) LOUIS VII (3)
(2) b.1120
1137-80

1160

Adela
of Champagne

Constance
of Castile
d.1160

Marie
b.1145

Henry
of Champagne
d.1181

Margaret
b.1157
m. Henry
of England
1155-83

PHILIP II
Augustus
b.1165
1180-1223

Isabel of
Hainault
d.1190

Alice
b.1150

Theobald V
of Blois
d.1191

Alice
b.1160
betrothed to
Richard of
England

LOUIS VIII
b.1187
1223-26

Blanche
of Castile
1188-1252
granddaughter of
**Eleanor of
Aquitaine**

PLANTAGENET DYNASTY IN ENGLAND

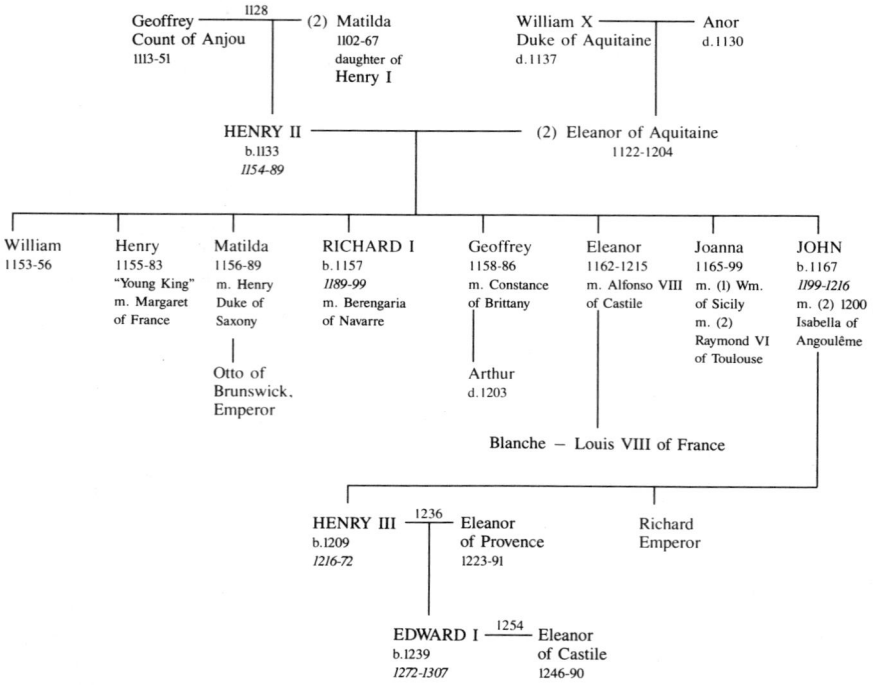

Geoffrey ——— 1128 ——— (2) Matilda   William X ——— Anor
Count of Anjou   1102-67   Duke of Aquitaine   d.1130
1113-51   daughter of   d.1137
                          Henry I

                    HENRY II ———   (2) Eleanor of Aquitaine
                    b.1133   1122-1204
                    1154-89

William	Henry	Matilda	RICHARD I	Geoffrey	Eleanor	Joanna	JOHN
1153-56	1155-83	1156-89	b.1157	1158-86	1162-1215	1165-99	b.1167
	"Young King"	m. Henry	*1189-99*	m. Constance	m. Alfonso VIII	m. (1) Wm.	*1199-1216*
	m. Margaret	Duke of	m. Berengaria	of Brittany	of Castile	of Sicily	m. (2) 1200
	of France	Saxony	of Navarre			m. (2)	Isabella of
						Raymond VI	Angoulême
						of Toulouse	
		Otto of		Arthur			
		Brunswick,		d.1203			
		Emperor					

Blanche — Louis VIII of France

HENRY III ——— 1236 ——— Eleanor   Richard
b.1209   of Provence   Emperor
1216-72   1223-91

EDWARD I ——— 1254 ——— Eleanor
b.1239   of Castile
1272-1307   1246-90

Bibliographical Note

This book is not the product of extensive research in unpublished sources. It is based on the comparative study of the best material in print, for the most part in libraries accessible to students in secondary school.

Among the satisfactory general accounts of the medieval world are Strayer, *Western Europe in the Middle Ages*, Tierney and Painter, *Western Europe in the Middle Ages*, and Stephenson, *Medieval History*, as well as the *Shorter Cambridge Medieval History*. An outstanding history, wide-ranging and profusely illustrated, is Lopez, *The Birth of Europe*. For ideas, philosophy, and religion, there are Artz, *The Mind of the Middle Ages*, and Taylor, *The Medieval Mind*. For social organization and daily living, there are Coulton, *Life in the Middle Ages*, Davis, *Life on a Medieval Barony*, and Power, *Medieval People*. Classical authorities are Gibbon's *Decline and Fall of the Roman Empire*, Bryce's *The Holy Roman Empire*, and Pirenne's *A History of Europe*. Many people learn about the Middle Ages from Durant's *Age of Faith* and Costain's vivid works, although they are suspect of professional historians.

Compilations of primary source material and notable secondary interpretations are less numerous for medieval than for modern history. Older ones, still valuable for breadth of coverage and highlighting crucial events, include Robinson, *Readings in European History*, Ketelby, *Readings from the Great Historians*, and the source books in English history of Beard, Cheyney, Kendall, and Tuell and Hatch. Mendenhall, *Ideas and Institutions in European History*, examines issues in depth and stresses controversy. Although highly compressed, Downs' *Basic Documents in Medieval History* is handy and useful. Also appropriate are parts of larger collections such as Bernard and Hodges, *Readings in European History*.

More specialized works provided material to be included in particular chapters. For the earlier centuries, Masterman, *The Dawn of*

Medieval Europe, and Oman, *The Dark Ages*, are useful, as well as Bainville, *Histoire de France*, and Pirenne, *Mohammed and Charlemagne*. Hodgkin's *Charles the Great* has copious quotations from Einhard; there are biographies of Charlemagne by Baker and James and, more recently, by Winston.

Knowledge of the Eastern Empire in the 6th century can be gathered from diverse sources. Popularizations are Graves, *Count Belisarius*, Lamb, *Theodora and the Emperor*, and Franzero, *Life and Times of Theodora*. More scholarly works are Diehl, *Byzantium, Greatness and Decline*, and *Theodora, Impératrice de Byzance*, and Ure, *Justinian and His Age*. The traditional authority is Bury, *History of the Later Roman Empire*; more recent is Jones, *The Later Roman Empire*, and more specialized is Barker, *Justinian and the Later Roman Empire*. All the modern authors draw heavily on the greatest classical historian of the 6th century, Procopius of Caesarea: on his *Wars* for history and geography, his *Buildings* for church architecture and public works, and his *Secret History* for personalities.

Freeman, *William the Conqueror*, and Haskins, *The Normans in English History*, are basic studies for the Norman Conquest. See, also, Maurois, *The Miracle of England*, Belloc, *William the Conqueror*, and good standard texts like Trevelyan's *History of England*.

With William and Gregory VII, we reach the times covered by Lees in *The Central Period of the Middle Ages* and Davis in *England under the Normans and the Angevins*. For church history, there are Creighton, *History of the Papacy*, and Dawley, *Chapters in Church History*; the best-known old work is Milman's *History of Latin Christianity*. Biographies of Gregory VII, by Mathew, Stephens, and Macdonald are somewhat dated.

The authoritative treatment of Bernard of Clairvaux is Morison, *The Life and Times of St. Bernard*. Other sources for this chapter were Newhall's *The Crusades*, Lamb's *The Crusades*, and Carlyle's account of Mohammed in *Heroes and Hero-Worship*. There are biographies of Mohammed by Muir and Dibble, of Gregory I by Gasquet, of Benedict of Nursia by McCann, of St. Augustine by Bertrand.

The most complete study of Eleanor is Kelly, *Eleanor of Aquitaine and the Four Kings*. Kelly tells a fascinating if slightly romanticized story of Eleanor and her contemporaries, several of whom were the chief opponents of Philip Augustus. She provides an exhaustive list of the relevant medieval chronicles. More recent biographies of Eleanor by Pernoud and Seward are to some extent derivative from Kelly's work. For Philip himself, there is Hutton's little biography, *Philip Augustus*. Adams' *Growth of the French Nation* and Romier's *A History of France* consider the new developments of Philip's era. For the capital and architecture, an excellent book is Temko's *Notre Dame of Paris*.

For the conflict between Simon de Montfort and Henry III, Davis and Trevelyan and Maurois are interesting, and there is valuable information in Green's old *History of the English People* and Churchill's newer *History of the English speaking Peoples*. The basic biography of Simon is Bemont's.

A good many works on special aspects of medieval history are available. Several by Painter and Stephenson and Baldwin are in paper in the Cornell University series, "The Development of Western Civilization." Others, like Pirenne's *Medieval Cities*, are Anchor books; still others, like Corbett's *The Papacy*, are Anvil Originals. More substantial works of this character are: Downey, *Constantinople in the Age of Justinian; The Cambridge History of Islam*; Gibb, *Mohammedanism*; Wallace-Hadril, *The Long-Haired Kings*; Heer, *The Holy Roman Empire*; Barlow, *The Feudal Kingdom of England*; Powicke, *The Loss of Normandy*; Jolliffe, *Angevin Kingship*; Tierney, *The Crisis of Church and State, 1050-1300*; Keen, *Chivalry*; Murray, *Abelard and St. Bernard*; Knowles, *Simon de Montfort, 1265-1965*; and Gillingham, "The Early Middle Ages" in *The Oxford Illustrated History of Britain*.

For many years biographies of prominent medieval figures were out-of-date or long out-of-print. About 1960, however, a resurgence of interest in historical personages stimulated publication of handsome, scholarly, and thoroughly modern accounts of some of the leading people of the Middle Ages. Examples are Barraclough, *The Crucible of Europe*, and Douglas, *William the Conqueror*. I am pleased now to report that similarly attractive treatment has been given to other medieval leaders in such publishing enterprises as the English Monarch Series of the University of California Press. I would mention, specifically, these biographies:

Browning, *Justinian and Theodora*

Watt, *Mohammed, Prophet and Statesman*

Daniel-Rops, *Bernard of Clairvaux*

James, *St. Bernard of Clairvaux*

Warren, *Henry II* and *King John*

Gillingham, *Richard the Lion-Heart*

Labage, *Simon de Montfort*

Unfortunately, many of these distinguished publications were not yet available when the original text of this book was being written. Some of them have been consulted in the preparation of this revised edition. The most informative and absorbing single book about the Middle Ages that I have read in the past year is Georges Duby's *William Marshal, The Flower of Chivalry*, based on the 13th-century biography in French verse of "the greatest of knights."

Index